The Cat
and the Curmudgeon

The Cat and the Curmudgeon

CLEVELAND AMORY

Illustrations by Lisa Adams

LITTLE, BROWN AND COMPANY

BOSTON   TORONTO   LONDON

First Edition

Library of Congress Cataloging-in-Publication Data

Amory, Cleveland.
    The cat and the curmudgeon / Cleveland Amory; illustrations by
Lisa Adams. — 1st ed.
        p.   cm.
    ISBN 0-316-03739-7
    1. Amory, Cleveland — Biography.   2. Authors, American — 20th cen-
tury — Biography.   3. Cats — United States — Anecdotes.   I. Title.
PS3551.M58Z4618   1990
818'.5407 — dc20   90-6419

10 9 8 7 6 5 4 3 2 1

HC

Published simultaneously in Canada
by Little, Brown & Company (Canada) Limited

Printed in the United States of America

This book is dedicated,
with as much affection as a curmudgeon can muster,
to everyone everywhere who has ever been owned by any animal.
And particularly to those who came to be so owned by rescue —
either in the woods, in the fields, on the streets,
from a public pound or a private shelter.

Contents

The Cat
and the Curmudgeon

I ○ *There Goes What's-His-Name*

"Some cats," Shakespeare said, "are born great, some achieve greatness, and some have greatness thrust upon 'em."

Actually, Shakespeare didn't say that about cats, he said it about people. And I suppose there will be some purists out there who will take me up on it. Technically they would have a point, but, frankly, it has always seemed to me that Shakespeare was overly concerned with people. His references to cats are really very poor. I believe if he had been more knowledgeable about them and had worked a little harder on his line, he might indeed have included them.

Note, though, that I use the world "them," not Shakespeare's " 'em." Cats are not notably fond of being referred to as "them," and they could hardly be expected to take kindly to " 'em." Ever ready as they are to pounce on even an unintended slur, they would consider the use of the shortened colloquialism on the part of a stranger — which to them Shakespeare certainly was — at the very least, unwarranted familiarity and, at worst, an affront to their dignity.

In any case I did not know whether or not Polar Bear was great when he was born. He was already a full-grown cat by the time I rescued him in a New York alley on a snowy Christmas Eve twelve years ago. But since the very first time I saw him and saw how, hungry and cold and wounded as he was, he had still not given up, that at least to me proved he had already achieved greatness, and he hardly needed any more of it thrust upon him.

He did not really get it, either. Because, however, of having had a book written about him and making the cover of *Parade* magazine and having hundreds of fan letters, what he did have thrust upon him, willy-nilly, was not further greatness but something which so often in our modern world passes for greatness. I refer, of course, to celebrity.

Once upon a time, before you were born, the world was very cold and dark. Just the same there were all sorts of creatures roaming the earth and in the ocean. There were, for example, dinosaurs. But one thing there was not, and that was celebrities. There wasn't so much as a one of them roaming around anywhere.

The word, you see, hadn't been invented yet. You could in those days say about one of the dinosaurs who was better known than the others that he or she had fame, or had celebrity, but if you said that he or she *was* a celebrity, that would have been just as odd as if you'd said he or she was a fame.

In the old days, too, people made a great distinction

between fame and what was then called notoriety. Fame was generally a good thing, but notoriety wasn't — in fact the word "notorious" was almost always very bad. A notorious dinosaur, for instance, may well have been a well-known dinosaur, but he or she would have still been a very bad dinosaur.

When the word "celebrity" as we know it today, however, came along, and you could both *have* celebrity and also *be* a celebrity, it seemed people just stopped making the old distinction between fame and notoriety, and from that time on it seemed a celebrity was a terrific thing to be. Just about everyone you could name wanted to be a celebrity. Gangsters wanted to be celebrities, and bank robbers, and stock manipulators, and real estate people, and even New York Yankee principal owners. Fathers and mothers wanted their children, if they couldn't grow up to be President, at least to grow up to be the very next best thing — a celebrity.

There was, though, one remarkable exception to this rule. His name, as you have probably already guessed, was Polar Bear. Polar Bear did not like anything about being a celebrity. For one thing, celebrities have to meet a great many new people, and Polar Bear did not like new people and he particularly did not like having to meet them. He had already met everyone he wanted to meet, and in fact he would have dearly liked to subtract some of these. For another thing, being a celebrity would mean a change in his life, and Polar Bear did not like change. He was, when you came right down to it, a very Republican cat — he did not like anything to happen which had not happened before. For still a third thing, Polar Bear would not, I knew, make the slightest distinction between genuinely famous celebrities and bad, notorious celebrities. To him any celebrity, good or bad, was a publicity hound — in all the bad senses of both words — and I knew if I argued with him about it, it wouldn't do any good. He would surely just have come back at me with the question of who ever heard of a publicity cat.

I could of course have come back at him and could indeed have given him a whole celebrity roster of Felixes and Garfields, Sylvesters and Morrises. But I did not do so because I knew what he would say to that. He always has answers for my answers. He would say that they were not real cats, and even if Morris was once real, the current Morris wasn't, and he would even probably add that he knew for a fact that the real Morris had died in 1978 — in his opinion undoubtedly from an overdose of publicity.

From the beginning I realized it was not going to be easy to open his closed little mind even to the idea of being a celebrity. But the way I went about it was, if I do say so myself, masterful. I did not start with the more difficult areas of celebrityhood. Instead I started with one relatively easy area — the recognition factor. I began with flattery. I couldn't very well start with professional flattery, but I knew cats liked personal flattery almost as well as celebrities liked both professional and personal flattery.

What I did, in a word, was point out how handsome he was — with his snowy white body (which it was after I'd gotten him all cleaned up after the rescue), his Winston Churchill–like lion head, his big expressive green eyes, and, at one end, his long, beautifully groomed whiskers and, at the other, his large lashable tail. I told him that just as he had some doubts about being a celebrity he should remember that many celebrities, too — and ones not half as handsome as he was — often harbored doubts.

In particular, I pointed out, they suffered from ambivalence in regard to the recognition factor.

On the one hand, I also pointed out, they liked to be publicly recognized and even enjoyed on such occasions the exchange of a few words and perhaps the granting of a reasonable number of autographs. On the other hand, there were also times when they did not like to be recognized, as, for example, when they were busy or going somewhere in a hurry or, for another example, when, though betrothed, they were eating in a restaurant with someone of the opposite gender to whom they were not. That is why, I told him, celebrities wore dark glasses. Then they could always be sure of some recognition as somebody or other but not necessarily recognition as somebody specific. Dark glasses also seemed to make it a little more difficult for people to approach them, in particular at those inopportune times when they did not wish to be approached.

I could sense that Polar Bear did not take to the idea of dark glasses at all — even when, although he knew we were just playing, I pretended to put a pair of mine on him. And so, to relieve his mind, I told him that, celebrity or no celebrity, I did not see any reason for his wearing dark glasses. In the first place, I said to him, they would probably not fit very well and he'd wear them all askew. And in the second place, I pointed out, frankly, he wasn't *that* famous. To make him feel better about this I told him that although I was the one who, after all, had made him famous, neither was I, and that the reason I didn't wear dark glasses was because I soon discovered that I was very rarely recognized and when I was it was too often a disappointment.

I gave him the example that, after two appearances on the Morton Downey Jr. Show, then at the height of its popularity, I had been recognized the next morning on the New York street by no less than four strangers in a row. All in all, by the time I met the fifth I was firmly considering running for President. With this person, however, after I was already halfway through my by then thoroughly practiced deprecatory wave, I suddenly realized that there was no necessity for it. Indeed, the man had nothing to say about my performance at all. Instead he made only a brief statement. "Your hair," he said, "looked fine." It was only then I at last realized who he was. He was my barber — a man who through the years had, as he often complains to me, apparently taken a good deal of criticism about my unwillingness to pay his growing rate for what he calls "hair styling." I really think if I let him have his way I would end up with my hair tied in a bow, and although I am a very secure person I am not secure enough for that, thank you very much.

In any case, after meeting my barber I decided not to run for President after all. But after telling Polar Bear that story I reminded him that, concerning this recognition matter, compared to any celebrity he would care to name he would undoubtedly be subject to meeting the least number of strangers. After all, I explained to him, he would never meet anyone on the street for the simple reason that he did not go on the street — except when he was being carried in a carrier or when he was on a leash on his way to the Park and even then, when we would cross the street, I would carry him in my arms and could take care myself of any necessary meeting or greeting people. As for the idea of his having to meet people on, say a trip, this was almost nonexistent. Basically, Polar Bear's idea of travel was strictly limited to my apartment — the kitchen on the south, the living room on the west, the bedroom on the north, and his balcony on the east — and these only when there was nobody else at any of these locations. When there was, he preferred being under the very middle of the bed, in the bedroom. And there he met no one but an occasional bug.

This balcony was, however, when you came right down to it, one place where he would have to learn to handle the celebrity recognition problem because he was, from it, highly visible to people on the sidewalk. Readers with good memories of my first book about Polar Bear will recall that the whole idea of this balcony was mine and mine alone. What I had done was to give up close to half of my balcony to him. I reached mine from a door, but his was reached only by bedroom window — and his half was securely chicken-wired in. The idea of this was so that he could pursue his lifelong interest in ornithology, but at the same time, while pursuing it — unfortunately, in all senses of the word — he would at least not fall off the balcony and plunge to the street.

Over and over I had told him that the whole thing was, if I did say so, superbly designed and entirely for his own protection. But he has, of course, adamantly refused even to try to see it from that point of view. In his blind little way he saw the balcony only as a prison — one which was not only no protection for him but also seemed to him solely for the protection of the pigeons — and furthermore he saw it as something which was manifestly unfair since it gave them total advantage over him. They could flutter around above him to their hearts' content and even let fly down on him their short-range missiles. Meanwhile he, of course, was utterly powerless to fight back — all because of something which in his opinion I had, in a moment of dangerously unwise strategical thinking, concocted — a unilateral nuclear freeze.

I realized that it was essential in my handling of his celebrity recognition problem that I overcome his prejudice about both his balcony and the pigeons and make him realize that, when it came to being a celebrity on this balcony, he would have to be on if not his best — I hesitated to say "party" behavior, because he was very bad at parties — then at least his best average behavior. He would have, in a word, to show the flag. The very least I expected, I told him, was that on the occasion when a stranger called from the sidewalk up to him he would give some kind of acknowledgment. A quick nod of the head or the wave of a paw, as long as it was done in deprecatory fashion, would do nicely.

I did not, of course, get what I wanted. If someone called his name he would either glare down at them — the very worst kind of celebrity recognition behavior — or, the next worst, he would totally ignore them. The problem was that he simply didn't have a single charming deprecatory bone in his body. It was just glare or ignore — that was his whole repertory. And on top of it, he would never even do me the courtesy of ceasing and desisting from his everlasting warfare with the pigeons. In vain I would reason with him that, no matter how he felt about its being his balcony and their being the aggressors, he could at least recognize the fact that a lot of people, myself included, not only liked our feathered friends but also found extremely distasteful his continuing to regard them as unplucked meals. There was, to being a celebrity, whether he liked it or not, a certain element of *noblesse oblige*.

That was a bad expression to use. It was hard enough to reason with Polar Bear in plain English. In a foreign language I might as well forget it. All in all I had to admit that, at the very simplest of all the jobs of being a celebrity, he had failed miserably.

Your average member of the cat-owned fraternity might have quit right there. But I am not, as any of you who know me know, your average member of any fraternity. It is just not in me to say "uncle" after one setback. All right, I said to myself, I had not yet won Polar Bear over on the celebrity recognition front. But I had really fought, when you came right down to it, only one battle, and I had lost it through no fault of mine. I had lost it through the pigeons, by having to fight on two fronts at once — something which has through the years tested the mettle of many another great commander. All in all, the way I assessed the situation — with, of course, my usual objectivity — was that I had lost one battle. I had not yet lost the war.

I had, it is true, lost many a skirmish with him — but these really had nothing to do with his celebrity. Once, I remember, when he wanted to go out on his balcony and he was, as usual, hollering "aeiou" at me — he has always been terrific at vowels but terrible at consonants — I decided that since it was snowing, and there was snow all over his balcony, I should put a sweater on him and fix little makeshift snowshoes. I did so. In fact I made the latter out of my own socks. Then he went out and was out there all of a minute, because, when I went back to his window to see how he was getting along he saw me and flew back in with his sweater and boots still out there. And, to top it off, he had the nerve to "aeiou" again over and over at me, clearly holding me responsible for the snow — which, for some reason, he obviously felt gave the pigeons one more advantage over him.

In any case, I started the next phase of my attack by freely admitting that I could see from his point of view that there was a down side to being a celebrity. I told him that I would be guilty of parting with something less than the unvarnished truth if I did not admit that from time to time he would have unwelcome intrusions from photographers trying to take his picture — I told him they were called *"paparazzi"* — and that there even might be gossip columnists prying into his private life. But, while admitting all that, at the same time I emphasized that there were many up sides to being a celebrity. Furthermore, I knew him well enough to know that many of these would surely appeal to him.

Patience, for example, never his long suit, would, I reasoned with him, now no longer be a problem. He would not have to sit and wait so much, not even in the place of all places he least liked to sit and wait — at the vet's. He would, on the other hand, shortly after arrival, be almost majestically summoned to the inner sanctum, and hence would not have to endure, in the outer waiting room, the disagreeable contemplation of other cats or, worse still, dogs. And there were many other up sides I mentioned. He could now get away with his seemingly everlasting bad habit of not recognizing people he ought to have known, because now people would excuse him on the grounds he must meet so many people he could hardly be expected to remember everyone. Also, he could with impunity now leave whenever he wanted to from any group anytime and from any place. He could pay no attention to people even when they were obviously talking to him. He could have, in other words, the same "celebrity fade" I had observed so often in the eyes of the many celebrities about whom I had so often written. Even, if he could believe it, when *I* was talking to them — and starting one of my best stories, too.

As if all this were not enough, I went on to point out that, as for strangers coming up to him and bothering him and using an inordinate amount of his time when he was busy looking out the window or washing or taking one of his morning, afternoon, or evening naps — well, this would no longer be the case. Such strangers would have to make an appointment in advance and I would handle all that. I would take care also of seeing that he had an unlisted telephone — even a cellular phone with an answering machine and speed dialing, if he so wished. But there was no need for him even to think of taking calls or making them. I would see to it that as far as any call was concerned, he was in a meeting. As for people who wanted to see him in person, I would make it my business to screen them thoroughly — particularly those who wanted to talk to him just to say they had. And, when it came to sending out his photograph, I would not only do it myself but I would also pay for the extra pictures and the postage as well. I even had an autoprint made for him and I did the stamping for him. He would never, literally, have to raise a paw.

Finally, although he was very bad at comparison, I endeavored to show him that, again, compared to any celebrity he would care to name, he would never have to give so much as a moment's worry to all the sordid financial affairs which so often beset such celebrities — the taxes, the agents, the endorsements, the requests for appearances, and so forth. I tried to show him how lucky he was to have someone like myself, for not even a measly ten percent, but for free, undertake all this for him. There was not even any necessity for him to lose any of his napping time for having to consider the ever-difficult celebrity decisions as, for example, what kind of new car to buy or whether to have a summer house in the country or on the shore, or even what to wear. After all, when it came to cars, he detested car travel, and when it came to homes, he did not like being anywhere except where he was. As for what to wear, he didn't have to give it a thought — he was always tastefully attired and could go anywhere just as he was.

Honestly, looking back, I really could not understand why he had not been able to see the whole celebrity problem in a more reasonable light — a problem which, for him, would be really no problem at all. I had done my very best, in my reasonable, optimistic way, to make him see the glass as half-full. But he, or course, in his irrational, pessimistic way, invariably saw it as half-empty. And, on top of it all, he obviously blamed me, of all people, for spilling the damned glass in the first place.

It was really, when you came right down to it, so unfair of him and showed so little gratitude. After all, all the time he was sitting around eating and washing and sleeping and enjoying himself, where was I? I told him just where I was — I was chained to a desk doing all the hard work in the trenches which had made his life of ease possible. I did not expect thanks, but I did expect an occasional paw on the back — and even, just once in a while, some slight recognition that he was at least trying to entertain the basic idea of being a celebrity. If I did not get this, frankly, I told him, I would have to take a different tack. I had played good cop long enough — I could also, I said, start playing bad cop, and if I did not get any recognition I would have no other option.

I did not get it, of course, and so, gently at first but with increasing firmness, I started to acquaint him with the possible consequences down the dangerous path he was taking. I said that, even if he could not warm up to all the aspects of being a celebrity, he could at least pretend to enjoy some of them. The public, I warned him, would not take kindly to his attitude. The public was by no means inclined to reclusive celebrities. There were exceptions, of course — a Garbo here, a Howard Hughes there, even a J. D. Salinger wherever — but, generally speaking, the public expected celebrities to be — well, celebrities. The public was also very fickle, I reminded him. The public knew it made celebrities, but the public also knew it could break celebrities. The public knew too that if it didn't get its way, all it would have to do would be to turn to some lesser celebrity and he would be consigned to oblivion. I even brought up the question of the "Where Are They Now?" columns. How would he like to be in one of those? I also mentioned the archetypical story of the five stages of Hollywood celebritydom:

      (1) Who is Hugh O'Brian?

      (2) Get me Hugh O'Brian,

      (3) Get me a Hugh O'Brian type,

      (4) Get me a young Hugh O'Brian,

      (5) Who is Hugh O'Brian?

Polar Bear wanted to know who Hugh O'Brian was. I told him, sternly, never mind who Hugh O'Brian was, that wasn't the point. The point was, how would he like that story not to be told anymore about Hugh O'Brian but about Polar Bear? I said for him to make no mistake about it, he was dancing on a very thin edge.

Even that, I warned him, lowering my voice, wouldn't by any means be the end of the road. Sooner or later he would die. And that, I said flatly, would be no picnic either. Dying nowadays, for an uncooperative celebrity, wasn't, I told him, what it was in the old days. It was a whole new ball game out there. Once people knew he was where he couldn't sue anymore, the floodgates would open. He would be fair game and it would be open season on him. I would be willing, I said, to bet my bottom dollar there would be a whole raft of terrible books about him. The writers of these books might not be able to make him out something currently fashionable, like a Nazi spy — he wasn't born in time for that — or even for being a rotten parent — he hadn't, at least to my knowledge, ever had any kittens. But that didn't mean he was out of the woods. He had, after all, been neutered, and what those writers would do to that just didn't bear thinking about. They would really go to town. To begin with, they would want to know why he'd been neutered and, after that, forget it. The cat would be out of the bag, whether he liked the expression or not. And he shouldn't think they would stop with what he'd done before, either — they wouldn't. They would pry into both his before and after, and, in the end, his whole sex life would be an open book — and at that he would be lucky if it was just one book.

Finally, I told him slowly and sadly, the whole thing would, also in the end, reflect on me. I would be the one held responsible for not steering him on the right celebrity path to begin with, and, afterward, for not keeping him on the straight and narrow. Even if he didn't give a wash of his paw himself how he went down in history he could at least consider that what he was doing was dragging someone else down with him — someone who, surely, deserved better.

I hadn't painted a pretty picture, but then I hadn't meant to do so. All I had done was to give him the plain facts of celebrity life today. In the end it was up to him. He could take it or leave it.

And, if you can believe it, he chose to leave it. All my logic, after a lifetime of studying and writing about the celebrity field, fell on deaf ears — indeed, he never even raised an ear. Really, I had to admit, stubbornness was his middle name, and once he had made up his mind about something — something which, incidentally, took him at the most a few seconds — that was it. Emerson said, "A foolish consistency is the hobgoblin of little minds," and while my dictionary defines hobgoblin as "a goblin represented as being mischievous, or ugly or evil," it also gives, as a secondary definition, "a bugbear." And make no mistake, Polar Bear, when it came to changing his mind, was both bearcat and bugbear. To him, celebrity in any way, shape, form, or manner was strictly for the birds. And when Polar Bear feels something is for the birds, he knows, as we have seen, whereof he speaks.

In fairness I should say that he did have the graciousness to grant the grand total of one television interview. This occurred on Entertainment Tonight, on the Christmas Eve following the publication of my book. And it took place, of course, in the apartment — Polar Bear would not have considered it anywhere else. From the beginning, however, I was apprehensive. I knew the whole thing would be touch and go — and indeed that is literally what it turned out to be.

The moment the crew entered the door was, of course, the exact moment Polar Bear disappeared. I eventually located him in the very middle of under the bed and finally hauled him out. But there is something about being in front of TV cameras which is Polar Bear's least favorite part of being a celebrity. I believe it is the rat-a-tat sound they make. In any case, to get him to even look as if he is looking at the camera I have to hold him in an ironclad grip with two hands on both sides of his jaw. And during this, no matter how hard I try to smile and make light of the whole thing, I promise you he looks as if he doesn't know what a television smile is. His expression is that of someone in front of a firing squad. As for the little "clucks" and "nice kitty-kitty's" from the cameraman, these not only did not make things better but made him look as if he had already been executed.

In any case, somehow we managed to get through — me holding Polar Bear in my viselike grip, trying hard to smile, chattering away about what a fun cat he was, meanwhile all the time trying not to turn whiter and whiter from the fact that his front claws were digging deeper and deeper into my knees and his back claws, which were even worse, were earnestly proceeding into areas where no claws should ever be. At first the producer did his level best to pretend it was all going well, but finally, by this time obviously concerned for the fate of his show, he signaled that the interview was over. He then quietly suggested that they should really have one other shot in which there would be more action. I explained that if there was to be much more action, it would be very doubtful if I should ever have children. But he ignored this. He was already looking for his other locations.

The next I saw of him he was out on the balcony. And not on my part of the balcony either, but Polar Bear's. He came in with a look of triumph. "I've got it," he said. With that, he explained that, for a final shot, Polar Bear should leap from the bedroom window. A cameraman would be waiting for him inside the balcony, and it would be just what the show needed for a close.

As a plan on paper it looked fine. In operation, however, I knew it would be very different. I pointed out that Polar Bear would see the cameraman and not only would he not go out, he would go as rapidly as possible in the opposite direction. And, although I did not know how he felt about sacrificing cameramen in the line of duty, the chances of his having, in this instance, to — well, scratch one — were, in my opinion, excellent.

The producer, however, would not hear of such negativism. He suggested I simply put Polar Bear out by reaching from the side of the window so that he didn't see the camera until he was already in full leap. It was just what the show needed, the producer pointed out again, and he was sure it would be a terrific shot.

And terrific, all right, it was. At first everyone seemed to have the whole thing in hand. The rest of the crew, at the producer's direction, made much noise — for Polar Bear's benefit — while they went out the door as if they were leaving for good. Meanwhile, just one cameraman, with his camera, sneaked into the bedroom and went out the window into Polar Bear's own balcony, where, crouching down, he silently took his post. Then it was up to me. Still grasping Polar Bear firmly in both hands, I took him into the bedroom and up to the side of the window. Here I awaited my crucial cue. When I received it I reached out toward the window and, with a firm fast movement, hung a sharp right with both hands. I had made myself as invisible as possible and yet I had given Polar Bear a launch which would have done credit to Cape Canaveral.

Touch and go I had said it would be, and touch and go it was. When Polar Bear saw that his sanctuary had been invaded and he was literally leaping into the very jaws of the enemy, he somehow managed, in midleap, an extraordinary variety of different moves in succession — all done so quickly they seemed in one motion. First there was the whirl of his body, next the turn in the opposite direction, then the brief touchdown of his left paw, after that with his right paw, a lightning right to the cameraman's jaw, and finally the leap back straight into my arms. He even managed to give me one good left hook to the stomach, too, just to let me know what he thought of my duplicity. Fortunately for my public, if not his, this never did show on camera, but his lethal right at the cameraman was there for all to see. And, this, of all nights, on the night of Peace On Earth, Good Will To Men.

Actually, individual interviews with no TV camera present were, as a matter of fact, hardly more successful. The trouble was that sooner or later a picture would be involved, and by this time Polar Bear regarded even a still photographer as a man up to no possible good. One day, for example, a woman reporter arrived from the *Toronto Star*. At first the interview went reasonably smoothly. Polar Bear stayed right in my lap and did not even make an effort to disappear. It was, however, the calm before the storm. The doorbell rang and it was, of course, the interviewer's partner, her photographer. Before the man had even taken out his camera Polar Bear had flown by him and repaired to his refuge under the bed. Here, as I carefully explained to the man as we visited the bedroom, he was literally unreachable except by crawl.

"Don't worry," the photographer said, "I have a cat myself. I know how to get him out." In vain I cautioned him once more. Even veteran crawlers, I explained, such as my late soldier brother, had failed. I even went so far as to emphasize the *late*. "Nonsense," he said, "I'll have him out before you know it." And, without another word, over the top — or, rather, under the top — he went.

Immediately Polar Bear began a dangerous series of steady hisses. Occasionally I would catch a glimpse of his nose or one of the man's shoes, but for some time there was apparently no actual contact. Finally I heard the smack of what I knew was the man's hand on the floor — obviously an attempted grab. This was at once followed by an incredibly loud whacking thump, and this time I knew it was not the man's hand but Polar Bear's paw. Although it sounded as if he had hit the floor rather than pay dirt, I couldn't be sure. In any case, after the thwack there was a long, ominous silence. I frankly feared the worst.

Finally, slowly and extremely sheepishly, the photographer emerged. I looked him over carefully and was relieved to see he was not visibly bleeding and still had the use of all his extremities. "You know," he said, "what I think I'll do? I think I'll get my camera and flash and photograph him right where he is. It'll really be a much more interesting shot."

I told him I couldn't agree with him more.

From the beginning there was, it seemed, a lively demand for Polar Bear to accompany me on what publishers call a "book tour." As a matter of plain hard fact there was considerably more demand for him than there was for me. Nevertheless, I did my best to grin and bear it. It was, after all, I told myself, the way of the world. People never look up to the person behind the personality. They just look up to the personality.

I know people have said I went on the book tour without Polar Bear because I did not want the competition.

I suppose that, when you're trying to do something on the field, there will always be those kinds of people in the bleachers. But the plain fact is, nothing could be farther from the truth. I am not afraid of competition. Man and boy, I have had competition out there on book tours that the kind of people who said things like that wouldn't understand if their lives depended on it. Why, on my very first book tour I went head-to-head with a Southern author named Harnett W. Kane. The tour was in Richmond, mind you, and my book was about Yankee Boston and his a biography about, as he put it, "the one woman outside my wife with whom I have ever been in love — Mrs. Robert E. Lee." And, if that wasn't bad enough, Harnett was probably the all-time champion book autographer. I've seen him stop people in the street if they had a copy of his book and offer to sign it. Finally, on our last stop on the tour, after I had sold maybe two copies of my book and he had sold a hundred of his, I asked him to sign one for me. He gave me one but refused to sign it. "You've got something of real value there, son," he said with some pride. "An unautographed Kane is a collector's item."

So, I repeat, it was hardly the competition that kept me from taking Polar Bear on the tour. It was the plain and simple fact, as I patiently explained to the publishers, that going with him from city to city, plane to plane, hotel to hotel, and even cab to cab, would be not only perilous in the extreme for him, but for me would be perilously close to certifiable insanity. I told them that, in Polar Bear's opinion, that kind of travel might be all right for dogs, horses, birds, mice, or humans, but it was far from all right for him.

I gave the publishers two examples. One was the occasion when I considered taking Polar Bear to another apartment while mine was being painted — the ordeal had been so awful that, in the end, I gave it up. In the ten years I had had Polar Bear, I told them, I had had the living room and even the kitchen painted but never the bedroom. Polar Bear stayed in the bedroom all the time the painters worked, loudly hissing beside the locked door at the noises in the next room, sniffing distastefully at the paint smells, and from time to time looking at me for all the world as if I had sold not only my birthright but his, too.

The second example I gave the publishers was that, although I had at one time briefly entertained the idea of a vacation with Polar Bear by taking a small house in the Hamptons, I did not so entertain it any longer. One look at the house brought the realization that the only room in which he could be safely confined without some access to going out making meals of the fish in the ocean was one small, hot bedroom and so I had no recourse but to abandon my summer vacation. New York, I decided, was really a terrific place in the summer. After all, a lot of people go away at that time, and all New York has ever really needed, when you came right down to it, is for about half the population to go away in the summer and not come back in the fall.

The publishers' final argument was that, while they knew I would do my best to sell the book, they really felt that, to put it candidly, Polar Bear would be a far better salesman. I answered this by saying they could not be more mistaken, that Polar Bear was bad enough at meeting people on his own turf but that off it he was a holy terror. As for his being a salesman, the mere thought was ludicrous. I had not at that time read *The Leadership Secrets of Attila the Hun*, because it had not yet been published, but later, after it had, I used it as what I considered an extremely apt comparison. I told them that in any carefully scored man-to-man contest between the original author of that book and Polar Bear in terrifying customers and not selling books, my money would be on Polar Bear. When they pointed out with some sarcasm that Attila was not the author of that book it was my turn to reply, with some hauteur, neither was Polar Bear the author of mine.

In conclusion I told them that if what they wanted was not to sell books, Polar Bear would be their answer, but that if what they wanted was to sell books, they should get themselves another boy. And, I reminded them, the sales manager never lived who could stand what he would see after Polar Bear had failed. I even patiently described this — which was, unfortunately for me, one of Polar Bear's favorite expressions — his own patented combination of sniff and curled smile which actually said "I told you so" better than any words could do the job.

Anyway, in the end the publishers reluctantly agreed to let me go "on the road," as it is called, on my own. Book tours for authors, I have learned from hard experience, are never easy. One thinks when one embarks, fortified by publisher encouragement, that one is going to take the country by storm. If so, one is usually brought up short. Publishers wisely warn authors that, when they get to a city, they should stay as far from bookstores as possible. The reason for this is that the chances of an author having his book in a bookstore when he is on tour is about the same as having a New York cab driver get out and open your door. It has happened, but it is not likely to happen again in your lifetime.

The trouble is, authors are inclined to fly off the handle and blame their publishers for not getting books in the bookstores. This is very unfair. The publishers, after all, cannot just put the books in the bookstores; the bookstores have to do that, and the bookstores can't put the books in the bookstores until they have bought the books from the publisher. But it is very unfair for the authors to blame the bookstores for not buying the books and putting them in the bookstores, because the bookstores cannot buy the books and put them in the bookstores until they know whether or not the public wants to buy the book. But it is very unfair of the authors to blame the public, too. The public, after all, doesn't know whether or not they want to buy the books because there are no books in the bookstores.

That is why, of course, not only reviews of books are important but also why it is important for authors to go on television and radio. The idea of this is that the host or hostess of the show can then tell the public to buy the book and the public can then go to the bookstores and tell the bookstores they want to buy the book and the bookstores can then go to the publishers and tell them they want to buy the book and the publishers can then send books to the bookstores and in the end there will be books in the bookstores and everyone will be happy.

What authors have to remember, however, is that television and radio hosts and hostesses have an awful lot of books sent to them and very few of these get to them. The reason for this is that when the publishers send the books to the television and radio stations, they don't go to the hosts and hostesses of the shows; they go to the mailrooms of the stations. The important figure here is the mailroom boy. The trouble is, the mailroom boy is very rarely a reader. He can read but he doesn't read books. He reads headlines and sports and comic strips and he looks at television, but when he sees a lot of books, they make him very nervous, and usually he either throws them away or gives them away. Your hope here is that one of the ones he gives away will be to his girlfriend. Of course if he does this, your book is no longer at the station, but just the same, if the mailroom boy's girlfriend likes the book she may tell the mailroom boy to take it back to the station and give it to the host or hostess.

Never, in other words, overlook the mailroom boy's girlfriend. However, even if everything works and she has made the mailroom boy take your book back to the station and give it to the host or hostess, this, if it happens at all, is likely to happen about an hour before the author is due to arrive at the station, and therefore the only thing the host or hostess has to go on is the jacket of your book. Even this presents problems because, although hosts and hostesses have to be fast readers, and usually do have a go at trying to read the book jacket, they are told an awful lot of things to remember before the show and apparently what the author's book is about is not one of them. I know that many times on my tour I had my book introduced as a novel. I also had it introduced as a new Christmas game. And, worst of all, not once, but several times, I had it introduced as a children's book. Fortunately only one TV hostess who did that had the temerity to suggest what ages she thought it was for. She suggested, as a matter of fact, twelve. I did not argue with her. Frankly, she herself looked just that age to me. All I told her, as politely as possible, was that to me there were three terrible ages of childhood — zero to ten, ten to twenty, and twenty to thirty.

There are, of course, many other features of an author's book tour besides television and radio interviews. There are also lectures, and again let me tell you from long experience these too can be no walk in the park. If you enter your auditorium and there is a very small turnout, your hostess will almost invariably tell you grimly that she had told the committee that people nowadays don't really want to come to hear people, they want to come to see people, and the only people they want to come to see are the people they see on TV. If, on the other hand, by some fluke there is a large crowd, rest assured you will not get the credit. Many times you will hear in such a situation, with the same kind of hostess grimness, some such line as "I only wish you could know how hard all of us have worked to get these people to come."

As for "book-and-author" luncheons, as they are called, these usually involve your being just one of at least four speakers. And if you sometimes wonder which is the best position to speak at these affairs, at least for the future selling of your book, wonder no longer. I have spoken in all four positions, and in each case I have been solemnly assured by the person in charge that my position was by far the most important. When I was the No. 1 speaker my job was easy. "You're it," I was told. "You're our leader. You make or break the whole lunch — that's why we put you there." Then, on another occasion, when I was the No. 2 speaker, I was equally solemnly assured that No. 2 was the most important. "You see," I was informed as we walked in, "you're really our lead speaker." This was followed by the hushed "You really wouldn't want to be the Number One. The waitresses will still be clearing the dishes and most of the time no one can hear a word." The same woman whispered the disadvantages of being No. 3 or No. 4. "They're getting tired by Number Three," she said, "and by Number Four so many people have to go. Babysitters, you know."

On the other hand, when I was No. 3 I was told that

that was the key slot. Again, the person in charge gave me the dishes problem of No. 1 and the babysitters problem for No. 4. "Number Two," she said, "is always our weak spot, but we have to put them *somewhere*." Finally, on the rare occasions when I got to be No. 4, I never heard a word about dishes, weak spots, or babysitters. "You're our main event," I was told. "You're the one everybody came to hear." This time, though, No. 3 got a different downer. "They *never* listen to Number Three," I was told. "They're all just waiting for *you*."

It was pretty heady stuff, all right, and they certainly had it down to a science. I did wonder, though, what happened when, as it occasionally must, they had an author come back for a repeat performance and be given, say, a different position in the batting order.

Even when it comes to sitting in front of a pile of books after the speeches, don't for a moment think you're home free. You never know, for one thing, when the author beside you might be another Harnett W. Kane. For another, you are almost certain to have some experiences which you will not soon forget. I remember three of these. One was the appearance of a woman in the line who debated long and hard as she stood in front of me. "Yes, I will," she said, firmly putting her book down for me to sign, "but don't sign it to me. Sign it to Mabel. Mabel loves to read. Mabel reads anything." The second was a woman who also stood in front of me for some time but did not put her book down. Greedily I reached for it to autograph. "Oh, no, don't," she said, "don't put anything in it. I may want to take it back." The third experience was a meeting with a woman who had not yet bought the book but who was obviously debating the purchase carefully. In the end, she put the book back on the table, shaking her head. "I just can't," she said. "I promised my husband I wouldn't buy a single nonessential between now and Christmas."

A final memorable experience and one which I am sure was mine alone occurred in Detroit. This did not involve a speech, but was simply a bookstore autograph, arranged by Doris Dixon, the Fund for Animals' longtime Michigan coordinator. It started out, of course, when I arrived. I noted that there was a reasonably long line of people and there were, mercifully, plenty of books. Of course there were no books in the other stores, and that's why the people were here, but happily I didn't learn that until later. With a modest wave I went to my assigned seat and sat down and signed people's books as they took their place in line. I did this as rapidly as possible, but it took some time because people not only wanted their names in the book as well as mine but they also wanted the name or rather names of their cats. Most had two or three but several had more — one had seventeen. The most popular name, incidentally, was Samantha. I tried shortening this to "Sam," but that was not popular. Nonetheless, I did my best not only to tell stories about Polar Bear but also to think of other ways to keep the line from breaking into open revolt.

Suddenly I noticed two women who, having bought the book, were both reading it together while they waited in the line. Now I submit that there are few authors alive, and I daresay few dead, who can resist approaching someone who is actually in the process of reading his book. In particular you always want to know where in the book they're reading. I had been a lecturer several times on cruise ships, where I have most often had this happen. Cruise ships are, after all, very close to the Promised Land for an author because here you have, first, a captive audience to whom, after your lecture, you can sell your book, and second, you can then walk around the deck and look over the shoulders of people, at least some of whom will be reading your book in their deck chairs. I remember on one occasion when, earnestly engaged in this pursuit, I noticed that one woman over whose shoulder I had looked the preceding afternoon had made only two pages of progress from my previous day's surveillance. I asked her sternly what seemed to be the trouble. "I went to the movies last night," she said. I told her graciously that I would understand that time but to please not let it happen again.

On this occasion in Detroit, however, seeing both those two women reading together, I got up as if to stretch and rest for a moment and then surreptitiously sauntered a few steps in their direction. The women were, I was first pleased to see, suitably engrossed, but then, as I got a closer look, I was brought up short with the realization that, having obviously just purchased the book, they were reading it, not at the beginning but at the very end.

In a loud voice I asked everyone in earshot if the police number in Detroit was, as it was in New York, 911. Immediately the bookstore manager appeared. She wanted to know what the problem was. I pointed to the two women — they were, I said, out of order. Indeed, they were reading my book out of order. I told her sternly that I did not permit my books to be read out of order and that I wanted them arrested. I told them I was perfectly prepared to read them their rights but they had to recognize my writing rights.

Actually I did make the women come up for interrogation. I told them I knew exactly what they were doing — they were reading the end of the book first to see if Polar

Bear had died in the end. And if he had, I continued my interrogation, they would have taken the book back, wouldn't they? Sheepishly they admitted they would have. It is not true, however, that I preferred charges against them. What I did instead was to make them stand in the corner until I had signed all the other people's books first, meanwhile explaining to the other people exactly why they were there and warning them they would join them if they so much as skipped a page.

Standing in the corner, you know, is a good old-fashioned punishment and in my opinion should not be confined to just children in school, where it is so often wasted. It is also, as I proved in the case of these women, very effective for adults as well. Frankly, I don't think any one of the people in that line will ever read one of my books out of order again.

On normal days when I get home I make a habit of going and lying down on the bed. I lie with my head north, whereupon Polar Bear jumps up and lies with his head south, right on my stomach. He then begins to knead away to his heart's content, which is of course good exercise for him and I feel I'm getting a good workout too — without all the trouble of getting on a bicycle or doing aerobics or anything like that, which can be so time-consuming. In any case, after this I usually initiate one of our regular biting fights. In these, during the cold weather I cover him with a blanket and in warm weather with a sheet. And then, while I come at him with my fingers from different directions from above, he bites from below. If I get him down with one hand before he draws blood, I win. If he gets a good finger bite lockhold, however — albeit a bloodless one — it's a draw. Whatever happens, afterward we go to sleep — which I like to do with one hand on him, wherever he is. But before we do, most of the time, particularly if he's won, he gives me a good-night lick.

In a book called *You and Your Cat*, by David Taylor, I have read, "The rasp-like upper surface of a cat's tongue is formed by hundreds of backward-pointing, small protuberances constructed of virtually the same substance as fingernails." I don't go along with rasp or nails. The farthest I will go is sandpaper, and at that it's the most wonderful, soft-feeling sandpaper in the world. But then Mr. Taylor even challenges that a cat is "communicating its contentment" when it purrs. All I can say is he never heard Polar Bear purr. Polar Bear's purr is pure chocolate syrup — and, remember, he's a vanilla cat.

I am going to ask you at this point, Gentle Reader — at least for all of you who remember when readers were called gentle — kindly to file and forget the above paragraph. I have two reasons for wishing you to do this. The first is that, being a curmudgeon, I am fearful that my fellow curmudgeons, on reading what they would surely regard as such an unseemly public display of affection, might well have cause to challenge my curmudgeonly standing. Indeed, I can see myself being actually drummed out of the regiment, my buttons cut, my sword, insignia, pen, and, for all I know, even my credit cards removed.

The second reason I have for wishing you to file and forget that paragraph is that when I have been on a trip not a line of it holds true. After a trip, indeed, I could go in and lie down on the bed and it would be hours before Polar Bear even deigned to come into the bedroom, let alone lie down with me. He has, in fact, just two policies with me after I've been away. After a short trip he gives me a hard time for a short time. After a long trip he gives me a hard time for a long time. The time after my book tour trip, however, he really outdid himself. He not only walked away from me when I tried to pick him up, he refused even to eat a bite of the delicious meal I prepared for him. Instead he first looked down at it, then up at me, and finally gave me one of his patented sneers. With that, he did not even walk away, he literally stalked away.

Finally I went to bed and, after a suitable interval, pretended to be asleep, thinking that no matter how mad he was he would get up on the bed and go to sleep, too. He could, after all, do this with me asleep and still not give up his principles. I waited a long time. At last I heard his familiar "aeiou," and felt his leap up onto the bottom of the bed. I could hardly wait for what I knew would be his next move — his slow walk up the bed, and his final flounce down on my stomach. At which point, of course, I would grab him.

I never, however, had the chance. Rather, he proceeded across the bed to the farthest corner away from my head. He, too, apparently had his idea of corner punishment and, if he couldn't put me in one, he had decided, when he knew I wanted him most, to go in one himself and stay there. He would show me once and for all that just because he didn't want to go away on any idiotic trip was no reason for me to go on one without him. All I had to do, which even I ought to be able to understand, was to stay where I was supposed to stay and then we could both be together without either one of us having to go anywhere. It was, when you came right down to it, just simple cat logic.

II ∘ *Cat Power*

The only area of being a celebrity of which I ever found Polar Bear to be even remotely fond was the increase in mail. Before this he never took much interest in mail, and I am sure he would have continued this policy had we lived in the country and had the mail been delivered, as it was in the Good Old Days, to your door.

The trouble would have been, of course, that Polar Bear likes very few people coming to what he regards as his door. Indeed, you can count on the fingers of one hand the number he does, and you would as a matter of fact have a digit or two left over. And, rest assured, these would not have included any postmen. Polar Bear feels about postmen the way postmen feel about dogs.

I know this for a fact because, even in a city apartment where the mail is just dumped into your box downstairs and then you have to get it yourself as you do everything nowadays, Polar Bear does meet a postman every once in a while. He meets them, for example, when they come up to the door for a signature on a registered letter or, for another example, when they appear just before Christmas. This they do not once but several times — Christmas is apparently a very meaningful holiday for postmen.

One such pre-Christmas postman visit was memorable. That was the day when someone who was not very good at wrapping packages sent Polar Bear some fresh catnip from a farmers' market. The postman had to bring it up because it was special delivery. And so, when I opened the door for him, there he stood with the flimsily wrapped basket which looked like a bouquet of flowers. I had no idea it was catnip, but Polar Bear knew it practically from the ring of the doorbell. As he leaped, I tried to place myself between the postman and the nips, and I think I did pretty well. If there was ever, however, a literal example of something being nip and tuck, this was it, and when it was all over there was no question but that Polar Bear was the winner. He had the basket, but the postman appeared to me, on first glance, as a basket case — albeit one who I'm sure had learned from then on to prefer even a dog to a cat after catnip.

This was a special occurrence, but, with increased mail and with very few postmen to contend with, Polar Bear did begin to show, as I say, increased interest. And the area of the mail in which he took perhaps the keenest interest outside of edibles was the arrival of new books. These were sometimes sent to me for a favorable comment for later use in a newspaper ad — a comment which is called a "blurb." When I opened such books — indeed, many times when I had not had a chance to do so because he had already done it for me — he would sniff them from cover to cover. In fact he often sniffed the covers right off them, which always seemed to me in itself an extremely favorable blurb. Certainly there was no question about his being, when it came to new books, a voracious reader. At the same time it hurt me very much that he ignored the older books I had written just because they weren't new. He wouldn't even sniff the covers to see if he would like them.

Polar Bear also liked something else about the increased mail. Somehow he seemed to be fully aware of the large amount which was addressed to him rather than to me. His character, I have always felt, leaves much to be desired in many departments but particularly in any department which involves any kind of competition with me. I remember, for example, one day when I brought up two packages — one addressed to me, and one to him. He opened his while sitting on mine. Whatever he did, his ability to spot the packages which were addressed to him was remarkable. Nor did all of these contain the telltale catnip or some other edible which was readily identifiable by smell. There were many others which were not so identifiable — toys, for instance, or food in cans — and to this day I've never been able to figure out how he knew what was in them.

Spot them he not only did, however, he also treated them all, not just catnip but even simpler items, as if, if he didn't move in on them tooth and claw, they might get away. I guarantee that on more than one occasion, having pried open a package containing a can, he would then start "aeiou"-ing around, batting me and making short runs in the direction of the kitchen. I always have the feeling that if I do not immediately follow him to the kitchen and get the can opener and open the can for him, he would either get himself a smart lawyer and take me to court for withholding rightful property or, almost as sinister from my point of view, develop his own capacity to pry cans open himself. He really is a great little prier — not only into his own affairs, but also into other people's and particularly mine.

My usual modus operandi was to open all the packages first and then, when he had sniffed and eaten to his heart's content, I could count on the fact he would want a nap and I could then enjoy the luxury of reading the rest of my mail without his sticking his selfish little nose into a lot of things which, whether he thought so or not, were none of his business.

One of the first of these was a letter from Mrs. Josephine Vernick of Southfield, Michigan. It was a very nice letter with one, to me, remarkable qualification. What, in a word, Mrs. Vernick told me she particularly liked about my book was my punctuation.

I was glad Polar Bear was asleep for that. I could just see him figuring out from my reaction that I had gotten a bad one, and it would be just like him in his rotten little competitive way to be pleased as punch over it. I had to admit, though, that in this case he would have a point. I submit that there is a wide variety of main reasons authors would like to be remembered after they have gone to their final reward, but I doubt that high on the list of any of them would be their punctuation. Just the same, I told myself, punctuation was, when you came right down to it, a basic element of one's style, and I could, therefore, at least take some satisfaction for the fact that I had received praise for this.

My satisfaction was, however, short-lived. This was

due to the very next letter I opened — one from Ms. Betty Stein of Fort Wayne, Indiana. Ms. Stein, a columnist for the *Fort Wayne News-Sentinel,* enclosed a review of my book. It began as follows:

> If you can ignore Mr. Amory's compulsion to write con-
> voluted sentences, as he does in two or three out of four
> in a row, and if you are in no hurry to go from the subject,
> which almost always is his cat named Polar Bear, to the
> predicate (that's the part of the sentence with the verb and
> the object, for those of you who have forgotten your
> courses in grammar, or maybe didn't have them because
> for quite a spell it was considered unstylish and unnec-
> essary to teach how to parse), and you don't mind going
> back to the beginning to find out what the author origi-
> nally intended the sentence to be about, you'll find . . .

Well, as I've always said, you can't win them all. But, hard as it is for me to admit, I should say that Ms. Stein was not the first to call attention to my predilection for convolution. My very first literary agent, Bernice Baum-garten, was also very narrow-gauge when it came to this. On one notable occasion, early in my literary career, she came perilously close to doing permanent damage to my writing psyche. First she gave me a stern lecture about style in general and then added that, of all her clients, I had the worst tendency to write, as she put it, "pretzel sentences."

How I have longed through the years to write just one book which would make her eat her words. Now, how-ever, after Ms. Stein's words I had to realize that that time was not yet.

One letter in particular seemed to sum up the majority feeling about cats from my correspondence. It came from a woman named Jackie Kamoroff, of Berkeley, California:

I sit surrounded by my Pervis, rescued at 3 weeks old from the jaws of a dog, Eloise, rescued from the cat incinerator known as the pound, and Bill, my 18½ year old senior citicat.

I noted that you described cat people as "cat owned." Around here we call it "cat power." I'm not sure I can define it but I can see you are definitely under its strong influence, as is my entire family, particularly my dad.

As for myself, since I got Pervis and Eloise my boyfriend and I are no longer able to stay at his house. We have to go to my house for a dose of cat.

I was not sure whether Ms. Kamoroff's boyfriend was un-under the influence of cat power, or may have had cats of his own who did not get along with Pervis and Eloise, or, failing both of these, perhaps Ms. Kamoroff's family would not allow Pervis and Eloise to leave and Ms. Kamoroff could not live without them. But one thing was certain: Ms. Kamoroff may have said she was unable to define "cat power," but she expressed the feelings of a very large number of other writers. Sandy Worley, of Spokane, Washington, for example, also like Ms. Kamoroff expressed the power in terms of a male/female relationship:

My husband was not a cat lover, but it was a "love me, love my cat" situation. So he has learned to love the cat. Even though he is allergic to the cat, he still allows it to have full run of the house. It has been quite a learning experience for him, and the only conclusion he has arrived at is that we are "cat butlers," whose only existence in a cat's life is to feed, pat, protect and jump at any demand!

Other correspondents found examples of "cat power" in some of my favorite quotations about cats I had used, including those from Leonardo da Vinci and Mark Twain. But, one I had also used was from the French philosopher

Alain: "Two things," he wrote, "are aesthetically perfect in the world — the clock and the cat." I had said that I was willing to go along with the cat, but that the clock stopped me. It did not, however, stop Anne Strong, of Shingle Springs, California:

> Bluemoon, the cat I belong to, just asked me to send his picture to Polar Bear, but when I asked him if he would look at Polar Bear's picture he walked off, so that's alright. One morning, however, jogging around the pond, I was struck with the word "clock" and built some positive associations with it. This surprised me since for as long as I can remember watches and such have been a bore. Well, that evening I read Alain's quote and your remark. May I suggest that a clock links one with the environment by its sound. Also, presuming it is working properly, it communicates nothing but the Here and Now or rather the Now-Here, Nowhere, the source of it all.

Frankly, just as I did not understand Alain's quote I did not understand Ms. Strong's explanation of it. The trouble is, I guess, I come from Boston and Bostonians are not very good with the Here and Now, the Now-Here, the Nowhere, or even the Source Of It All. Just the same, that doesn't stop us from maintaining California girls are fun to talk to even if they are not easy to listen to.

Fortunately, many other letter writers gave me additional cat quotes which were far easier to decipher. I had one favorite — one which came to me from no less than four different correspondents. "Being owned by a cat," this read, "is a liberal's introduction to conservatism." Since Polar Bear is as Republican as they come, this quotation appealed to me very much. And, on top of this, it was fortified by Linda Upchurch, of Arlington, Virginia, who favored me with the extraordinary news that she had adopted a cat which she had decided to name, of all names, Liberal:

> I did not then know the quotation you mentioned. But I heartily subscribe to it. My cat is black and white. At first I wanted to call him BW, but that was too rednecky for me. So I decided to go the reverse and let my cat make a statement of my own politics. I admit I fudged a little by nicknaming and calling him Libby, or just Lib, but I stopped this when a friend said you should never nickname cats — that they don't like the lack of formality in it. The irony of it all is that Liberal may make a statement for me, but his name has not made the slightest impression on him. Frankly, he is Old Guard to the core. A few months ago when I moved to another apartment he was sick for a week and angry with me for a month and now, in the new apartment, he will not permit any change at all. The other day I timidly attempted to move just a few pieces of the living room furniture but he literally went into a funk and just sulked and skulked around until I put back every single piece I had moved.

Second only to Liberal's introduction to conservatism was a quotation sent to me by Mrs. Schuyler Pardee, of Winter Park, Florida, who informed me it came from none other than the late Adlai Stevenson. "Cats do not practice witchcraft," Stevenson said, "in areas where people do not believe in it."

My third and final favorite came from Aida Zinc, of Malvern, Pennsylvania. "Cats," she said, "are like Baptists. They both raise hell, but you never catch 'em at it."

Until I received that letter I never knew what religion Polar Bear was. I feel I do now, if for no other reason, because more times than I wish to tell you in the dark of the night when I am sound asleep he goes into the kitchen and, with dastardly quiet, upsets everything, even carefully wrapped garbage. Then, in the morning when I go into the kitchen with him I of course find the carnage. He gives me a look which I promise you contains nothing but a remarkable combination of surprise and innocence — both mixed with what I can only describe as a firm determination to join with me and search the premises to find the perpetrator.

Polar Bear, after eating his mail, spent, as I mentioned, a good deal of time sleeping through most of mine. And, as I have also said, when it came to difficult letters this was fine with me, because I was certain, deep in his rotten little soul, he would be very fond of these. The letters were, after all, part and parcel of the whole celebrity thing which he detested. And, if some of them were critical, then, from his point of view, I had received, also from his point of view, my just deserts.

And some of the letters, make no mistake, were indeed critical — beginning, if you can believe it, with what I had named him. "This is not meant to be a carping letter," began Auriel Douglas, of Los Angeles — another California girl, and one who then, of course, proceeds to carp — "but rather one which aids and instructs someone who desperately needs guidance and lessons in the art of naming a cat. I do concede you did attempt to link your cat's color to the word 'Polar' inasmuch as those regions are generally covered by white snow, but to name a cat after another animal! No, no, never! It's not the done thing."

Not the "done" thing — now, really. But unfortunately Ms. Douglas was not done yet. "When naming a cat," she went on in her infuriating way, "if one's imagination is totally at a loss, start with a good encyclopedia. Look up names of emperors, empressesses, kings and queens.

Cats, particularly male cats, like very strong names which link them to majestic feats.''

Empres*sesses,* indeed. Another thing about California girls is that they never finish school, on the theory presumably that, since out there there are no finishing schools, there is no point in it. Anyway, Ms. Douglas suggested that if I did not find anything desirable in royalty I should have moved on to artists. She mentioned Renoir, Modigliani, and Cézanne and then added patronizingly, ''Picasso is a very nice name for a multi-colored cat, while Mondrian would suit one with two or three different colors. As for other names, there's absolutely nothing wrong with — in fact there is something quite distinguished with — a simple 'John,' or 'James' or 'William.'

''I do hope,'' Ms. Douglas concluded, patronizing to the end, ''these tips will help. What must your cat's friends *think* when they hear him called 'Polar Bear?' I'd rather you called him 'Roly-Poly,' which, judging by your description, he is fast becoming.''

That last personal remark seemed to me totally uncalled for — particularly since at the time I read it Polar Bear, having each day for more than a week eaten a hearty mail, was definitely more out of shape than ever. And, as I looked at him, still stunned to the quick by Ms. Douglas, I had an almost eerie feeling that he was hugely enjoying my discomfort. I might have been making it all up, but I doubted it. After all, he has never been fond enough of his name to deign to recognize it in the company of anyone else — which he well knows is especially embarrassing to me — and the fact that he now seemed to know I had received at least one especially critical letter for the name was surely not out of the realm of possibility.

The next letter, I was happy to see, was far more civil.

It was from Emily Johnston, of Westminster, Maryland, a woman who, while obviously not enamored with Polar Bear's name, rather gently suggested the name "William the Conqueror." She added that she too had a white cat whom she had named "Wilfrid Hyde-White." At the same time, she also admitted she had what she described as "a 16-pound cowardly red tabby." To him she had affixed, of all names, "Truman Kapuddy." However, the names suggested by Sarah Bizzell, of Fayettesville, North Carolina, to me deserved the prize. She named one of her cats Samuel Moses Beauregard Napoleon Bonaparte King Tut I. "Moses," she added helpfully, "for short."

Finally, Eugene Sheehy, of New York, favored me with a passage from Ivy Compton-Burnett's *Mother and Son* about a cat named Plautus:

> "Why do you call him 'Plautus?' " said Miss Burke. . . .
>
> "Oh, because he *is* Plautus," said Miss Wolsey. "Because the essence of Plautus is in him. How could he be called anything else?"
>
> "Who was Plautus in real life?"
>
> "Who could he have been but the person to give this Plautus his name?"
>
> "He was a Latin writer," said Miss Greatheart, as Miss Burke left a second question unanswered. "I think he wrote plays; not very good ones."
>
> "Why did you call the cat after him?"
>
> "Well, he has not written any good plays either," said Miss Wolsey.

Second only to my naming mistakes I was criticized for one particular error of my ways with Polar Bear. And this was one in which I knew he would take the greatest pleasure. It was, not to beat around the bush any longer, my ineptitude in getting pills down him and my final reliance on a sneak night attack when he was sound asleep. For this I was even taken to task by a stern memorandum which arrived right from my own Fund for Animals office. It was signed by Lia Albo, who is chief of the Fund's New York rescue service and a veteran of many cat-owned years. "The trouble is," she wrote, "you did not psyche yourself. You must first psyche yourself to believe you're going to be able to get the job done. Then, after you're all psyched up your psyche will spread to the cat."

I tried to explain to Ms. Albo that we Bostonians had a very poor record when it came to psyching ourselves, let alone spreading our psyche around to other people. Nonetheless, when she graciously offered to come to my apartment and do the first psyching job on Polar Bear herself, I could hardly refuse on his behalf. And so, on the very next day, Ms. Albo appeared. With some misgiving I picked up Polar Bear and placed him in her arms. She held him firmly, and I did not interrupt her while she was obviously at work in the psyching department. Then, when this was apparently concluded, she next deftly plopped the pill in his mouth and, as she did so, I noticed she blew hard on his face. "Blowing hard on his face," she explained, "is very important, too. Now, you'll see, he will *have* to swallow."

Polar Bear, however, whether psyched or not, had apparently never had anybody blow hard on his face. To say he did not like it was putting it mildly. What he did, in a word, was blow right back in Ms. Albo's face. Furthermore he did so with his mouth pursed, so that he managed a foreshortened but still remarkable replica of a Ubangi blowgun. Suffice it to say that his aim was perfect. The pill was returned to Ms. Albo directly between the eyes.

Afterward, I thanked her for her trouble but said that, all things considered, whether my critics liked it or not, I intended to return to my sneak night attack when he was fast asleep.

In fairness to Ms. Albo I should say that there were several other believers in the blow-to-swallow method. One was Rosalie Gleim of Florence, Kentucky, who also advised me not to get discouraged. "I have had cats since my childhood," she wrote, "but I did not learn to pill one until I was forty. The worst advice," she added, "was to put the pill on the eraser end of a pencil."

That was helpful, at least in reverse. On the other hand, Roberta Little, of Carmel, California, a long time Manx-catter, wrote me at some length of what she said was a foolproof method — which apparently had worked with the toughest of all her cats, one named, aptly enough, "Thumper":

What is it about white cats? The Thump is a copper-eyed white Manx who suffers from lockjaw every time he hears me uncork a pill bottle. But after years of suffering, I have finally found a way to pill him effectively. You have to be smarter than they are and that's not easy. I literally have to sit on him! You don't want to try this when any other people are around because it's not a very dignified position to be in. Kneel on the floor and stuff your cat between your knees, facing the same way you are, with just his head poking out between your thighs. Behind you, make sure your feet are crossed to prevent a rear exit. It took me a couple of tries at this before I realized cats have a reverse gear, too. Then "sit" on them gently, just enough to keep them where you want 'em. You can confuse them by pretending this is a new game, but that only works a few times. If you can catch them in the middle of a plea for help, grab the scruff of the neck, thereby freezing their mouth open, you can stuff that pill in, then slam their mouth shut and stroke their throat . . . if you have more than one cat I think it's best to do this away from the others. I think it makes them laugh, and that could be embarrassing for the cat you're pilling.

Finally, the simplest advice of all came from Lenore Clifton, of Carmichael, California. "Our vet," she wrote, "fills a syringe with vitamins and, in front of Shaddow, and before giving it to him, takes some of it himself." Mrs. Clifton did not, however, say whether or not her vet administered pills to Shaddow in the same manner, but she certainly implied as much. And, frankly, ever since she sent me that letter I have been very curious to know what Polar Bear's reaction would be if I decided to emulate Shaddow's vet. Somehow, however, what with one thing and another, I have never gotten around to trying.

There were many letters which named other errors I had committed in my first year with Polar Bear — the year which the book encompassed. But one letter stood out because it did not stop with just one error. Instead it contained a veritable litany of them. Furthermore, it came on the letterhead of none other than a doctor of sociology:

> I have read your book and I want you to know that you have managed, in one short volume, to violate every known cat taboo. Indeed, you forced P. Bear into a situation of ceremonial uncleanliness that must have driven him almost into a nervous breakdown. People don't realize that cats come from a "pride" culture full of rigid taboos that cover face-to-face interaction and rules governing statuses based on age, sex, profile, long or short hair, color and pattern. Their social structure is identical to that of the Navajo people in that it is matriarchal and contains extremely strong taboos.
> Cats hunt with the lead cat, who is female, bringing

down the prey. Only after that do the other cats participate because if they jumped in on the chase they would interfere with the timing of this. When you tried to get P. Bear to fetch the ball of yarn, you interfered with his role as lead cat and, naturally, he backed off and allowed your gross bad manners to appropriate his work. In the future, your proper role should be to stand back admiringly while he brings down the yarn, and only then approach it.

Also, when P. Bear didn't provide a welcome for Kamikaze, the kitten you took in, your attempt to force him to "be nice" (1) violated his role behavior *vis-a-vis* a younger, female, different color animal where the adult must be passive and long-suffering but dignified until the other cat has calmed down enough to be trained, and (2) you violated the strongest taboo in the cat world when you forced him to look you in the eye while you explained things to him. The most hostile thing a cat can do is look another animal in the eye, and you forced P. Bear not only to violate his taboos over the kitten but to make eye contact with his best friend when all he was trying to do was to obey the deepest set of norms in the cat world. Shame on you.

Sincerely,

Curtiss Ewing
Arlington, Vermont

First "Shame on you" and then "Sincerely" — really, it was too much. I simply could not believe the unmitigated gall of such a terrible woman. I am a very fair-minded person and have always, even in difficult circumstances, been able to mitigate my own gall. Nonetheless this drove me to my limit. Furthermore, when I reread the letter, I decided that it fairly reeked of profemale, antimale prejudice — the "matriarchal Navajos," "the lead cat, who is female," "the role behavior *vis-a-vis* a younger female," and all the rest of it.

I did have, however, one consolation about the letter. It arrived on a day when Polar Bear was away on business. He was, as a matter of fact, in the other room engaged in extremely manly business — the manning of the barricades against Rosa, the cleaning woman, and what Polar Bear regards as an enemy-filled armored personnel carrier: i.e., the vacuum. I really was very happy he did not see my reaction to that letter — I don't think I could have borne the satisfaction he would have taken in it.

What I did do was to devise a plan of action which would put Dr. Ewing in her place and at the same time not descend to her level and put the whole thing on a male-versus-female footing. In a word, I resolved to comb every letter I could get my hands on to find examples of men being just as damned capable of looking after their cats as any "matriarchal" Navajo she could find.

Frankly, it took a little time because there were only two or three letters on my side as opposed to perhaps a hundred or so on hers. But I saw no necessity of counting or even taking votes. When I am right about something I am right and that is that. I wasn't, after all, running a poll, and if I did, I'd do it the way they do those idiotic television polls and charge fifty cents for every call.

In any case, the letter I chose to use as the best example of cat husbandry being superior to cat wifery came from Lynn Goldsmith, of Oneonta, New York. I quote the letter at the same length I gave that awful Ewing woman:

Dear Mr. Amory:

On February 14, 1975, my husband of seven months brought me a Valentine's present in his pocket. It was a tiny white kitten with the biggest pair of green eyes, and the biggest ears I had ever seen. She was from the humane society, and since Rob had never owned a pet I suspected from the beginning that the present for me was really for him.

I wish I could say that it was love at first sight, but nothing could be further from the truth. I didn't like cats after a childhood trauma of watching one devour a chipmunk. Our apartment didn't allow cats, so we were in danger of being evicted if our landlord saw her. I was trying to write my Master's thesis, and the kitten had an annoying habit of mistaking my legs for a tree, and trying to climb on my lap that way. Once there, she would bat at my moving pen, scatter my notecards, and otherwise cause havoc and chaos in my already chaotic notes. Besides, she kept us awake at night, not crying for her mother, which I could have sympathized with, but trying to entice us to play.

Weren't cats supposed to sleep a majority of the time? I presented my case to my husband, explaining that we could have a pet, preferably a dog, once I was out of school, and we had a place of our own. She was a cute kitten, and I was sure that she would be very quickly adopted. Rob doesn't very often refuse to compromise, in fact I can get my way a surprising amount of the time, but he refused to return the kitten. I attributed his decision to sleep deprivation, and assumed that he would eventually see the logic in my argument.

Well, we were eventually evicted for having a cat, and I finished my thesis in the University library. Abbey became firmly ensconced as a member of our family, and eventually grew to fit her large eyes and ears — in fact I venture to say that she rivaled Polar Bear in size. She lived for ten years, and I can't imagine what our lives would have been without her. We do have another cat now, as well as a child who has learned responsibility and respect from our dignified, and somewhat less tolerant, elder statescat.

Having, with the assistance of Ms. Goldsmith and her persistent husband, put Dr. Ewing in her place, I now turned to the task of putting Polar Bear in his. The very next time we opened the mail together I pointed out to him letters about cats who regularly did all kinds of things I had tried in vain to get him to do. The first and foremost of these were letters from people who regularly walked their cats on leashes with harnesses — letters which indirectly criticized me for the fact that I had failed in my efforts to make Polar Bear ambulatory. I told him the next time I went to play chess in the Park he would jolly well go with me and, whether he liked it or not, on a leash. He gave me, of course, a look that all the cat-owned know — the look which says, so very clearly, not only lots of luck but also that you will need it.

I showed him letters too about cats who regularly watched television shows with their owners. I tried to do this with Polar Bear but I had noticed that as he grew in age he grew more and more critical of television fare. The more he saw of young cats in commercials the more he obviously disdained them. They simply, he obviously felt, had not learned their craft. As for shows in which there were other animals, these also receive poor ratings with him. As far as I could see, he liked only bird shows and fish shows, and this not only made me annoyed because he clearly liked them for the wrong reasons but also afforded us extremely slim pickings on the tube. He never even made an effort to understand why I liked so many sports on TV. The only sport I ever found him really interested in was Ping-Pong. My feeling about this was that he liked not only the quick back-and-forth of it — which he followed intently — but also felt the sound of the ball was just the right amount of noise. The trouble was that Ping-Pong was just big on TV during the Olympics — which gave us a good watch all right but one that came on, after all, only every four years, and certainly wouldn't help them in their sweeps.

I felt so sorry for Polar Bear about this that I was very glad when another letter writer, Geri Colloton, of New York, wrote me that I should get some videos which were specially designed for cats and which Polar Bear and I could watch together. I did this, and was pleased to see the first one which came was called *Video Catnip*. This I felt would do the trick because Polar Bear could, like the rest of us, both watch it and enjoy a snack with it. The video, put out by PetAvision, however, had no catnip. Instead it came in three long sections entitled, in order, "Cheep Thrills," "Mews and Feather Report," and "A Stalk in the Park." I was not crazy about those titles but I immediately sat Polar Bear down and turned it on. Actually I enjoyed it very much — birds chirping around and eating, squirrels chattering around and eating, chipmunks clucking around and eating — but frankly, I did get sort of hungry. So I went to the kitchen and got a snack for both Polar Bear and myself. When I brought it to him, though, I realized he hadn't been watching at all — he was fast asleep. I woke him up immediately. I didn't mind him sleeping through regular TV, I told him, but what he was watching was what I'd bought and whether he knew it or not this was pay TV and he could jolly well watch it whether he liked it or not. Whereupon, of course, after my outburst, he went back to sleep again.

I had almost exactly the same experience with the second video I tried, entitled *Kitty Video* and put out by Lazy Cat Productions. Finally I realized the trouble. I am not good at reading instructions, and, sure enough, I hadn't read the pamphlet which came with the *Kitty Video*. The first part was entitled "How to Teach Your Cat to Watch

TV." "Most cats," it began, "are not accustomed to watching television and will need some assistance to learn this human skill."

I'm not an easy man to stop once I've started reading something but I want to tell you this time I came close. "Human *skill?*" They had to be kidding.

But they were not:

> Loud music, too many people in the room and other animals can be disrupting and can cause a lack of concentration on the cat's part. Next, place your cat on your lap and begin the tape. Pet the cat and position his head toward the television screen (strategically scratch under the right cheek to aim head left). Never force a cat to watch the TV. He will have to discover it on his own. Tapping gently on the TV screen can help bring the cat's attention to the video.

I tried everything they said on Polar Bear — even that "head left," which I didn't understand. But nothing worked. Maybe, I thought, he should be watching the television alone, without me. But a large "caution" on the instructions quickly disabused me of that:

> Do not leave your cat alone while the video is playing. If the cat should leap at the screen, it could cause damage both to furnishings and to the cat. Your cat will need to learn to watch TV passively. With practice, your cat can become a harmless couch potato.

Polar Bear was their boy for that, all right, except for one thing — this time he was asleep before I even finished reading the instructions. Finally I put aside the cat video. And, I was relieved to find, my very next letter revealed there were far more than couch potato cats out there. There were cats who actually Did Things. There was even one cat, owned by Florence Davis, of Willow Grove,

Pennsylvania, who not only played the piano but also, when Ms. Davis played a selection of which he was not fond, would jump up and sit on her hands until she stopped.

Ms. Fields' cat was not the only one who took matters into his own hands. My favorite of these was a cat named Bogart, who, his owner, Carol Clausen of San Jose, California, wrote me, was so impossible that when she and her husband took in a stray he forced them to pay an extraordinary price. "We ended up," she wrote, "having to keep them separated and my husband and I had to sleep in separate rooms so that each cat had someone to sleep with."

This was meaningful stuff for a bachelor like me to read, and, as I looked at Polar Bear, knowing all too well how awful he could be about other cats, I wondered if he realized to what sorry ends his selfishness could lead. Just when I was trying to get through to him about this — which was difficult because his eyes were fixed on the balcony — suddenly he jumped up, raced around through the bedroom, flew out the window to his balcony, and smashed right up against the wire at a darling pair of pigeons — pigeons who were, mind you, billing and cooing.

He was, I decided, incorrigible — nothing to him was sacred, not even true love. My only recourse was to turn to a group of letters I'd filed under the heading "Cat Smartness." If there was anything on cat earth about which Polar Bear prided himself it was how smart he was, and I thought it would do him good to learn that there were cats out there who, when it came to smartness, could give him cards and spades.

To me the most remarkable of these was a letter from

Lenore Evans, of San Diego, California, about her cat named José. Mrs. Evans, an elderly widow, wrote me that one fall she was, as usual, engaged in stripping off the dead leaves from her fruit trees preparatory to raking them up when she realized she could not reach the top leaves. "Well," she said aloud to herself, "I can't reach those — I guess I'll have to wait for them to drop naturally." With that, and without hesitation, José, who had been watching the process, immediately ran up to one of the top branches of each tree in turn and, holding on with his hind legs to the trunks of the trees, proceeded with his front paws to reach out and shake the branches until all the top leaves had fallen. "Does this cat know the English language?" Mrs. Evans asked. "Is he a reincarnation of someone I once knew? Do you know I lowered my intelligence secretly to ask who he was? With that question, he just rubs his head on me but doesn't tell me anything."

Judging from the rest of Mrs. Evans' letter, however, José may have had good reason not to answer:

When he tries to awaken me for his breakfast, I play a game with him by pretending I don't hear him "meowing." He does something different about this each time. But one day, when he had finished reaching under the blankets and tearing at me, he suddenly stopped jumping up and down on me and rubbing his face against mine. Instead he very carefully put his mouth into my ear, took a deep breath, and positively screamed his loudest. How did he know my hearing was there? At night, when he wants in with me, he jumps on the screen — I leave a big window open all night — and "meows." Once I decided he didn't need to come in right then, so I tried ignoring him. I looked at him and said, "there's nothing you can do to get me out of bed." With that he raised one foot, extended his claws, and brought his nails slowly down the screen. It was the old "nails-on-the-blackboard" bit, and of course I couldn't stand it. I got up and let him in.

I certainly didn't want Polar Bear to get one of his big ideas from that letter. A big boy at school used to do that, and I *still* hate it.

But again, just when I finished that letter Polar Bear, back from his pigeon breakup, happened to push on the floor — he loves to push things on the floor — a letter I had not yet filed under "Cat Smartness." As I looked at the letter I noticed it was one not addressed to me but to him — one purporting to be from a cat named Chris Kitty. Ms. Kitty parted with the information that her veterinarian had said that in all his years of practice he had come across the occasional dumb dog but never once in his life a dumb cat.

Polar Bear ate that up, of course — even though, as I recall, there was no cat food or catnip in it. But I would not be deterred from my effort to prove that he was far from what he thought he was — the smartest cat in the world. It really was curious that, as little interest as he had in being the most famous cat in the world, he had a terrific interest in being recognized as the smartest cat in the world.

But to do this, I realized, I would have to call up my big guns and all my ammunition. This meant, in a word, going to my Siamese file. From even a cursory reading of this file there was no question but that most Siamese owners consider Siamese the smartest cats there are — there was just the question of whether they or their cats should write the letters proving it.

My favorite letter on this subject did come, though, from

a person — Mary Ruth Everett, of West Chester, Pennsylvania:

For twenty years we had a Siamese named Arthur (with his approval), and the only thing that cat could not do was speak English. While he lived he, of course, ruled the household. This fact was accepted by everyone. There are dozens of Arthur stories I could tell, but one I think especially you would enjoy is about what he did to visitors.

Our unique old house (called the Gingerbread House in West Chester) was planned and built well over a hundred years ago by an eccentric university professor, and above the huge high mantle is a captain's-walk type railing with a central curved-out area in which, we think, he undoubtedly kept the bust of Shakespeare. Against the chimney it is warm and perfectly sized and shaped for Arthur to be curled up in. It was his place. There he stayed until someone knocked on the door. In an instant he sat up, perfectly straight and perfectly still — a statue. No *new* person ever spotted him. He waited until people were settled, drinks in hands, nibbles being nibbled and conversation going nicely, to his satisfaction. Then, with a Siamese rebel yell, he would leap down into the center of the room. Even the most dignified (sometimes stuffy?) victim/visitor jumped out of their seats, scattering food and drink and uttered, among their screams, some of the most undignified expletives on record. We smiled and said, "Oh, you haven't met Arthur" — which turned the conversation, no matter how serious previously, to Arthur-talk, which was just what he wanted. He then sat, calmly, washing and loving every minute of it, sizing up the people and spotting unerringly a *non*-cat loving one; into that one's lap he flatteringly (?) jumped, curled up, and purred loudly.

My second favorite letter on the Siamese came from Mrs. Althea Huber, of Bourbonnaise, Illinois, a lady who lives with a husband and nine cats, seven of whom are strays and two who are Siamese. She claimed the latter, Biggety and Cinderella, not only ruled the roost but regarded all other cats as, in their opinion, servant cats:

> I am really not sure that Siamese are smarter, but they certainly talk more and they are most likely to behave in a "human" way. Biggety can open any door, even difficult kitchen cabinet ones. As for Cinderella, she not only thinks the sun rises and sets on my husband, she regards him as the person who, in the morning, is responsible for turning on the sun. If Charles doesn't do it, and it is a dark, cloudy day, Cinderella accepts it — but only after that special Siamese look of distaste, accompanied by a stream of conversation which clearly says, in extremely patronizing fashion, "It really is so hard to get good help nowadays."

Convinced as I was of Siamese smartness, there was one large exception I would make to their being the smartest of cats. This included almost any female stray of any breed with kittens. My mail brought me several remarkably convincing examples of this, of which I shall choose just two. The first came in a letter I received from Jeanne Baggot-Guise, of Mystic Island, New Jersey, a woman who rescued, one winter's night, an extremely wild stray whom she named Lady Jane:

> One night I heard a kitten's distress call; I thought it was a bird at first. I went out front to look, and there was Jane. About eight feet away was a kitten, eyes open but not yet walking. "Jane," I said, "is this your baby?" "I never saw that kitten in my life," she replied. "Jane, there's no other cat around right now, and this kitten did not get here by itself." "Nope," she said, "not mine." So I sighed and took the kitten inside. A little while later, as I showed my husband The Latest, I heard that piercing cry again.
>
> I went outside again. This time there were two more kittens, and Jane was much closer to them. I looked at

her, she looked at me. I said, "Jane, if you think I'm going to nurse three babies when you have all the facilities right at hand you're nuts." I picked up the kittens, picked up Jane (the one and only time she let me) and marched into the house. Jane said, "Oh, there's my other baby!" Mother and children took up residence in what was then our green room (you'll never guess what color it's painted now) and, in a word, throve.

The second example came from Donna Hess, of Palm City, Florida. Her husband's and her story also began with a wild stray, this one named Shadee. At the beginning, however, Shadee was not about to give up her freedom. She would appear at the Hess home for an occasional meal and would once in a while allow herself to be groomed, but that was all. She would not stay overnight. Soon, however, it became clear to the Hesses that Shadee was pregnant. Then, one night, she disappeared. Finally, many nights later — and four hours late for dinner — she reappeared once more, this time slim and trim. And, again, each night after dinner she would disappear again, obviously going to her kittens.

The Hesses searched everywhere for Shadee's kittens, but with no success:

As time passed we began to wonder if the kittens were even alive. Then, exactly six weeks after her delivery, Shadee arrived at our house at a very unusual hour, 8:45 AM. Following closely behind her was the most beautiful, fat, fluffy and furry female kitten we had ever seen. She brought her offspring directly to us, meowed for breakfast, and ultimately decided to spend the afternoon. And that evening, after leaving her kitten, she once more disappeared.

My husband and I came to the conclusion that there was only one kitten. Time would prove us much in error.

The next time, she brought two more kittens. The final time, three more. At long last Shadee, too, stayed for good.

The Hess story was not, however, over. Two of the kittens were deformed. One was missing a right front leg, the other a right hind leg. The Hesses' veterinarian declared that the two deformed cats were not adoptable, and should be destroyed. The Hesses went to another veterinarian — in fact they went to four other veterinarians — and then ended up with five unanimous opinions. The deformed kittens should be destroyed. The Hesses did not agree. They placed ads in the local newspapers, and put up posters everywhere:

> One of my clients at the beauty shop where I work noticed one of our posters with a picture of the two deformed kittens. She called and agreed to stop by to see them.
>
> She informed me that she and her family had recently moved from a "no-pet" condo and were looking for a small pet for their twelve-year-old daughter. They arrived as promised, and fell in love with Peg and Chester. At this point, after a family discussion, it was decided to adopt both "unadoptable" kittens. We later learned that the husband in the family is an amputee. He had only one arm, and the daughter who wanted Peg and Chester had never known the father any other way.

In the end, however, I rested my case on cat smartness on neither a Siamese nor a cat mother but rather on two tomcats of uncertain origin whose claim to cat smartness came from one single act. The first story was sent to me by Diane Benedetto, of Boca Raton, Florida. It concerned a tom whom she did not even own — he was instead owned by a friend of hers. The cat, it seemed, regularly disappeared every Tuesday night and at exactly the same time, 7 P.M. Then, at exactly the same time each Tuesday — midnight — he returned and meowed to get in. Ms. Benedetto's friend became more and more curious about his cat's Tuesday nights — so much so that he decided, one Tuesday, to follow him, thereby becoming perhaps the first man ever to put a tail on his own cat:

> It was not easy, as the cat went through backyards, over fences, and down alleys until he came at last to a large two-story building. He then went up the fire escape of this building and settled down by a window. Somehow his owner managed to keep up with him but finally with the cat just sitting there on the fire escape and looking inside the owner decided that his cat had a friend in there and was waiting for it to come out. In any case he decided that was the place for a stakeout and he waited, too. He looked at his watch — it was ten minutes to eight. The wait seemed to go on and on. Suddenly the cat's tail began to twitch. The man looked at his watch — it was exactly ten minutes past eight. Almost immediately a voice from inside the room rang out. "Bingo," it said.

The second story was perhaps even more memorable. It was sent to me by Frederic Wyatt, of North Hollywood, California. His report was brief:

> We bought our home in California in October, 1965. With the purchase we acquired a lovely, affectionate cat who had obviously resided there for some time. Our relationship was ideal until the day of the California earthquake in the San Fernando Valley. During it, our cat disappeared. In time he reappeared — but not at our house. Instead he took up residence across the street. Never again did he darken our door.

Obviously that cat had gone to his final reward before the major San Francisco earthquake of 1989, but it is entirely possible that one of the smaller quakes following the '65 one may well have necessitated still another move for him. In any case, as I thought of these two stories I wondered what Polar Bear would do in similar situations. I did not play Bingo, but I wondered if I did and he came to watch me he would not find it a very dull game when compared to one of my good, crisp two-hour chess matches. As for the earthquake theory, I knew that Polar Bear did not regard me, as the Siamese cat Cinderella regarded Mr. Huber, as the person responsible for turning on the sun in the morning. On the other hand he did hold me responsible for every kind of weather he didn't like. If it was too cold in the winter, and there was snow on the balcony, it was my fault. If it was too hot in the summer, and there was a thunderstorm, it was my fault, too. All noisy holidays were my fault — the Fourth of July and firecrackers, Halloween and people at the door in crazy costumes, St. Patrick's Day, and Memorial Day, Labor Day and any other day when they had parades with brass and drums were my fault. Was I really sure he would not regard an earthquake too as my fault? And even if he did, would it then be possible for him, in his hard little heart, to forgive not just the earthquake but such an awful pun?

III ∘ *First Dog*

One thing I have never known about Polar Bear, and do not know to this day, is how old he is. Since I rescued him ten years ago he has not gotten any younger but, I repeat, I do not know his age exactly. I do know, however, that whatever age he is, he doesn't act it. He jumps and pounces around and plays with his toys and bats the ball of yarn under his scratching post almost the way he did when he was a kitten. I presume this, because of course I did not know him when he was a kitten.

That actually is one of the fascinations of cats — they play practically their whole lives the way they did as kittens. But, frankly, I think some of Polar Bear's behavior nowadays is, for a cat of his years, on the unseemly side. I sometimes wish, indeed, that he would spend a little more effort trying to emulate me in learning how to age gracefully.

At the time I rescued him, Susan Thompson, his vet, thought he was about two, but she has lately amended this upward and she now feels he could have been, at the time of the rescue, as much as five. Therefore, as I write this, as I say ten years later, he is somewhere between twelve and fifteen.

I on the other hand, am somewhere between sixty and seventy. I am very secure about my age. I tell close friends exactly how old I am except of course for the irritating kind who are always adding a year on you behind your back — the kind who will tell you that if you were born, say, in 1920 and it is now 1990, you're seventy. You're not, of course. You weren't *one* in 1920, for Pete's sake, you were *zero* in 1920, and you weren't anywhere near one until 1921. And so you're not seventy, you're sixty-nine. It's just simple mathematics. A child could figure it out.

The only time I take a year or two or even a few years off my age is when I'm with some younger woman, and I want to make her feel more comfortable. Of course I'm careful — you have to be nowadays. Some women will go rummaging around on or in your dresser for your passport or driver's license or go prying into some old article about you which, it will be just your luck, will turn out to be one which is full of inaccuracies about your age.

Actually the only thing that makes my blood boil about this whole age business are those television and radio people who mention your birthday when it comes around every year. They wish you a happy birthday, which is very nice of them and all very well, but then, for Crow Mike, out of a clear blue they blab out exactly what birthday it is. That really gets my dander up — and I'm sure it would get Polar Bear's up, too. Of course they're probably very young children themselves and don't know the first thing about age, but to be allowed to get away with doing that on the public airways is just beyond the pale. What is the FCC for? — after all, you and I are paying for it.

Anyway, as I said, I'm very secure about my age. And I only wish Polar Bear would be more like me and not go charging around the apartment when I have company as if there was no tomorrow. I had even hoped that, as he grew older, he would grow more mellow. The trouble is, he has not grown more mellow, he has grown less mellow. In fact he has become a curmudgeon, and even if you know very little about curmudgeons you should know that the word "mellow" is not in the vocabulary of any self-respecting curmudgeon you would care to meet in this world or the next.

Actually at first I thought it was very interesting that Polar Bear had become a curmudgeon. I remember very well just where I was when I first noticed it, the way we do about famous historical events. I was in the kitchen, in fact, and I had just taken his can out of the refrigerator — the same one he had refused to eat in the morning. And, instead of the cross "aeiou" I expected with the usual argument I knew we'd have to follow, I heard instead, unmistakably, a growl. I turned and looked at him. I told him that I could not believe my ears, whereupon, as if he knew perfectly well what I was saying, he looked first at the food and then at me and then, if you please, he growled again. This time I was totally nonplussed, and, frankly, I am never totally nonplussed. Once in a while I may be a little nonplussed. But usually, if I do say so, I am plussed. But this time I wasn't. The fact was incontrovertible. He had growled — and since he was a cat and not a dog, there was only one thing he could be. And that, of course, was a curmudgeon.

As I said at first, I thought it was very interesting that he had become a curmudgeon. Frankly, I'd never heard of a curmudgeon cat, and I thought it added to his uniqueness. But, as I thought about it some more, I also realized that it posed a problem. This was that, since I was already a curmudgeon, it meant there were now two curmudgeons under one roof. And that was, I knew, basically an untenable situation. I will tell you very candidly that two curmudgeons under one roof is one curmudgeon too many — and this holds just as true when one curmudgeon is a curmudgeon person and the other is a curmudgeon cat as it does when both are curmudgeon persons or, for that matter, I would assume, when both are curmudgeon cats.

I have had personal experience with two curmudgeons under one roof and I have never forgotten it. They were two Boston uncles of mine and they lived in the same apartment house. But even though they did not live in the same apartment, it still didn't work. They didn't speak to each other. And they hadn't spoken for years.

In fairness, on family occasions such as Thanksgiving or Christmas, they would occasionally speak through a third party such as me. If the salt, for example, was in front of one of them and the other wanted it, they would ask me — Mother always had me sit between them — to ask "your uncle" please to pass the salt. They never, I should add, split infinitives. And it worked fine — the other uncle passed the salt — not to the first uncle, of course, but to me, and then I passed it to him. In fairness, too, one of the uncles at least tried to set up some operative public ground rules when they passed each other on the public street. One day outside Boston's Somerset Club, that venerable institution to which both of them of course belonged, one broke their then-standing ten-year no-talking streak, which I believe was the Boston record at that time. "Sir," he said to the other uncle, "do we bow when we meet or not? It is a matter of complete indifference to me — it is for you to decide." The other uncle was taken so totally aback by this river of conversation after so many silent years that he apparently made what the first uncle construed as, if not a whole bow, at least a curt nod. In any case, from that time on they did, on passing, indeed curtly nod to one another. But they never did speak to each other and, shortly before their deaths, they established what I believe is the still-standing Boston record — one in which my entire family has taken, and quite pardonably I believe, quiet pride.

The Boston in which I grew up was a fertile ground for the breeding of curmudgeons, as well as for their care and feeding. I do not remember exactly when I became one, but I believe it was in the latter years of my late marriage. I also believe the reason for it was that it suddenly dawned on me one day, when I was reading in the paper about a woman wrestler, that being a curmudgeon was the last thing in the world that a man can be that a woman cannot be. Women can be irritating — after all, they are women — but they cannot be curmudgeons. Nowadays they can be truck drivers and weight lifters, hammer throwers and jockeys, firepersons, frogpersons, and even, I presume, Teenage Mutant Ninja Turtlepersons. But they cannot be curmudgeons. This is not to say that women have not tried to be curmudgeons — they have indeed. In fact I personally knew one — my aunt Lolla, who was, as a matter of fact, the wife of my Uncle Bagnalls, one of those uncles I mentioned. Aunt Lolla tried all her life to be a curmudgeon, but all she succeeded in doing was making Uncle Bagnalls a bachelor.

Even the dictionary defines curmudgeon as "a gruff and irritable elderly man." This is, of course, not entirely accurate. All right, maturity is part and parcel of decent curmudgeonry, but *elderly*, for Pete's sweet sake, that's nonsense. The reason is simple — dictionaries are obviously written by young people — who else would have the time? But you would think some older person would have caught the error and also taught them that there's a world of difference between being elderly and being mature. Many's the time I have asked a young person if he or she has the slightest idea of what a curmudgeon is, and you simply cannot believe some of the answers I've received. I remember one young man who told me he thought it was some kind of medieval weapon, and another one who thought for some time and then blurted out he thought it was a large fish. For all I know, they both worked on the dictionary.

Nonetheless, giving the devil his due, the dictionary does at least have the decency, where curmudgeons are concerned, to confine them to men. But when Polar Bear became a curmudgeon, I could not help wondering if curmudgeonry among cats was confined to male cats. Frankly, between you and me and the gatepost, now that I think about it I've met more unfriendly female cats than I have male cats, and it may well be that many of these were trying to be curmudgeons, too, just like my aunt Lolla. Whether they would be successful at it, of course, is another story. The fact is it takes, if I do say so, a lot of hard work to become an all-round curmudgeon. And, although Polar Bear took to it like a duck to water, I very much doubt if your average female cat would be able to master the art — if she would excuse that expression — as well as he had. They well many have, within the limits of their gender, but so far, until I see one with my own eyes, and watch her in operation, I'm from Missouri.

Anyway, to go back to where I was, I'm not from Missouri, I am from Boston. And, as I said, Boston has many curmudgeons and in particular it has many curmudgeon writers. I have often wondered why this is so, and one reason I have come to is that they get sick and tired of answering people who ask them how they write.

For myself, I don't mind telling people how I write except I am not inordinately fond of other writers telling me how *they* write. Indeed, over the years I notice I've come to prefer dead writers to living writers. I am particularly irritated by young writers who tell me they write on word processors. As a person who began his difficulties with the modern world with trying to operate a Venetian blind, I feel that to try to take up a word processor would be, for me, both foolhardy and probably dangerous. I did have a woman who came to my apartment one day and who, for a charge of $50, tried to explain to me the operation of a memory typewriter. I got as far as watching that typewriter grab the paper and roll it around when I asked her to please take it away. It was not only frightening me, it was also frightening Polar Bear. He doesn't like anything working by itself, and, frankly, he's not much on working in general.

Actually, the way I write is in longhand. I don't know how many people are still familiar with longhand — from the letters I've received I would gather very few. But I find it the best way to write a first draft because, since even I can't read some of it, it is at least not too definite and I do not get discouraged by it. Later I try to put it on a typewriter but not on any word processor or memory typewriter or anything like that. It is an old-fashioned typewriter where you can at least see every word you put down, and not one of those awful little ball things where you can't see anything until it's too damn late to do anything about it.

People also ask where I write. The best place for a writer to write, my friend the late Ring Lardner once said, is in a hotel room that is too expensive for you. I have tried this and I agree with Ring up to a point — but this point comes when all these modern hotels decided to have all their windows permanently sealed. The idea, as I understand it, is not to keep writers from jumping out the window — which is, after all, none of their business — but rather to keep down the air-conditioning costs in the hot weather, when people open up their windows and forget to turn off the air conditioner. Whatever it is, it's an outrage. I think writing in a sealed-windowed hotel room might be satisfactory for writing a history of submarine disasters or perhaps a new ending for the opera *Aida,* but otherwise I would not recommend it.

There are many other reasons why writers become curmudgeons. First and foremost of these are editors. The first letter I received from the first book I ever wrote came from the very first editor I ever had, at the old *Saturday Evening Post*. His name was J. Bryan III and he has since become a fine writer and, I presume if he still edits, is still a terrible editor. In any case, he wrote me a single-sentence criticism of my whole book. "The world 'only,' " he wrote, "is an adverb and should immediately precede the word it modifies — it should not be thrown into a sentence at random.'' To this day I'm terrified of the word, and only use it on only the rarest possible occasions.

At the present time I have another editor, Walter Anderson of *Parade* magazine, who is equally terrible but for an entirely different reason. All editors, I have noticed through the years, have a plethora of phobias and Mr. Anderson is no exception. His particular phobia is length. I do not know whether this was because, as a child, he was not allowed to wear long pants until after the other boys in his class wore them, or whether, in growing up, he aspired to the basketball team, but I do know that whatever you give him to read he would like it better if there was less of it.

It is extremely difficult to work for such a man, but through the years what has sustained me is that I have found numerous instances of far more illustrious writers than I who have also suffered under this same heartlessness. My favorite example of this was the late, great James Thurber. In his early days as a reporter, Mr. Thurber was forced to labor in the vineyards of a newspaper editor in Ohio who wanted every article as short as possible. Furthermore, he wanted both the opening paragraph that way and even the opening sentence. Dispatched one evening to cover a murder, Thurber dutifully turned in his story within the requirements. "Dead," he wrote. "That's what the bullet-ridden body of the man found outside the Elm Street Saloon last night was.''

There is, I would believe, only one thing worse for a writer than having such an editor. That is having an editor who edits at the source. I have now two of these. The first, as all faithful readers of my last book will recall, is my assistant, a woman named Marian Probst. Ms. Probst came to me during the Spanish War and, as far as I'm concerned, is still on trial. And, make no mistake about it, a trying woman she is. As I've told you, I write my first drafts in longhand, and in the old days I used to give them to Marian to type. If Marian did not like a sentence or some line, she had three policies — one was to change it, the second was to leave it out, and the third was to leave out the whole paragraph. Worse, she never gave me back my first copy at all — I think, like Polar Bear, she ate it. In any case, one day, after finding wholesale changes, I said to her, "Women are better at simple, repetitive tasks." In those happy days, I hasten to add, we men could sometimes get away with saying things like that. But not, even in those days, with Marian. "Yes," she replied, "like listening to simple, repetitive jokes." Marian really is one of the many crosses I have to bear. Fortunately I have the patience of Job.

And, as if this were not enough, Marian is not the only editor-at-the-source with whom I have to cope. The second is none other than Polar Bear himself. Polar Bear sits, you see, on the shelf of the typewriter table on the left side of my old-fashioned typewriter, where the bar goes out as you type. And, as he has gotten older, he has become less and less inclined to move even when the bar runs into him. Remember, I do have a bell on the typewriter, and the bell is supposed to ring toward the end of the line and well before the bar runs into him. But either Polar Bear's hearing isn't as good as it was or he doesn't like bells. Whatever it is, he doesn't move, and what I have is not only the messiest right-hand margin you could imagine but also, on occasion, the necessity of actually having to change to a shorter word to accommodate him. If that is not editing at the source I do not know what it is — really, it's a wonder this book gets through to you at all.

Being, as I am, put upon so much of the time during the week, you may be sure that when it comes to my weekends I do what I please. This is not only not writing but it is also actually doing something which is as far from writing as possible. This is playing chess. It is only a short walk from my apartment to a place in Central Park which is called the Chess House. It is on a hill near the old Carousel — which plays, incidentally, just three awful tunes over and over — but it is otherwise a very pleasant place. It features stone tables with chessboards on them which were donated by the late New York philanthropist Bernard Baruch. Of course some people of lesser mentality also use these tables to play checkers and make entirely too much noise while they are doing so, but what we regular chess nuts do is to bring our own chessmen in bags and meet there and play. There is also an inside house to which in very inclement weather we repair, but very seldom. Often I have played outside with rain pouring down, and if you're ahead you don't notice it and ignore it. Your opponent, of course, if he's behind, does notice the rain, and always wants to declare a draw or quit. But you just have to ignore him, and make your move.

In any case, on one particular Saturday I was, as usual, determined to go to the Park and I was also determined, after reading all those letters from people who had successfully taught their cats to walk in harnesses on leashes, to take Polar Bear with me.

The minute he saw me take the harness out Polar Bear decided he didn't want to go and, as usual, went under the bed. Afterward, when I had routed him out, he lay around gasping and feigning various illnesses such as having swallowed several huge hairballs. I am used to this, however, and, taking no prisoners, soon had him in harness — whereupon I picked up both him and my chess pieces and went down the elevator and across the street and into the Park. Here I put Polar Bear down and gave a gay little skip which I thought would indicate to him that it was now walking time. Instead, he just glared at me as if he hoped nobody else was looking.

In vain I pointed out joggers and bicyclists and all sorts of people doing all sorts of exercise. We were in a world, I told him very firmly, which every day grew more and more conscious of fitness — even I walked back and forth to my chess every Saturday and Sunday, rain or shine, and yet there he was, just like a prairie dog or a mole, not willing to make anything but a tiny little circle around the end of the leash. All right, I said, if that was what he was going to do, he could jolly well just spend the rest of the afternoon sitting on my lap and watching chess and getting fatter and more out of shape by the minute.

One of the exciting things about playing chess in the Park is, you never know until you get there with whom you're going to play. You know their faces and their styles of play and even some of their first names — after all, you've been playing with them for years. But you really never learn much else about them because chess is so engrossing that there's really no place for unimportant social amenities like last names or occupations. Once in a while you look forward to playing someone in particular — he might have lucked out on you last week and won a game — and then when you get there you can't find him and you ask around and find he died. It really can be very irritating, especially if he won that last game from you, but of course there's nothing you can do about it except play someone else. Once in a while one of us regulars will even take on a newcomer, if we've just won a game from a regular and we're in a bonhomous mood. Of course we know it probably will be a very short game, but at least it gives the new fellow a chance to learn something.

On this particular Saturday, still carrying Polar Bear, I walked up the ramp to the Chess House and, to my amazement, I saw nobody outside at the stone tables. I couldn't believe it — on a Saturday afternoon, too. I knew they couldn't all be inside the Chess House because it wasn't raining. And they couldn't all have died at once.

I realized I had to find out what was the matter, so I proceeded right up the Chess House door. There they all were, inside, rain or no rain, and there was also a young woman from the Parks Department. She told me that the reason everyone was inside was that there was going to be a special Park event — a Hungarian Grand Master would be coming who had agreed to play us all simultaneously. As she asked me if I wanted to participate, I noticed that she had a curious smile on her face.

I told her I would indeed like to participate. I also implied that she could wipe that smile right off her face — I would give that Hungarian Grand Master a game he would not soon forget. Meanwhile, at the same time I informed her that I would like to make a call to my assistant, because Polar Bear did not like to be inside the Chess House and, anyway, I saw no reason to give that Hungarian Grand Master the advantage of my having to hold Polar Bear and play him at the same time.

I went and called Marian and told her there was an emergency. A Hungarian Grand Master was coming to play me in the Park and I had Polar Bear with me and she would have to come and hold him and take him until I got through. I told her that it shouldn't take me too long. The fellow might be a Grand Master but I was at the top of my game.

Marian was reluctant — she has never understood that, in the Good Old Days, everybody worked half a day on Saturday. And everybody was happier, too. I had to wait quite a while, but at last Marian appeared and I gave her Polar Bear and went inside and joined the others at the long table which had been set up with perhaps twenty boards. There were seats for all of us beside the boards on one side, and on the other side there were no seats because the Grand Master would walk from board to board playing us all.

As I waited for him to appear, I realized I had something of an advantage over him. He would probably think he was up against just an ordinary player, but he would not be — he would be up against Yours Truly. I do not say I am a Grand Master, or for that matter a Master, but I am an Expert, which is the next category, and I surely could have been a Master if I had started my chess career earlier and had had time to read all those damned chess books which those awful young Masters I'm always running into at tournaments are always reading. Remember, too, I'd gotten sidetracked into getting married, which can be a terrible time-waster.

Not that I wanted to make any excuses. There is no luck in chess. You start even and you can't say that the wind was against you or you had the sun in your eyes or anything else you can say in practically any other sport you could mention. Even the excuse that you haven't played for a long time is perilous — an experienced opponent will know soon enough whether there is any truth in this. As for saying you are suffering from some kind of illness, the establishment of this as a preamble for a match was put to rest for all time by the great English champion, Alexander. Late in life Grand Master Alexander was faced with a young whippersnapper who said he was sorry, he didn't believe he would be able to give him a good match — he had been ill. Alexander fixed a steely eye on the young man — the steely eye is very important to this story — and spoke slowly. "Young man," he said, "in forty years of tournament play I do not believe I have ever defeated a wholly well man."

One thing I did resolve to tell that Hungarian fellow, whoever he was, was that he should know he was up against a man who had played not one game but two games with Bobby Fischer. Actually the match had not occurred in a tournament, but I saw no reason to stress that fact. What had happened was that Fischer, then sixteen years old, had come to the office of Norman Cousins at the *Saturday Review* at a time when I was also there. So, too, was Fischer's mother, who had decided that Mr. Cousins was the person to persuade her son to go to college — something which Fischer did not, apparently, want to do.

Mr. Cousins undertook his task with his usual determination. "I understand, Bobby," he began, "you don't want to go to college." "Nah," replied Fischer. "Bobby," Cousins pursued, "is there some reason none of us may understand that you don't want to go to college?" "Yah," said Fischer. Cousins smiled — he was zeroing in, he knew, on the crux of the matter. "Why, Bobby?" he asked gently. Replied Fischer, "Too much homework." Still Cousins refused to give up. "Bobby," he said, "I think you don't understand college. College isn't just books and study and homework. College teaches us who we are. Wouldn't you, Bobby," he asked, "like to know who you are?" Fischer looked at him curiously. "I know who I am," he said. "Who are you?"

The discussion was over. But afterward, as I said, I played two games with the then-new champion. As it happened I didn't win either one. But then, I hadn't played in some time and, as I recall, I was not feeling well.

At long last the Hungarian appeared. I could not believe my eyes. Immediately I knew why the Parks Department woman had smiled when she asked me to play. "Your opponent," she said, as the introductions were made, "is twelve years old." But that was not the final straw. The twelve-year-old was not even a *he* — he was a *she*.

The whole thing was too ridiculous. I am a very broad-minded man about women taking up chess. I think it's good for the game and I have several times gone out of my way to play one and help her with her strategy or in any other way I can. But a twelve-year-old — really, that was going too far. Just the same, I had agreed, and to back out then would not only be ungentlemanly but for all I knew might cause some kind of international incident.

Dutifully, albeit reluctantly, I sat down and waited until the child approached my board. I tried not to be patronizing or too smug but it wasn't easy. Honestly, she was an infant. She could hardly see over the table and her eyes were on a level with the pieces.

Anyway she moved pawn to King 4. And as I waited — you do not make your move until she comes back to your board — I decided on a traditional Sicilian, to which I would later add the fianchettoing of not just my king-side bishop but also my queen-side — so that I could later sweep the diagonals across the board. There was no doubt in my mind that before the game was over I would make that little girl mind her *p*'s and *q*'s. And I didn't mean the old-fashioned *p*'s and *q*'s, either — I meant pawns and queens.

Something — I don't know what it was — went wrong. First I lost a pawn. I wasn't happy about that, but I attributed it either to overconfidence or condescension or perhaps both. Anyway, I quickly pulled myself together. Surely I could spot that child a pawn, and somewhere in the middle of the game my male logic would come to the fore. But somehow, in the middle of that middle game, I suddenly and unaccountably lost a knight. I really couldn't believe the predicament I'd let myself into. It was some kind of mental aberration, I felt, caused undoubtedly by my subconscious being sorry for my little opponent. Finally, out of the blue, on her nineteenth move, I heard a tiny-voiced squeaky whisper say something like "shah," by which I assumed she meant "check." And, sure enough, it was a perfectly good check. Then, as I moved out of check, on her twentieth move she reached what seemed her whole arm length with her queen and, still in that ghastly voice, said gently, "Shah mat." I couldn't believe it. I had been checkmated by a twelve-year-old girl.

Now, I want to say here and now that I am as good a sport as the next man when it comes to losing a chess game. In other words, I do not throw the pieces or strike my opponent physically. I may, after a game in which I made a blunder and lost — we always lose, the other person never wins — kick a few trees on my way back from the Park, but I try to do it so that nobody sees it. This time, in view of the situation, I was the soul of chess sportsmanship. I even stood up and shook hands with that damned little twerp. And, afterward, I stood around graciously and watched, one by one, all my pals also lose. I don't say I was hoping for this to happen, but Somerset Maugham's statement did cross my mind: "All of us like to see our friends get ahead," he said, "but not too far."

It is true that, as I walked outside the Chess House, I did kick the door — but the plain fact was, the door was in my way. And, once outside, I put my mind on doing some good, sound positive thinking. What *was* chess, after all, I asked myself. It was just a game, for heaven's sakes. It was just plain damned foolishness to think it was a test of intelligence or logic or anything like that, or even — I hesitated to admit this on that particular occasion — a test of one's masculinity. And, I went on thinking, when you come right down to it, a child has a huge advantage over an adult. A child has nothing else in his rotten little mind except winning, whereas a person like myself has dozens of other far more important things to think of. And, as far as the him being a her, well again, carrying the whole thing to its logical conclusion, that just added to the strength of my argument. Being a girl, she undoubtedly had even less on her mind than a boy would have.

In other words, as I thought the thing through, I felt, if not all myself again, at least better. At this moment I saw Marian sitting with Polar Bear at one of the tables in the sun. "I went in and watched for a while," she said, "but you never saw me. You never even saw Polar Bear." I told her chess was like that — you never really notice anything when you're playing chess. "How," she asked brightly, "did you come out?"

Marian is always asking things like that brightly because

she's not bright enough to know not to ask them. It's really infuriating. She should have known that if I'd won I would have told her. Reluctantly I grunted something about losing. And Marian wouldn't let it go. She never lets anything like that go, which is why I should have let her go long ago. "You lost!" she exclaimed. "To that little girl! The one playing you all at once!"

I asked her to please keep her voice down. There was no necessity for broadcasting the whole damned thing all over the Park. And anyway, I told her, it wasn't really playing all of us at once. It was what was called "simultaneous," which was very different. I started trying to explain it, but I gave up. I wasn't feeling very well, I told her. I think I'm sick. But Marian, of course, wouldn't let that go. "Well, at least," she said, "you didn't say that before you started. And so she couldn't say that in forty years of tournament play she'd never defeated a wholly well man. She wasn't old enough."

One of the really terrible things about Marian is her memory. She remembers everything. I have never really seen why God gave so many women so many good memories and so many men so many rotten memories. They not only don't need them as much as we do, they are also always remembering things that are very embarrassing to us. What happened that day was a perfect example. It's bad enough Marian remembers every one of my favorite stories by heart, but to bring one of them up at a time like that — particularly when she has never learned the first thing about chess — was really too much. If women have such good memories, why in heaven's name can't they use them to remember when *not* to remember things?

In any case, on the walk out of the chess place, I tried

to explain to her that playing a group of players simultaneously is actually an advantage for the man — or, in that particular case, a woman — player. In the first place, it meant that the person gets the white pieces and therefore had the first move, which is an advantage. In the second-place, that person doesn't have to make a move until he or she gets to your board, whereupon you have to make your move the minute he or she arrives. In other words, the pressure really is on you and not on the person playing you.

I was just warming up to my explanation of the whole thing — it was not easy, because Marian just does not have my kind of logical thought process — when, all of a sudden, with one bound and one bounce, something leaped into our midst which at first seemed, not only to Marian and to me but also, I'm sure, to Polar Bear, a huge sheep.

All right, we were at that moment at a part of the Park which is called Sheep Meadow, but there hasn't been a sheep in Sheep Meadow since anyone can remember. Actually what had jumped into Marian's and my lap was not, of course, a sheep. It was, in fact, an Olde English sheep dog — an almost exact replica of my very first dog. As I hugged and patted him, I did so with some difficulty, because as the dog had leaped, Polar Bear had also leaped and had taken up a position literally on top of my head with both paws digging, respectively, into both my ears. Nonetheless, I could hear well his steady stream of hisses. I think that the real trouble was that he had never in all his life seen anything like an Olde English sheep dog and he had not the slightest idea of what it was. But to him, whatever it was, there was entirely too much of it, and it certainly did not belong with any civilized cat. Indeed, I had the distinct impression that he regarded it as a very bad cross between a giant sloth bear and the Creature from the Lost Lagoon or whatever the name of that movie was.

Certainly lost the creature was, and whether or not Polar Bear regarded it as belonging to some kind of remote wilderness, and the more remote the better, our immediate problem was to try to locate its owner. Marian suggested that, since the dog did not have a collar or a leash, I use my belt for both of them. I protested. Despite my fitness program, which I've already said entailed regular walks to and from my chess, I very much doubted that my trousers could be counted on to hold up without my belt, particularly when I had both hands on Polar Bear.

Marian would not hear of this. Taking Polar Bear from me, she motioned me to proceed with the makeshift collar and leash. And so, in short order, with the Creature leading the way — we hoped in the direction he had come from — and with me hanging on for dear life, with one hand on the end of my belt and with the other on my trousers, we began our journey. On the way I gave Marian, for her edification, a brief synopsis, based on the memories of my first dog, Brookie, of the wonderful qualities of the Olde English sheep dog. I mentioned how friendly they were, how good with children, and how, because they didn't have any tails, they invariably wagged their whole back ends. I also pointed out that, while they didn't seem to have any eyes in their face underneath all that hair, they really did see very well or at least were supposed to. I did tell her, though, that actually Brookie never did see very well and was always barking or growling at good things he came up on or were coming at him and was always panting happily and licking at bad things. Finally I mentioned how brave they were, and loyal to their people, but that despite this they were terrific wanderers and were always going long distances and getting lost. I also reminded her that the "Olde" in Olde English sheep dog was always spelled with an *e*, which showed how really old they were. This one was not, however, olde at all. He was, in fact, still a puppye.

The good news was that since we knew there weren't many Olde English sheep dogs in the Park we stood a very good chance, even if we did not locate the dog's owner, of at least locating somebody who knew the dog and would lead us to his person. The bad news was that it was starting to get dark, and Central Park is a very large place, and it became clearer and clearer that we had less and less chance of finding either the dog's person or even someone who knew him or her. Actually all we found were critics. One lady was very cross — "You ought to be ashamed of yourself," she said to me. "That leash is too short for a big dog." And one man was not happy about Marian and Polar Bear. "That cat is terrified of that dog," he said. "You ought to take him home."

In the end we decided to take that man's advice. The owner, we decided, might well be, for all we knew, home, too, and already calling up shelters and reporting a Lost Dog. We too should probably be back in my apartment reporting a Found Dog.

For Polar Bear the next-to-final straw was entering the apartment building, going up in the elevator, and realizing that the huge beast, which to him was at best an outside dog, was now going to be admitted into his sanctum sanctorum. But the last final straw for him came when we actually entered. Marian still had Polar Bear in her arms and I still had the creature by the leash, but neither of us had either for long. The dog leaped off the leash from me and made a beeline for the kitchen. First, with one slurp, he drank all of Polar Bear's water and then promptly moved on to Polar Bear's favorite — his bowl of niblets. At that point Polar Bear let out one loud hiss and, using Marian's breast as a springboard, dove, both claws extended, for wherever he assumed would be the sheep dog's eyes — if indeed he had any.

I want you to know that here was another crisis, and here again I was not found wanting. Not for nothing had I been one of Milton Academy's great catchers — the catcher who, if I do say so, was always called upon to warm up our great pitcher, Slim Curtiss. All right, they might use another catcher in the actual game, but when it came down to seeing how much "stuff" Slim had on that day and to handle those warm-up pitches when he was fresh, you can imagine on whom they called. And this crisis, I knew in a flash, was no warm-up — it was a game situation. The game was on the line, and there was going to be a play at the plate — the crucial test for any catcher worth his salt.

I forgot my trousers completely. I dropped down and with all my instincts working threw one leg out. This was to guard the plate — i.e., the dog's head — still down in the bowl. At the same time, I put both hands out in a ball-catching position to meet the onflying runner — i.e., Polar Bear. And, as I say, I did my job. Polar Bear never reached that plate or bowl at all — he was out by a mile, and only my leg mashed into the sheep dog. And remember, I caught Polar Bear without even one of my trusty old catcher's mitts in my hands. When you came right down to it, I caught a Bear bare-handed. And, make no mistake, I paid for it in the palms of both hands.

Of course, as I raised Polar Bear over my head, I told

Marian it was nothing — just a scratch. I did not even receive my proper moment of triumph, because the dog, having finished the niblets, was obviously determined to leap up and have a turn at bat, with both his paws, at Polar Bear. I had done my duty, however, and, with my trousers still in a precarious position, I graciously allowed Marian to do the mopping up. She did a very good job, too — for her — of placing herself between the dog and me. "You take Polar Bear to the bedroom," she commanded, taking the sheep dog again by the end of the belt and hauling him over in front of the fire. "I'll keep the dog here and start making some calls about him."

At this, almost docilely, the sheep dog made a typical dog circle in front of the fireplace and lay down. I honestly think he was fast asleep before Polar Bear, watching from my shoulder, could believe what he was doing. Actually, I think in some ways his going to sleep infuriated Polar Bear even more than the attack on his provisions. In any case, Polar Bear not only resumed his hissing but also, if I was not mistaken, began spitting with rage. Still holding him firmly, I told him to mind his manners — that, whatever the situation, he was still the host and the dog was our guest. But this time I was just going through the motions. Where Polar Bear and the Olde English sheep dog were concerned, what you had was Iran and Iraq. I know a lost cause when I see one, and without further ado I took him to the bedroom and shut the door. There, leaving him to fuss and fume at the door, I went over to the bed and lay down. I could feel a nap coming on. Chess is very tiring, you know — particularly when you lose.

Almost immediately, it seemed, I was in Dreamland — literally. And here I would like to say a word about my dreams. In my younger days I didn't always have good dreams, in the sense of their coming out right. I don't know anybody who always does have them that way unless they're some damn saint or something. But what I almost always did have were good dreams in the sense of well-written dreams. They had a beginning, and a middle and an end. You had somebody to root for — usually yourself — and they didn't skimp on the production. You had a large cast and you went to interesting places and you had attractive girls and particularly one *very* attractive one. You didn't always get her in the end, but so what? You can't win them all, and at least you got a good run for your money. Indeed, in some of those dreams there was so much going on you got what amounted to a double feature, and not one of those one A, one B jobs, either. Often you got two straight A's.

Today, like so many things nowadays, at least to my experience, dreams are not only not as good as they used to be; most of them are not worth dreaming. They're just a waste of good sleeping time. Maybe they think they're trying to make us old-fashioned "escape" dreams, because they think that's what the public wants. Whatever they think, they're not doing the job. What they're making are dreams which are always putting you somewhere where there is no way out, or where you're trying to get up a wall with nothing to get a purchase on. My guess is they're just trying to turn them out too fast to meet some deadline for some production schedule or something. Whatever they're doing, what you get is one little low-budget job after another. The casts are minimal and the acting, what there is of it, is nothing but overacting. Frankly, I haven't dreamed a single dream in years that couldn't use more work and a complete rewrite, a new director, and probably a new producer as well.

That afternoon's dream was typical. I expected to have one about chess, but I wasn't looking forward to it because I knew they'd probably spend the whole dream on my blunder in losing to that damned twelve-year-old girl. In the old days, of course, they wouldn't have done that. They wouldn't have mentioned that blunder, and they would have given me a good old-fashioned dream I could get my teeth into — like playing Bobby Fischer for the World Championship, for example. I could even help them with the dialogue, if they didn't know chess.

I didn't get that, of course — in fact I didn't get a dream about chess at all. What I got instead was a dream about my Olde English sheep dog. That would have been perfectly all right with me if they'd done me the courtesy of giving me a good old-fashioned dream. But I didn't get that either. What I got instead was a dream that from start to finish was nothing but a comedy of errors. It would have been funny if it was meant to be a comedy, but it wasn't. What it was was really libelous, not only about me but about Brookie, too. All in all it was just a perfect example of rotten dreamworkmanship and probably no dream research department. For all I know, they probably economized on them, too.

Anyway, the dream started with Brookie jumping off the back of a truck and knocking me down and attacking me. Attacking me, mind you! A dog who never in his life attacked me or anyone else who didn't deserve to be attacked and whom I loved from the very first moment I saw him, every day of his life and for that matter still love. What the dream was obviously trying to show was what happened the day Brookie first arrived, but it didn't happen anything like the way they showed it. What really happened was Brookie arrived in a big crate on the back of a pickup truck one Christmas morning when I was eight years old. My grandmother had given him to me after I had picked him out from a picture book she had of dogs. When she and I and the whole family ran out to see him and when I saw the man prying off the slats of the crate with a hammer and screwdriver and got my first sight of Brookie, I was so excited that I had an asthma attack. My mother made me lie down, and the next thing I knew Brookie was on top of my stomach licking my face. But an attack, really! It just wasn't like that at all. It was, as a matter of fact, the happiest moment of my childhood.

The next scene I remembered in my damned dream was just as off-base and in my judgment perilously close to libel. Anyway, what it showed was my brother and me robbing the cook in the kitchen at gunpoint, and right after that we were being tried in court for stock fraud — as if we were Ivan Boeskys or Milkens or something.

This was really outrageous. The trouble was, the people who wrote the stupid dream didn't take the trouble to give any background to whoever they thought would dream the damned thing in the first place. And their writers didn't know the first thing about Boston, or the textile business. The fact is that the textile business in Boston, in which my father worked, was in those days either a feast or a famine. When it was a feast we had a gardener and a chauffeur and maids and a cook. When it was a famine we had boarders. The dream picked one of the feast times, of course — you'd know they would — but to have it that, my brother and I went around robbing the servants like reverse Robin Hoods or something. Really, it was so far from the truth that when it wasn't libelous it was ludicrous.

In the actual facts of the matter, my brother and I were blameless as the driven snow. What happened was that we were low on funds one summer and, knowing my father was flush that year, we went to him to get a bigger allowance. But Boston fathers, then or now, aren't New York fathers — what my brother got was thirty-five cents a week and what I got was twenty-five cents. And we didn't get our raise, either. So, after that, we decided to take a trip into Boston and see my uncle who was a stockbroker to see if he could do anything about the problem. He suggested various stocks for us to buy, but on thirty-five and twenty-five cents a week we realized it was going to be a long haul, particularly when my uncle explained that stocks could go down as well as up. We thought our uncle looked as if he was doing pretty well, so we asked him what stocks he bought — we thought that might be quicker. But when he confided to us that he made money whether stocks went up or down, that did it. There and then we decided that that's what we wanted to be — stockbrokers.

The only trouble was, of course, we didn't have any stocks to sell, so we did the next best thing — we made up stocks. But for the dream to imply that we went out and robbed people was really below the belt. We spent a lot of time painting up certificates and even went to the trouble of putting out stock listings, which we gave out to all our customers free. We even had some of the stocks paying dividends — Family Foods, for example, a stock which we put up or down depending upon whether or not we liked our dinner, paid one cent a week, and we paid it right out of our own pocket. We also had a stock called Pet Food, in honor of Brookie. We started putting that up or down, too, depending on whether or not he liked his dinner. But since Brookie always liked his dinner, we decided to put that up or down, too, depending upon whether or not we liked our dinner. After that, we had a whole raft of other stocks — Weather, and Good Housekeeping, and General Automobile, and School, and we even had the Red Sox and the Braves and the Bruins, which were the easiest to put up or down.

Naturally we had to have customers for our stocks and, far from the way the dream had it, instead of robbing the servants we gave them the chance to get in on a good thing on the ground floor. We sold the cook, for example, Family Foods — she learned very quickly what we liked best to eat — we sold the gardener Weather, and the chauffeur General Automobile, and we even got the upstairs maid into Good Housekeeping, even though she took a lot of persuading because she'd never heard of stocks before. As for our friends at school, we got several of them into School, and even more into our sporting stocks. And in less time than it takes to tell about it, we had no measly thirty-five or twenty-five cents in our pockets — we were rolling in dough. Every now and then some spoilsport would want to sell his or her stock and, although we carefully explained to them that this was not how America was built, we always let them if they absolutely insisted, as long as they sold it to someone else and didn't bother us about it and we got a small commission. Meanwhile, we didn't behave like a couple of nouveaux riches with our money — we just bought necessities. I remember, for example, the time we bought, C.O.D., two new baseball gloves. We were out having a catch with Brookie that evening when my father drove up and saw the new gloves and asked us where we'd gotten them. We told him the truth — we told him we'd sold stock for them.

What the dream really made a mess out of was the ending. What really happened, when you came right down to it, was just plain rotten luck. The upstairs maid, the same one to whom we had so much trouble selling Good Housekeeping, had an emergency in her family and came to my father for a small loan. Like any good Bostonian, my father asked her why she hadn't saved for a rainy day — whereupon she burst into tears and said she had, but that it was all in the stock. He patted her on the head and told her not to worry, she could sell the stock. Whereupon she burst into tears again and said she had tried to, but no one would buy it. Then my father asked her who had sold it to her, and that was when she had to mention us, and that we wouldn't buy it back from her.

She had no business bringing that up, of course — and that's where I suppose the damned dream got its Ivan Boesky idea, but I repeat we never robbed anybody — not even after we decided, after consultation with our father, to give the servants back their money. My father's attitude toward this was very poor, we thought, particularly after we'd explained to him that what he could be doing was to start a crash which could spread to our friends at school. At that point he made us give them back their money, too. The final straw was when he made us sell our gloves. This time we told him frankly that what he was doing was killing private initiative. Even today, looking back, the way the dream told the story of robbing the servants — that seems to be really rotten journalism. Actually, what we had done was to teach those servants, firsthand, the economy and to make them a part of a real dream — the Great American Dream, in fact.

But, to get back to that dumb dream of mine that day, I want to say here and now that the third part of it was just as bad as the first two. This part had Brookie and me at sea — in fact it had me ramming an enemy ship, one which was moored and anchored — and Brookie falling overboard. This was just plain slander. In the first place, the boat I rammed was a powerboat, and since as a sailing man I hated powerboats, wherever it was, even moored, it was still an enemy ship. In the second place, Brookie never fell overboard. He almost did, it was true, but he didn't. The dream was really sloppy here. In the third place, I didn't just purposely ram a moored boat — I was much too good a sailorman for that. There was a reason I did it. I did it to save Brookie, and there was just simply no excuse for the dream not giving me the credit for that.

The real story began at Peaches Point, near Marblehead where, again in one of our flush years, we went in the summer. My father had a large racing yacht, a "Q," as that class was called, which came complete with a man who polished the brass on the wheel and the winches and the turnbuckles. I, on the other hand, had a tiny catboat — a Brutal Beast, as that class was called. And that summer I had made a bet with another Brutal Beast captain that, whoever won the next race, the other would have to be his man for the rest of the summer. And, to make a long story short, I won.

Even after I won the race, however, and had won my man for the summer, I was still not out of the woods. The trouble was, there was no brass on my boat for my man to shine. To a lesser skipper this might have seemed an insoluble problem, but not to me. With Brookie on board

I hoisted sail on the *Eagle*, as I had named my boat, and set out for Marblehead harbor and its famous Graves Yard.

As I pulled into the dock, Selden Graves himself, the owner of the Yard, came down to greet me. He was the archetypical Marbleheader — tall and taciturn, lanky and laconic, but with a hint of a smile lurking in a granite face. "Hello, Cap'n Amory," he said, patting Brookie. "What can I do you for?" I told him I wanted a wheel on *Eagle* with a lot of brass on it because I had won a man in a bet and there wasn't anything for him to shine. Solemnly, Graves looked over all twelve feet of the length of *Eagle*. "Well," he said, "I don't think we've ever put a wheel on a Brutal Beast, but I see no reason why it can't be done. You and Brookie, though, will have to mind the wire. It'll cross right here." He showed me where the wire in the center of the boat would cross *Eagle*'s entire beam and feed right back along the sides to the rudder. I told him that I would mind the wire, and I was sure that Brookie would, too.

That very afternoon I had my wheel, and was sailing back with a good stiff breeze behind me and with Brookie, sniffing the wind as usual, wedged into the small space between one of the forestays and the mast. Frankly, I felt like the captain of a Cup Defender. By the time I reached Peaches Point, however, the wind was really strong and, as I turned into it with my sail flapping, I realized for the first time that it wasn't quite as easy to steer with a wheel as it was with a tiller. I also realized that with the wind that strong I wasn't going to make it to my mooring, and I had to veer off and try again. The trouble was that, as I did so, I was headed straight for a large powerboat which was owned by the richest inhabitant of Peaches Point. I don't know what its real name was, but it was orange and we called it the Tangerine Terror.

But for the dream to say I purposely rammed the Terror was an outrage. I didn't have any alternative. If I'd tried to slack off and go around the stern of the Terror, with those gusts of wind I'd never have made it. And if I'd tried to tack, Brookie, wedged up there as he was on the leeward side, would have fallen overboard. Anyway, what happened was we hit the Terror. You have no idea how hard a sailboat in a good breeze can hit — particularly since a wave from another damned powerboat rode under us just before we hit, and *Eagle* was riding down that wave so we hit the Terror right at her waterline. Brookie bounced first into the Terror, and then back toward me. He would have hit the wire, too, if I hadn't grabbed him. In any case, as I held him and we kept bobbing and banging into the Terror before drifting astern of her, I had a chance to assay the damage. There was no doubt but that *Eagle* had placed a hole in the Terror — and not a small hole, either. In fact, water was gurgling in.

Like any good sailorman, I knew my duty and headed straight for the dock. Dropping sail, I did not hit the dock too hard, but at this point I couldn't have cared. I just threw my bow line around a cleat in the dock and, with Brookie racing beside me, ran for the house of the owner of the Terror.

He himself came to the door. "Oh, hello, Clippie," he said genially, using my childhood nickname, "and Brookie too," he said, giving him a pat. "Why don't you come in and have a cold drink?" And, he added, "I'll see that James gets Brookie some water." I told him quickly that I wasn't thirsty, and neither was Brookie, but I had to talk to him about something that was the matter. He patted me on the head. "Oh, that can wait, Clippie," he said. I told him it couldn't wait, and while he was telling James about the drink, I blurted out that I had put a hole in his boat. Even that didn't seem to concern him. "Oh, don't you worry," he said. "I'll tell my man, and he'll fix it in the morning. Here, sit down." This time I did more than blurt. "Sir," I said, "it can't wait. Your boat is sinking!"

At this he ran to the window and looked out at the Terror, which, by this time, was indeed, if not actually sinking, at least listing very badly to port. "God!" he said, ignoring me and running for the dock. At this moment James, having brought some water for Brookie and put it on the porch, handed me some orange pop. Frankly, though, I wasn't all that thirsty, and neither was Brookie. Brookie knew when something was the matter, and the dream never gave him credit for that any more than it gave credit to me.

The fourth part of the dream was just as inaccurate as the rest of it, but this time they went too far. They showed Brookie and me on Death Row, and the reason we were there, apparently, was we had both been convicted of murder. And the person we were supposed to have murdered was, of all people, our governess.

Again, the dream didn't give any background to the whole thing. I hadn't murdered the governess — all I had done was to try to put her out of commission. The background was very important. What had happened was that my parents had decided, after our last governess had left, to get a new governess. My brother and I could not abide the decision. Governesses, we felt, were all very well for sissies, and even for my sister — she was four — but for two grown men of eight and three-quarters, which I was, and eleven and a quarter, which my brother was, it was an insult.

The way my parents went about getting a new governess was to interview them in the living room, and so, after my brother and I held what we called a Council of War, my brother decided that what we had to do first was to send a reconnaissance party down the stairs, close to the living room, where we could hear the new governess being interviewed. "We've got to listen for Achilles' heels," my brother told me sternly. "They've all got Achilles' heels. All we have to do is find them."

I didn't know what an Achilles' heel was, but I felt that if I could get the governess running, and I had Brookie with me, I could sic Brookie on her because he loved to run after people and nip at their heels. If the governess had a bad one, I figured, Brookie, with a little practice, could at least make it worse.

Anyway, our war plans worked out perfectly with the first two governesses. One left after one day. We had learned from our reconnaissance that she was afraid of dogs, so what we did was to tell her she ought to stay away from Brookie, because he didn't like women, and he'd been a War Dog. The second governess took us longer. She didn't mind Brookie, but she told my parents while she didn't mind working in the daytime, she wanted her nights to herself and didn't want us bothering her. Our war plan for this one involved a friend of ours named Joe Burnett, who had had a disagreement with his family and had decided to run away. He was going west, my brother explained to me, and he was going to have to live off the land but he was going to stop at our house first and it would be up to us to provision him.

Even though it was a long way from Southborough, Joe's home, to our house in Milton, Joe was going to be there very early in the morning, and if we weren't up yet, he was to throw a pebble at our window to wake us. What my brother, who was very versatile in his war planning — he would later become Deputy Director of the C.I.A. — decided to do was instead of telling Joe which window was ours, to give him directions to the governess' window.

The plan worked beautifully. My brother hadn't overlooked a single detail — he had found out, for example, that the governess was a very sound sleeper — and, just as he figured, when Joe got tired of throwing pebble after pebble with no one waking up, he finally threw a rock. Right through the governess' window, too. And though sadly it was very bad for Joe's escape, because our family called his family, it was perfect for us. That governess was out of the house by noon. It was all careful planning, my brother explained to me, and having Right on your side.

The third governess, though, was a tough one. She was English, and her name was Miss Quince, and she didn't seem to have any Achilles' heel at all. She didn't even dislike Brookie. Indeed, the only thing Miss Quince did really dislike, we learned from our reconnaissance, was playing games. And, though hour after hour we Parcheesied her and dominoed her and mah-jongged her and chessed and checkered, and even croqueted her, it did no good. But again, to get back to that dream, that Brookie and I had killed her and that's why we were on Death Row, was just plain absurd. What actually happened was that late one afternoon, just before supper, my brother and I were playing croquet with Miss Quince, and I had just knocked her ball into the bushes and had two shots for the last two wickets on the stake. At that moment — Miss Quince was really a very poor sport — she suddenly announced it was suppertime and the game was over. All I did was tell her what I thought of her decision, when she started running at me, and that was when I took my mallet — we had just gotten nice new ones, with heavy heads — and swung it around my head, and let fly at her. I didn't aim for her head at all — what I was aiming for was her Achilles' heel, but since she was coming at me I could hardly have been expected to hit it. Anyway, my mallet kind of whirled around, with its heavy head making it pick up speed, and where I hit her was just below the knees. She went down like a stone. She just stayed there, too, face down, right in the way of my wicket. My brother and Brookie reached her first. My brother just looked at her for what seemed an awful long time. "I think," he said matter-of-factly, "you've killed her."

Well, I hadn't, of course. The dream just blew the whole thing out of proportion and it totally ignored the all-important fact of the whole matter — that Miss Quince may have lost the battle, but my brother and I had won the war. Miss Quince left the next morning, and my parents decided that they would just get a governess for my sister — that my brother and I were really too old for governesses. All right, on the short side of the whole thing I did get the worst spanking I ever had, but that was a whole lot better than being executed. And as for Brookie going to be executed, as the dream had it, that would have been a terrible miscarriage of justice. While my brother and I just looked at Miss Quince when she was down, it was Brookie who dug around and tried to find her face.

And that was what finally got Miss Quince up. As I said, she didn't dislike Brookie, but she didn't much like his idea of artificial respiration.

The finale of the dream was really the worst part of all. This time, once again Brookie and I were going to be executed — the writers of those dreams must have had sequels on their brains. But this time, if you please, we were being executed in front of a whole firing line of nuns. They were all dressed in black, and one of them was coming up to us with two handkerchiefs to tie around our eyes.

The dream had it that she tied those handkerchiefs, too — which was absolute nonsense. In a spot like that, neither Brookie nor I would have ever accepted those handkerchiefs. We would have just shaken our heads with sardonic smiles the way we'd seen the hero in *Beau Geste* and lots of other movies do it, and then we would have looked the firing squad right in their eyes.

And, once more, they missed the whole background and the whole real conflict. The problem was that this dream occurred at my first school, the Brush Hill School, one which was not only right near my house — that was why Brookie was always down there — but it was also right near a convent. And that was the problem — the nuns were always complaining about the noise we made at recess. The whole thing came to a head one day in our regular game of prisoner's base. Brookie and I had just made a heroic dash down to our prisoners without being tagged — which meant we had rescued them as they were reaching out, hand to hand from the goal line, and we had brought our team dead even. Then suddenly there was this Mother Superior and those nuns talking to our recess teacher, and the next thing I knew the recess teacher was telling us the game was over.

Of course, the dream didn't go into any of that. And, re-member, it was now a tied ball game. I'm not talking extra innings here, mind you, I'm talking a flat-out tie in reg-ulation time with two minutes left on the clock before the end of recess. And they had the gall to call the game over.

All right, our side had made some noise, but so had the other side. What are you supposed to do in a close game like that — take the Vow of Silence? Anyway, since I was the captain of my team, it was up to me to lodge a protest. The other captain, as I recall, didn't do a damn thing. Whether he was a very religious person or just some idiot who was satisfied with a tie, I don't remember. In any case, in no time at all Brookie and I were surrounded by nuns and Brookie was barking — no dog likes being sur-rounded by people in black — and I was giving my side of the whole thing, but before I could even marshal my arguments, the next thing I knew we were in Miss Pitts' office — the Mother Superior and all the nuns and every-body except Brookie. They wouldn't let Brookie in.

It really was a kangaroo court in there, and that dream was just as kangaroo as they come. It had terrible writers, too, because they let a great character slip right through their fingers. That character was Miss Pitts, the head of the school. Man and boy, I've known my share of for-midable women in my time, but I'll tell you here and now I've never known one of them who could hold a candle — if you'll pardon the expression in this particular situa-tion — to Miss Pitts. I don't want to make personal re-marks, but I'll tell you Miss Pitts' breastworks would have made the Army Corps of Engineers want to get into some other line of work. And, when she looked down at you over them and through her glasses, which she wore 'way down over her nose with long black tapes around her neck, she was really terrifying. You felt awful small in front of her — many's the time I saw even Brookie look like a Chihuahua.

But Miss Pitts should have been ashamed of herself, the way she conducted that trial. She believed anything and everything the Mother Superior and those nuns said and wouldn't take my word for anything — even when I asked her, as politely as possible, who the hell's field they thought it was. They also said, not counting that time, that I'd taken the Lord's name in vain nine times. I didn't argue about that. All I argued was that it shouldn't have been in vain — that of all times in life when you needed to appeal to a Higher Authority, certainly one of them was when you'd had a rotten decision called on you for no reason at all. Remember, in those days there was no such thing as Instant Replay. The final straw was when one of the nuns said I had said something about kissing her. I never said a word about kissing her — all I said was that a tie was like kissing your sister, and of course I meant your sister sister, not a nun sister.

I was ten, as I recall, when it all happened. And I certainly learned then there are times when there is no justice in the world. But the whole execution thing in the dream was, as I say, just ridiculous. I do know, though, where they got that handkerchief idea from. They got that because Miss Pitts decided my punishment would be that every single day before recess I would have to go to her office and she would tie a handkerchief around my mouth and I would have to wear it every day until Christmas.

But the point is, it was never over my eyes. And I really didn't mind it over my mouth once I got used to it. It made it a little difficult for me to give commands to my team, but they soon learned to come up close, which I particularly didn't mind when they were girls. Actually what I told everybody — and particularly the girls — was that I had a very sensitive mouth and I wasn't supposed to let the cold weather get on it. I didn't do it for sympathy or to be a hero or anything like that. I did it because I wasn't going to let Miss Pitts or that Mother Superior or those nuns walk all over me.

As I woke up, I seemed to be pushing something away from my eyes or my mouth, I don't remember which. In any case, I looked around and saw Polar Bear still obviously pawing at the door. For a while I just lay there wondering how long he'd been doing it — I had heard you can dream incredibly long dreams in an extraordinarily short time. If so, this was at least one good thing about that dream. I certainly wouldn't have wanted to waste a lot of time on a dream that had blown as many opportunities as that one had.

At that moment Marian came in. She was very excited. It turned out that among the calls she had made about the sheep dog had been one to the Fund for Animals hotline, and the woman who owned the sheep dog had later called that line about her dog being lost, and Marian had called back, and now it was just a matter of time before the woman would come and get her dog.

Marian suggested she would stay with Polar Bear until the woman came, and why didn't I go in and say good-bye to the sheep dog? I thought it was a great idea, particularly after the dream had done so much injustice to sheep dogs. The only trouble was that, in the course of our Changing of the Guard, Polar Bear saw his opportunity and, in a flash, he was out the door, around the corner, and after the sheep dog. I rushed out there, but I knew he would reach the dog long before I did, and I was also sure that there would now be another *mano a mano* with no me to thwart the first *mano*.

But, amazingly, nothing like that happened. As Polar Bear charged toward him, the sheep dog merely raised a playful paw. At this, Polar Bear put on the brakes and slid to a stop. The sheep dog sighed and gave every indication of continuing his sleep. Polar Bear surveyed him crossly for only a brief moment, then with a sigh of his own — which I was sure he meant to appear resigned but which I actually think contained more than that — he turned around and snuggled, his back up against the stomach of the sheep dog, stretched out, and, to my astonishment, closed his eyes, and went to sleep too.

For a long time I just stood and watched them. Then, very quietly, I lay down beside them, and gently, so as not to wake them, I began patting them both at once. I thought about the wonderful times Brookie and I had had together, but I also thought how wonderful it was that Polar Bear should now decide to make friends with this sheep dog. I also made a firm resolution that sometime in the future I would once more have a dog like Brookie and a cat like Polar Bear. But I would get them both at the same time, or as near to it as possible, and have them grow up together.

As I watched them, both the sheep dog and Polar Bear were obviously in Dreamland. The sheep dog's paws started moving, and so did Polar Bear's. I just hoped they were having good dreams and that theirs at least weren't full of the kind of sloppy modern workmanship that ruined so many of mine. But of course I couldn't be sure. For all I knew their dreams, too, weren't what they were in the old days.

IV ∘ *On the Cusp*

There are three kind of door cats. There
are indoor cats and there are outdoor cats and there are
also indoor and outdoor cats. Indeed there is probably
every kind of door cat except shut door cats. I have never
yet met a cat who liked a shut door. Polar Bear dislikes
shut doors so much that I have even seen him start a two-
front war against both my closet doors at once. He won
the war too, of course, because I opened them knowing
full well what he wanted to do was see if there was any
new footwear in there which needed being whipped into
biting shape.

But, I digress. Of the three kinds of cats I mentioned,
Polar Bear is strictly an indoor cat. Except for forays to
his balcony and an occasional trip with me in his carrier
he stays indoors. Nonetheless I know, of course, that there
are also outdoor cats. By this I mean cats who are looked

after by people who feed them — cats who live outside and have only inside access to some barn or other shelter. I admire these cats and I also admire the people who look after them and, hopefully, get them neutered or spayed.

Besides indoor and outdoor cats, however, there is that other kind of cat I have mentioned — the cat who is both an indoor and outdoor cat. These are cats who basically live indoors but who go outdoors whenever they feel like it. I object to these indoor-and-outdoor cats — or rather I object to the people who have them, because they do not confine them in chicken-wired runs on the order of the balcony I had built for Polar Bear. All right, his balcony isn't the biggest balcony in the world, but neither is mine — and remember, he took half of that.

I object on two grounds to those of you who do not confine your cats. One is that they kill birds — yours and, worse still, your neighbors', people who, after all, are entirely entitled to like their birds as much as you like your cat. The second ground I object on is that the chances of your cat getting injured or killed either by automobile, dog, or other animal are not only good — they are, in your cat's lifetime, an odds-on bet.

People have written me that my chicken-wire-run idea is too confining for the cat. My answer is that it does not need to be — it can be a long and interesting run and even include a tree or two. Indeed, it can be anything you want it to be as long as your cat can't get out any way but the same way he got in — the best way being a swinging door to your kitchen. The important thing is that not only are your birds and your neighbors' birds safe, so is your cat or cats. And again, not only from automobile, dog, or other animal but also from disappearance. This can be just as bad as the other fates which befall your cat, because you will, in all probability, never know what happened to him. All you can do is guess and hope — and, once more, your hope is a long shot. Barbara Diamond, in *Cat Fancy* magazine, printed the stark statistics. She put the average life of the indoor cat at twelve to fifteen years, the average life of the outdoor cat at two to three years.

Which brings me to another point — the matter of declawing. On this I am as adamant as I am about the indoor-outdoor matter. Cats should not be declawed, period — end of argument. I know there are veterinarians who maintain that, if they do not declaw the cat as the owner wishes, the owner will "get rid of it" — my very least favorite expression — and therefore they do it. My answer to this is they should not do it. They should keep the cat, and get a home for it and get rid of the owner.

I say this even about cats who, people will tell you, never go out and therefore seemingly have no need of their defenses — i.e., their claws. But the fact is there is always the chance your cat will get out. Maybe it is not a very good chance, but it is there all the same — the ill-opportuned opened door, the ill-screened window, the carrying case which flew open, or that automobile trip when you stopped and someone got out the door and so, unnoticed, did the cat. Your cat may even get out, ironically, at your vet's. And, when and if one of these occasions happens, your cat is not just virtually defenseless, your cat is hopelessly so.

I say this knowing full well cats are destructive of furniture. All the scratching posts ever produced and all the remedies ever devised to stop cats scratching to the contrary notwithstanding, sooner or later your cat will scratch your furniture. You can cut his nails, even his back nails, to your heart's content and even to his hissing discontent, but some day, some night, he will have a go at your favorite antique.

But do you then declaw him? Of course you don't. You don't even punish him. Punishment not administered at the moment, and most of the time even then, is, with a cat, not an option. Instead you should just stop and think one thought — is that piece of furniture or even all of your furniture put together as important as your cat?

The answer is, of course, a simple one. And, in my case, therein, as they say, hangs a tale. This tale, as you have probably already guessed, was about Polar Bear having a go at my own favorite piece of furniture. It is, or rather was, a beautiful chess table which was sold to me by an antiques dealer in Charleston, South Carolina. It also was, or at least so the dealer assured me, the chess table owned by that late great Confederate, Robert E. Lee.

In any case it is a table so important to me that I do not ever use it for play with my regular chess friends — the kind who might spill something on it or, worse still, burn it with a cigarette. I use it only when I am by myself, working out some chess problems. From the beginning, however, Polar Bear never understood how important to me this table is — I think he is a Yankee at heart. And, one day, as I was working out a chess problem, he leaped upon the table and skidded — i.e., dug — his way to a stop. I looked at the table in horror. I do not know how many of you remember, in the good old days of marble-playing how, if you didn't yell "No Roman Roadsies" before your opponent yelled "Roman Roadsies" — well, your opponent dug a road all the way to the hole. In this case Polar Bear had dug a Roman Roadsie in Robert E.

Lee's chess table. But did I do anything about it? Of course not — I did nothing.

Actually I am not being entirely accurate when I say I did nothing about it. What I did was think about something — about the time when I too had been in a somewhat similar situation to Polar Bear's at that particular moment. It all happened many years ago when I was visiting in Scottsdale, Arizona, at the home of the father of Miss Nancy Davis.

I had met Miss Davis in the early fifties at a time before she had met Mr. Ronald Reagan. She was at that time an actress living in New York and was a close friend of the late Betsy Barton, a writer friend of mine of whom I was very fond. Miss Davis and I started seeing each other from time to time, and one day after the publication of my second book I chanced to mention to her that I was about to go on a book tour. Immediately she wanted to know if I was going to Arizona. I said yes, as a matter of fact I was. She wanted to know if I would be in Phoenix. I consulted my schedule — I told her I would indeed be in Phoenix. And, as a matter of fact, for a weekend. "Well then," she said, "you'll have to stay at my father's house. He has a home in Scottsdale."

The very next day Miss Davis called, told me she had called her father, and said that, although he could only see me on Friday night — he had to go back to Chicago that weekend — he had insisted that I come and stay the whole weekend because the maid and cook would be there and they would have nothing to do and the house would be mine. In vain I protested all the trouble she and her father were going through, but she would not hear of it. Her father, she said, was looking forward to it.

I had never met her father, although I knew he was an

extremely eminent neurologist who had, among other achievements, raised millions of dollars for his Northwestern University Medical School. When I arrived at his house late Friday afternoon, he himself met me at the door, and I could see immediately that he was an exceptionally formidable fellow. Nonetheless he greeted me cordially and, as we talked about his daughter, he not only introduced me to what he said would be my room but also took the trouble to show me the rest of the house. Although Scottsdale would later become one of the nation's most fashionable suburbs, in those days it was just a relatively simple place out in the desert. The Davis home, however, was far from simple. Indeed, as one of the showplaces of Scottsdale, it was both luxuriously furnished and also had an extraordinary collection of both fine art and antique furniture. Dr. Davis was particularly proud of the desk in the den — one which he told me had once belonged, as I recall, to Alexander Hamilton.

Over cocktails I soon learned that Dr. Davis himself also seemed to belong to Alexander Hamilton — at least as far as his politics were concerned. And by dinnertime our conversation had begun to flag. Indeed, before the soup course was concluded, I had the distinct impression that, as a dinner partner, to interest Dr. Davis for very long, I was neither bright enough, successful enough, famous enough, rich enough, nor Republican enough. Suffice it to say that in ensuing years I was not in the least surprised when Dr. Davis would join a group of Californians in the inner circle of the country's right-wing conservatives. During that dinner, however, I remember that he seemed to have much curiosity about my relations with his daughter — relations which, he seemed very relieved to find, had not progressed to the point at which he surely would have become exercised. Indeed, before retiring, he bid me both a cordial good night and also what seemed a rather final good-bye, explaining that he would be leaving early the next morning but that I was to enjoy myself and that the maid and cook would be at my disposal.

Accordingly, when I arose the next morning I immediately headed for the kitchen. Here the maid informed me that Dr. Davis always took his breakfast in the den, and would I like to do that also? I said that would be fine and, in short order, she brought me a tray. In short order, too, I fell to the fine breakfast. I also began, however, to make some phone calls which the publisher had instructed me to make, and soon there were incoming calls as well. Altogether, accepting and turning down engagements, I was in the midst of that brief period of celebrity that authors on book tours enjoy to the fullest. And, meanwhile, with the pressure and excitement of it all, I was smoking like a well-fired chimney.

All of a sudden, after finishing a phone call and starting to light up another cigarette, I noticed that my previous cigarette, which I had totally forgotten, had missed the ashtray. It had also missed the breakfast tray. It had not, however, missed Alexander Hamilton's desk. It was not a minor burn, either — it was a Roman Roadsie.

For a long moment I just stared at it in horror. At that moment the maid appeared with more coffee. As she approached, I had only one option. This was to drop head down with my arms extended over the charred battlefield. "Oh, Mr. Amory," she said, "you must be so tired — all those calls." Without moving from my position, and trying to look as weary as it was possible to do at that early morning hour, I nodded wanly. I told her it wasn't easy being on a book tour — it was really exhausting.

After the maid had gone, I worked on other options. I could, of course, summon the maid and admit what I had done, but she was not a young maid and I feared a possible stroke. I could also have covered the whole thing up, stayed over until Dr. Davis returned on Monday morning, brought myself to my full height, and said, "Sir, I have something terrible to report. I have burned a furrow in Alexander Hamilton's desk. I am terribly sorry, sir. I shall of course pay every cent of the repairs."

I did not even consider this option. Dr. Davis was not the sort of man to whom you could say such a thing. He would have only one answer, which would have been to summon his chauffeur, march me out to the desert, and shoot me. There was actually only one possible option — somehow to get the desk repaired before the return of Dr. Davis. But this demanded getting rid of the maid and the cook. Bravely, first once more assuming my supine position, I summoned both of them. I told them that I was going to be away all that day and probably all Sunday too and they should take those days off. I wouldn't need them back until Monday. Immediately they protested that they could not do that, that Dr. Davis had instructed them to take care of me. I argued with them. I told them that it was absurd for them just to stay there and sit around when I would not even be there.

Our discussion went on and on, but finally they agreed, saying they would be back first thing Monday morning. Please not the first thing, I entreated. I might be coming in very late Sunday night, and I would like to sleep Monday morning. I told them I would be terribly tired by then — even more tired than they could see I was now. Nonetheless, no matter what I tried, the very latest I could get them to agree to appearing was Monday at 9 A.M.

The moment I heard their car go out the driveway, I grabbed the Yellow Pages. I tried Furniture Repair after Furniture Repair. There was no answer after no answer — it was, after all, Saturday morning. Finally I found one that was open. I have a desk here, I said as casually as I could, which I saw seemed to need a small repair. They asked me to explain. "Sounds to me," they said, "as if we'll have to sand it down and refinish the whole top." I said they could do whatever they had to do, but they had to have it look as close as they could to the way it was before. "OK," they said, "we'll pick it up Monday and have it back within the week." I told them they didn't get the picture at all. They would have to pick it up today, I said, and return it on Monday. Early Monday, I emphasized. Very early Monday. Crack of dawn Monday. "Two overtime days?" they exclaimed. "Do you have any idea what kind of money the boss would be talking?" I told them money was no object. I did not even haggle, although the price we finally agreed upon would have allowed me a weekend penthouse at the Arizona Biltmore. A condemned man in the desert does not haggle with the proprietors of an oasis.

The moment I put the phone down I made an exact diagram of everything on the desk. I then placed each item, carefully marked, on another table. When I had finished, sure enough I heard a truck in the driveway, and two large men arrived to pick up the desk. Before one of them started to pick up his end, however, he whistled. "Whew," he said, "what we've got here, Sam, is a torch job." I ignored this but made them promise, torch job or no torch job, dead or alive, the desk had to be back by the crack of dawn Monday. They looked on their order slip. "Right," they said.

Furniture Repair was as good as its word. Literally at dawn Monday, the same men in the same truck chugged up with the desk. I looked at it carefully. The furrow was not only no longer visible to the naked eye; it would not have been visible to Dr. Davis even with a neurological X-ray eye. What had obviously been done was that the whole top of the desk had been reduced by the exact size of the furrow. But the matching and coloring were really remarkable. By the time the maid and the cook appeared, I was sitting behind the desk with every item as it was. The maid asked me if I would like breakfast. I told her indeed I would — a large one. She noticed that I did not have an ashtray. "I'll get you one," she said. I shook my head. I told her I'd given up smoking, and she should, too — she might burn something if she wasn't careful.

Ever since then I've watched the career of Miss Davis with keen interest. I am always saddened when a woman I once dated sees fit to be so unwise as to settle for a secondary choice as marriage partner rather than me, and I often think how sad it is that in later years they are consigned to live to regret their ill-considered decision. When I read about Mrs. Reagan going on to be first First Lady of California and then First Lady of the Country, I had to admit that, under the circumstances, she'd done as well as could be expected for someone not at that time farseeing enough to see the possibilities in me. Often as I read about her, however, and particularly after Dr. Davis's death, my thoughts kept returning to Alexander Hamilton's desk. Did it go back to Chicago with the Davis family there? Or did it go with the Reagans to their ranch in San Ysidro? Or did the desk stay with them all the time and go first to Sacramento and then to the White House and finally to Bel Air?

Wherever it went, I often thought about someday having a chance to see it again — at which time I would tell Mrs. Reagan the truth about it. Not the whole truth, mind you — Mrs. Reagan is too much like her father for that — or even nothing but the truth. Rather I would choose to tell her just some of the truth. Something casual, say, like Mrs. Reagan, you certainly have a beautiful desk there, but, frankly, I know furniture and I think I should tell you that I just don't believe the top of that desk is the original top.

For years, as I say, I have wanted to do that and finally I thought the time had come when, a few years ago, I was asked by Walter Anderson, the editor of *Parade*, to go to Washington and interview Mrs. Reagan. I accepted with extraordinary alacrity. At last, I thought, I would have my chance to speak my piece to her about — well, the piece. The interview took place, too, but somehow, what with one thing and another, I never got the chance to do what I had set out to do. It was not that Mrs. Reagan was short with me. She was not — in fact, I was granted a full hour. But what I had envisioned — some airy persiflage and then a casual walk around the rooms until I spotted Alexander Hamilton's desk — never came to pass. It did not even come close to pass. Throughout the interview I was not only not alone with Mrs. Reagan but in the additional company of two of her secretaries as well as a Secret Service man and a stenographer who took down every word either she or I said, not to mention a video cameraman. When I quietly asked him what he was there for, he did not answer. The stenographer, however, quickly and quietly explained to me that he was there so that if, for example, I wrote that Mrs. Reagan had laughed and she had not, they would then have evidence of my error. Altogether, to have suggested a short stroll in search of a piece of missing furniture in such surroundings would have taken the kind of nerve which, against the Davis family, either *père* or *fille,* I just never seemed able to muster. It would have taken, I guess, a trained actor, which probably explains why she chose Mr. Reagan.

After the interview was over, reluctantly I realized that my great opportunity had come and gone and I had been found wanting. There was no question but that I had failed. Nonetheless, I simply could not go to my final reward with the secret of Alexander Hamilton's desk locked away forever. Before I left the White House I stopped at the desk of Mrs. Reagan's secretary and told her the story. Would she, I asked her, when she had the chance, please tell Mrs. Reagan the story and would she also mind asking her where the desk was now? The secretary agreed. And, in a few days I had a letter from her. "In regard to the Scottsdale story," she wrote, "Mrs. Reagan has asked me to inform you that she has no recollection of such a desk being in that room."

No recollection! Could it be possible, I wondered, that I had dreamed the whole thing and that it was just one more dream I had had which, like so many of the others, needed more work? Or, on the other hand, could it be true and was Mrs. Reagan unwilling to admit that one of her priceless antiques was ersatz? Or, for a third possibility, could she have consulted one of her astrologers, and had the astrologer told her to give me that answer? Or, for a fourth and final possibility, could I have uncovered still another White House cover-up — one in which the desk had been destroyed but no one would admit the fact? I finally decided that this was my favorite answer to the riddle, but somehow, deep down inside, I sincerely hoped the whole affair would not end up in court. I just could not picture Nancy Reagan having to testify, like Fawn Hall, that she had shredded Alexander Hamilton's desk.

I was not thinking of Alexander Hamilton's desk when I received one of the most curious letters from my first book about Polar Bear. I was, however, thinking about Mrs. Reagan, if for no other reason than that the letter concerned astrology — a subject of which Mrs. Reagan was not only perhaps the country's most famous devotee, but also one in which she saw fit to devote the whole first chapter of her latest memoir. In any case, the subject of the letter I received was that I should see to it that Polar Bear had his horoscope done. The woman who wrote the letter obviously knew not only a great deal about astrology but also a good deal about the character of Polar Bear. She suggested in fact that if Polar Bear did not like his horoscope being done by an outsider, I could do it myself. There were many books about cat astrology which could help me.

Frankly, before I got that letter, I didn't know there was such a thing as cat astrology and I certainly didn't know there were many books about it. As a matter of fact, despite my relationship with Mrs. Reagan, I didn't know much about astrology, period. It was true, of course, that there are people in the Fund for Animals offices, as I guess there are in most offices, who talk a lot about astrology and ask their friends what sign they are and so forth, but, as I think I had mentioned previously, I am not very big on things like that and indeed am on the small side with most ologies which have to do with making decisions, romances, and other problems. We Bostonians just don't seem to have problems like that. We just have problems with other people.

Actually one of the problems I had with other people was with a young lady in the Fund's New York office. She was a very strong believer in astrology. One day she announced to us that she had cast her own horoscope, and she also parted with the information that she would have to leave us. The horoscope, she said, clearly indicated that the best place for her to live would be in Oregon. We were trying to work out the possiblity of transferring her to Roger and Cathy Anunsen's Fund for Animals office in Oregon when, not long after, she informed us that she had decided not to move there after all. She told us that she had done another horoscope, and this one had produced the information that Oregon, as well as California — and indeed everything west of the Mississippi — was going to fall into the sea. She had, therefore, decided to stay with us in New York. It is not easy nowadays, as I believe I've said before, to get good help.

The experience, however, had left me somewhat soured on the subject of astrology, and I had put off the matter of answering the woman who wanted me to have Polar Bear's horoscope done. Finally, though, I bit the bullet. Indeed, I had already planned a letter in which I proposed to tell the woman that as for her having doubts about an outsider doing the job, she could not have been more right — I had never yet found anything Polar Bear liked an outsider doing except going away. As for my being able to do the job, I also proposed to tell her that in this she could not have been more wrong. I had never understood astrology even when people took extreme patience trying to explain it to me.

In the middle of putting off writing this letter, however, I received a call from the woman. I told her I was sorry that I had not answered her letter sooner and then explained what I was going to say. "I told you," the woman said sternly, "there are many books. You don't have to know the first thing about astrology yourself."

That made me cross. I do not feel I know everything, but I do feel I know the first thing about everything. As a matter of fact, most writers know the first thing about everything — the trouble comes when they have to go on to the second thing. In any case, to prove my point, I told her I very well knew that the first thing I would have to know to do Polar Bear's horoscope would be the exact date and time of his birth. I informed her that even the vet couldn't pin down the date of his birth within three years and, as for the time of it, we didn't have the faintest idea. He had been, after all, a stray.

Nonetheless, the woman persisted. "You don't have to know the exact date or time of birth," she said. "You'll see — just go get yourself some of the cat astrology books I mentioned." She paused — I had already learned she was a very meaningful pause woman. "And while you're at it," she continued, "you might pick up a couple of astrology books for yourself. Honestly, I think they might help you."

I ignored what she was irritatingly implying, but I couldn't stop her. "I've looked you up," she went on, "and you're a Virgo. I also know that your birthday is September second. The thing I don't know is what time you were born." Two A.M., I said. She wanted to know what authority I had for that. I told her my mother was the authority because I had asked her. I did not tell the woman that it was also because this was not the first call I had had on the subject.

"Aha," she said. I didn't like the sound of that because I was pretty sure what was coming next. "What year was it?" she asked. I pretended I hadn't heard her, but it did no good. "Aha," she said again, "remember, I can find out. They did you last year on your birthday on the radio and they said what year you were." I told her that if they did, they were wrong, and if they did it last year they were wrong by a year — which by my count was at least two years wrong now.

That at least stopped her. Just the same, after her letter and her telephone call I was intrigued enough by the idea of there being books about cat astrology that I decided the very next morning to go out and get some. And, because I was right there in the bookstore, I also picked up some people astrology books. I did not do so, I wish to make it clear, because the woman had told me to. I did it only because I had made up my mind that the next time that woman or somebody like her called they'd soon find out they didn't have an amateur on the other end of the line — they'd have Yours Truly.

That very afternoon, in fact, I turned to one of the people astrology books I had picked out. It was called *Sun Signs,* by Linda Goodman. I turned first to the list of "Famous Virgo Personalities":

Prince Albert	Lyndon Johnson
Lauren Bacall	Elia Kazan
Robert Benchley	Joseph P. Kennedy
Ingrid Bergman	Lafayette
Leonard Bernstein	D. H. Lawrence
Sid Caesar	Sophia Loren
Maurice Chevalier	H. L. Mencken
Theodore Dreiser	Walter Reuther
Queen Elizabeth I	Cardinal Richelieu
Henry Ford II	Peter Sellers
Greta Garbo	Robert Taft

Arthur Godfrey   William Howard Taft
Goethe   Roy Wilkins
John Gunther

Actually, I didn't think much of that list, not just because I wasn't on it — I could see the list wasn't up-to-date — but also because, as far as I could see, there was only one well-known cat person in the whole lot. And that one, after all, was Cardinal Richelieu — a man who certainly was a big cat person in France but was a pretty tough baby in other ways. Nonetheless, I plowed on — into a chapter, apparently written for women, called "The Virgo Man":

> We may as well get this out into the open right away — don't pin your hopes on a Virgo man if your heart is hungry for romantic dreams and fairy tales, or you'll find yourself on a starvation diet. . . . A pleasure-seeking, self-ish, mentally lazy woman will never make it with a Virgo man, even if she's fairly oozing with sex appeal. This is the very last man in the world you can expect to find running off with a Go-go girl, though he might loan her his sweater if she's chilly.

That really infuriated me. It was, I felt, close to libelous on all us good Virgos. And what about Joseph P. Kennedy, for Pete's sake? Can you picture him loaning a topless Go-go girl a sweater? At any rate I decided at this point to give up *Sun Signs* and have a go at a book called *Moon Signs*, by Donna Cunningham. "This book," said the introduction, "with its Moon Sign tables and Moon descriptions, can help you prevent lunar burnout and keep you from baying at the Full Moon."

Frankly, I didn't see how I could have lunar burnout when I'd just started on the damn subject, and I couldn't imagine either Polar Bear or myself going around baying at the Full Moon, but I doggedly kept on. And, I soon learned, it was not just a question of baying at the Full Moon, it was meditating on it — indeed, Polar Bear and I should apparently not just meditate on the Full Moon but on the New Moon as well. I didn't know what Polar Bear was to bay at or meditate on, because after all I didn't yet have a sign for him, but what was evidently expected of me to do, as a Virgo, was what Ms. Cunningham described as "Meditations and Affirmations for the Lunations":

I AM COMPASSIONATE TOWARDS MYSELF AS WELL AS OTHERS.
I LET GO OF IMPOSSIBLE STANDARDS OF PERFECTION.

I saw no reason why I couldn't have a go at baying at that. Indeed I had already decided, when I started on this astrological exercise, that I wasn't going to try to set any impossible standards of perfection for myself, but neither was I going to give up easily. And so, with firm resolve, after *Sun Signs* and *Moon Signs* I went on to another of my books. This one was called *Astrological Guide for You in 1990*. It was by Sydney Omarr, but it had an introduction by Raymond Mungo, a man who in turn was introduced by Mr. Omarr as having "Pisces sun, Scorpio Moon and Cancer rising sign — a grand Water trine." Mr. Mungo, in his turn, was equally flattering about Sydney. "You've chosen your guide well," he wrote. "Omarr is Mr. Astrology to the world, perhaps the cosmos." Mr. Mungo warned us, however, not to try to bother Mr. Omarr in person. "Sydney Omarr's whereabouts," he wrote, "are not for public knowledge."

If Mr. Omarr was as tough on Virgos as some of the others, I could well understand why he was on the lam. But, however he felt about Virgos, I was relieved to find he had something nice to say about us in a chapter he had included by another astrologer, Marsha Rose Emery, Ph.D. The chapter was entitled "Your Erotic Nature in 1990," and I really don't know how I chanced on it — the book just seemed to open to it. In any case, Dr. Emery had this to say about us Virgos and — well, our nature:

> Anyone you allow to get close to you this year will find out that Virgo is anything but a puritanical virgin. . . . This year people see you as far more sexually dynamic than anyone could have realized from your outward conservative stance.

That was more like it, and I eagerly embraced more of Mr. Omarr — particularly what he had to say about what was going to happen to me in 1990. At that time, he had done my whole 1990 month by month. For June, for example, he said, "Now is the time to dig in and deal with details. Read between the lines, if necessary."

That sure brought me up short. Reading between the lines is not an easy thing to do in your own book. Under August he said, "You'll pull strings from behind-the-scenes." Frankly I just don't think he had any idea how hard that would be for me to do with Marian and Polar Bear around. Nonetheless, under November he had good news: "One page of your life," he wrote, "is coming to an end while another more fulfilling chapter is beginning."

One thing I did hope — that it would be a more fulfilling chapter than this one had been so far. For the plain fact was, as far as getting Polar Bear's horoscope done, I wasn't getting anywhere. But that did not stop me. As I've always said, when the writing gets tough, the tough get writing. And some of us are not only tough but smart, too — smart enough to know that when we're not getting anywhere, we ought to get some help.

The help I got, through a friend's advice, was to call a woman named Robyn Ray — one who, my friend told me, was a consulting astrologer. Normally I'm a little leery about consulting consultants but in this case, astrology being a pretty leery subject to begin with, I decided to put my leeriness aside. I called Ms. Ray and asked her if we could do lunch. In New York, you will recall, we don't have lunch, we do lunch.

Ms. Ray was, it turned out, a charming woman — one who, before doing lunch with me, had been doing what she called a "power breakfast" with what she described as "a spiritual support group." I told her spiritual support was just what I needed at this stage, and I was sure we could really do a terrific power lunch. I also told her she seemed to me to be just what the doctor ordered. "It's funny you should say that," she said. "Nostradamus, you know, the most famous of all astro-predictors, was a doctor as well as an astrologer." She paused. "So were all doctors until just before the beginning of the seventeenth century — they were all astrologers as well as doctors. Nostradamus, in fact, avoided the Inquisition by writing his predictions in astrological terms. Otherwise he would have been accused of consorting with the Devil, and would have been executed."

I told her I would be careful to write my predictions in astrological terms, too. I knew there were millions of believers in astrology out there who might not execute me but they would certainly not take kindly to anyone making fun of them. Anyway, I next told Ms. Ray what my problem was, and I asked her if she had ever done such a thing as a cat horoscope. "No," Ms. Ray told me, smiling, "but I did do my dog's." How, I asked her nervously, did he like it? I reminded her Polar Bear was very critical. "He liked it fine," she said.

Relieved, I proceeded on to my difficulties about solving my problem — that I didn't know what year Polar Bear was born, let alone what time. Ms. Ray sighed. "You'll miss a lot," she said, "because you won't get the ascendant." It was my turn to sigh. I didn't want to admit I didn't know what an ascendant was. But I did tell her I was finding astrology very complicated in general and in particular I was getting pretty fed up with what they said about Virgos. "Don't get discouraged," Ms. Ray smiled, "Virgo is a sexy sign — particularly if you've got the moon and eight other planets affecting you."

I told her that was good news indeed and I would try to be on the lookout for the affections of any of those planets, and also would try to reciprocate them. I did mention, however, that I was concerned with reading lists of other Virgos — there seemed to be a lot of them, I said, with whom I didn't have anything in common. "Don't worry about that either," she said. "Other Virgos have different planets and different signs in different houses." Oh, I said. Finally I told her that I really didn't understand signs, or planets, or houses or even cusps. "Don't worry about cusps," she said; "they're just the edges. Remember it's not just the planetary influence on us — it's how we realize it. The problem most people have with astrology is that they think everything is predetermined, but it's not. That's my approach to astrology. I'm not taking responsibility for your own life away from you — you always have the choice. If somebody says something personal to you, you can either be insulted or you can take it in stride. For example, if an astrologer tells you that you seem to have a need to be destructive, you can handle this by going out and helping people tear down old buildings."

I told her that I had never thought of that, but New York was surely the right place for it. There were half a dozen buildings being torn down right on my block. I added that Polar Bear was pretty destructive around the apartment, but I didn't know how he'd be about going after a whole building. Ms. Ray smiled again. Then, gently, toward the end of our lunch, she explained to me that the astrology books I had been trying to read were too difficult for me at this stage of my astrological development. And, suspecting that that might be the case, she said she had brought along a book she thought I could handle. As we said good-bye she handed it to me.

The book was called *How to Learn Astrology*, by Marc Edmund Jones. And, later that very afternoon I started on it. The first thing I was relieved to find was that it was not a children's book — I had been a little nervous about that from what Ms. Ray had said. It was, however, a beginners' book — indeed, Mr. Jones mentioned beginners in his very second paragraph. Moving on for a moment, I went to see what he had to say about Virgos. "The symbol is the Virgin," he wrote, "represented by the 'M' of primitive matter, with an added stroke to suggest a chastity girdle."

A chastity girdle! Was there no limit to the insults to us Virgos? And even in a beginners' book! What if some child got ahold of it? How would you like to be a Virgo father and have to explain a thing like that to your child? Or, for that matter, how would you like to be a Virgo child asking your father what his "M" meant? Just the same, by this time pretty well inured to Virgos having to take so many slings and arrows of outrageous fortune, I just rose above what Mr. Jones had to say about us and went on trying to find out what "houses" and "planets" had to do with everything. "Most simply," Mr. Jones wrote, "a 'house' is a place where someone lives and in the horoscope it is a place where a planet, or group of planets, is located."

As I understood it, the planets were getting into our houses and the houses were getting into our signs, and that was why all Virgos, for example, weren't the same. But don't think for a moment there are just a couple of houses or anything like that — there are, apparently, twelve of them. Mr. Jones suggested that I learn each of their "fundamental meanings." The "First House," he explained, for example, had as its fundamental meaning "personality." The "Second House" had "resources and money," while the "Third House" had a whole slew of fundamental meanings, which he said were "Environment, Brethren, Communication and Short Trips." Yet not until the "Ninth House" did you get to "Understanding, Religion and Long Trips."

It really wasn't easy but I plowed on, because once I had those houses down pat, Mr. Jones suggested that I go on to the planets and what he called their "Simple Meaning." He had arranged these, he wrote, "in order of practical convenience":

Sun	Purpose
Moon	Feeling
Mars	Initiative
Venus	Acquisitiveness
Mercury	Mentality
Jupiter	Enthusiasm

Saturn	Sensitiveness
Uranus	Independence
Neptune	Obligation
Pluto	Obsession

Mr. Jones then proceeded from houses and planets to aspects and ascendants, conjunctions and oppositions, quadralures and sextiles, and even T-crosses and trines. If this was a book for beginners, I began to feel, Mr. Jones had the wrong boy. He stopped me, finally, on page 162:

> The beginner is learning to use an ephemeris and a Table of Houses without any necessity of mastering the mathematics behind them, and in the same fashion he can use the special type of logarithms prepared of astrological operations without need to concern himself over the mechanics of applying geometrical proportion to irregularities. He has been dealing on the one side with the daily or twenty-four hour motion of the planetary bodies, and on the other with the extent to which each planet must move to reach its horoscopic position. He has seen that the factor determining the latter is the time elapsing from midnight or noon of the ephemeris to the moment of birth, and by the simple device of adding the special logarithm of this lesser time span to the special logarithm of the zodiacal movement of a particular planet in a whole twenty-four hours he has the logarithm of the zodiacal span the planet in question must traverse to reach its horoscopic place.

For beginners, mind you. In the end, reluctantly, I had to say that astrology was just too tough for me. But I had not yet given up on it for Polar Bear. Polar Bear is tougher than I am — frankly, he's one tough cat — and remember, I hadn't yet tackled so much as one cat astrology book. But neither that nor the fact that I did not know what year Polar Bear was born, much less what time of day, did not now worry me. The main reason for this was that the more I read of astrology the more I realized that an awful lot of it is backward. East in astrology, for example, is west, and west is east. North is south, and south is north. Planets and houses don't move clockwise, they move counterclockwise. Indeed, the more I read the simple horoscopes in the astrology books, the more I realized that what the astrologers had really done was to take the lives of famous people, the details of which were well known, and then fit their signs and houses and planets and ascendants and all the rest of it into those already known facts — so this too was really backward.

If they could do all they did backward, I suddenly thought, in one of those flashes of inspiration for which I wish I were better known, why couldn't I? Maybe I too had another career ahead of me — after all, Nostradamus had been dead a long time and how many people are there out there who can name the No. 2 man in the field? Maybe also, of course, I wouldn't make it, but, whether I did it or not, I wasn't getting too far in my astrological studies going forward — I could hardly do any worse going in the opposite direction. One thing was certain. There and then I determined that was the way I would do Polar Bear's horoscope — with no holds barred and the Devil take the hindmost. I realized this was hardly an apt expression, considering the problem Nostradamus had with the Devil as well as the direction in which I was now determined to go, but my die was cast. I would start by taking Polar Bear's traits of character, both the good and the bad — I wanted, after all, a true astrological portrait, warts and all — and then I would go back and find out into which sign, with similiar character traits, he best fitted. And, in the end, I would know exactly what sign he was.

And, who knows? By the time I got to the ascendants and the aspects, conjunctions and oppositions, quadralures and sextiles, the T-crosses and the trines and even the cusps, I might be able to pinpoint the exact day and even the time he was born. Greenwich Mean Time, of course, is what I mean. Those astrology books give you not only Greenwich Mean Time but also Sidereal Time, and, frankly, at my age, I really didn't have the time, either Mean or Sidereal, for that kind of thing. That could be done, after all, by some child with a computer or something.

I had four books on cat astrology. And the very one I turned to first was easily the most remarkable — if for no other reason because it was written by a cat. It was called *Horoscopes for Pussycats,* and its author was a cat named Bootsie Campbell. The brief "About the Author" section told us that Ms., or for all I know Mrs., Campbell "had a father who was an all-white Maine Coon cat named Snowball," and a mother who was a "beautiful tortoise-shell." Bootsie herself, this section said, was "a Gemini." There was also a picture of the author which seemed to be taken front-on at night, and showed her looking out a window, deep in concentration, presumably at the stars.

I showed Bootsie's picture to Polar Bear, to which he gave his usual "so what" sniff. He really is very bad about other cats' pictures. This time, though, I did not let him get away with it. I pointed out to him in no unmistakable way that, while he was going around eating books, this Bootsie was writing them. I felt I did not have to add that, while I was hard at work doing all the writing of these books, what he was doing when he wasn't eating them was lying around living off the fat of the land from them.

The second book was called *The Cat Horoscope Book* and was written by a man named Henry Cole. He was described as "a nationally known astrologist." "Not only will this book," the jacket promised, "answer your most pressing problems, but it will also present you with a complete personality file on your cat based on privileged information."

This was particularly good news, because it would mean I would now have not just a complete personality file on Polar Bear but I would as well have one based on privileged information, which, if I could keep him from either digging around or prying into, I was determined to keep that way. I knew I had one thing going for me. In strong contrast to Bootsie, when Polar Bear went out on his balcony at night he was so interested in the pigeons that I would be willing to bet he didn't give the stars, let alone what they could be telling him, so much as a passing thought.

The third book was called *Cat Astrology*. This one was written by Mary Daniels, who was both a friend of mine and also a feature writer for the *Chicago Tribune*, as well as the author of a book about the cat Morris. Mrs. Daniels wrote in her introduction of a "chance encounter with a young Buddhist priest in a dark and dusty bookstore." She recounted the incident as follows:

> "Buddhists believe pets are in their last incarnation before becoming human and probably will reincarnate in their next life as humans; they are learning how to become more like people by associating with them.
> "All living things have karma (one's fate in one's

existence as determined by behavior in a previous)," continued the gentle Buddhist priest.

"Animals' perception of right and wrong is 'very dim,' " he added, "and their capacity for choice is less than ours. But if they respond to it properly, the general trend is upward."

Whether doing Polar Bear's horoscope, even if backward, would be an upward trend toward his perception of right and wrong I couldn't be sure. As for helping him on his way toward being a person in his next incarnation, I wasn't at all certain that that would be, for him, an upward step. I was, after all, as all faithful readers of my first book will recall, a Mark Twain man where this sort of thing was concerned. "If," said Mark, "Man could be crossed with a cat, it would improve Man but it would deteriorate the cat."

It was, in the introduction to my fourth cat astrology book — one called *Catsigns*, by William Fairchild, an English novelist and playwright — that I at last found something into which I could get my teeth. In fact here I found the first real backup I had yet had of my whole idea of doing Polar Bear's horoscope backward. I want you to remember, though, that I had the idea first, before I had read this. In any case, here's what Mr. Fairchild said on the subject:

> If you haven't the vaguest idea of his birthday, or, if he's a stray who's walked in without any identity papers and adopted you, just decide on his principal characteristic, find it under one of the Signs, and then read the rest of the information contained therein. If it doesn't check out for him it could be that he's been putting on an act to fool you, or that love has partially blinded you to his true strengths and weaknesses. Take a long cool look at him and try again. His Moon Sign won't tell you everything

about him. . . . It *will* tell you, however, a very great deal that you will *need* to know for your mutual wellbeing and accord. After you've read it once for yourself you might try reading it a second time to him.

I knew this wouldn't be easy. Polar Bear is hard enough to read to the first time, and frankly, I had never tried doing it a second time. But I did try it anyway. And, of course, it didn't work. For Polar Bear, nothing works when it's something that to him is too much like working.

One thing I did learn from Mr. Fairchild was his dos and don'ts about how to handle cats of different Moon Signs. If, for example, you cat was an Aries cat, his "do" was to develop a keen sense of humor; his "don't" was not to question his belief in his own brilliance. If, on the other hand, you had a Cancer cat, your "do" was to smile at your wife/husband when he's looking, and your "don't" was to be a martyr — one is enough, Mr. Fairchild said. If, on the third hand, you had a Leo cat, your "do" was to let him think he's on the throne, whereas your "don't" would be to let him treat you as a devoted subject. Finally, if your cat was a Sagittarius, your "do" was to realize he thinks he's a genius, and your "don't" was to admit you're not a genius.

I thought a lot about these suggestions as applied to Polar Bear, but, helpful as Mr. Fairchild was, the fact remained I still did not have Polar Bear's sign. Accordingly, I proceeded to put all four cat astrology books in a row. After that I took their comments on the characters of the different cat signs, and compared them sign by sign with what I knew of Polar Bear's character. It wouldn't be easy, I knew, but then, what about astrology was?

I decided to score Polar Bear sign by sign — on a 0 to 5 basis, and then the sign on which he scored the highest would be his. I started with Aries (birthdates March 22 to April 19) because I had learned by this time that astrology books never started with something like Capricorn (December 22 to January 19), which would coincide with the year as we know it. Instead they always started with Aries. Frankly, I had my suspicions that the reason they do this is that this way they include April Fools' Day, but, putting these suspicions aside, I went along with it.

Actually I found much unanimity of opinion on Aries cats. Mr. Cole, for example, called the Aries cat "the egoist of all felines. Don't," he advised, "try too hard to adapt your Arian to the human condition for he views humans as merely a means to an end — his own." That sounded like Polar Bear. Mrs. Daniels called the Aries cat the "Godfather" and the "boss cat," and pointed out that he was ruled by Mars, "the red planet of War." There was a lot of Polar Bear here, but what Mrs. Daniels said made me concerned about female Aries cats — of whom I had a nervous picture as Amazons. "This is the cat," she went on, "that heads unerringly toward the very guest who hates cats." Again, she was right on the money about Polar Bear. As for Mr. Fairchild, he declared that the Aries cat's habit of "continually fizzling out of great enterprises can be ascribed to the effect of the Moon (water) on the fire sign (Aries)." Finally, when it came to the cat Bootsie, she spoke directly to Arian cats. "Your heart is easily moved," she said, "although you don't show it quite so intensely." She also gave these cats some party advice. "Don't arch your back," she said, "and ignore guests."

That last and the boss cat idea, as well as several other points, made me at least consider Polar Bear as a possible Aries — in fact, I was about to give him a 4 out of 5. But what stopped me in my tracks was the fact that Mr. Cole had called the Aries cat not only the "egoist of all felines," but also the "hippie of the cat kingdom." Polar Bear a hippie! The very thought was intolerable — he wasn't even a long-haired cat. Without further ado I scored Polar Bear only a 1 as an Aries.

Taurus (April 20 to May 20) was, according to Henry Cole, "the sign of the Bull — a naturally female sign" — something I found totally mind-stopping — but which he went on to say was "a fixed sign ruled by Venus." One thing was certain — that part of it, at least, ruled out Polar Bear. Nonetheless, when Mr. Cole went on to refer to the Taurian as a "hibernating bear," and a cat whose favorite sound was "the click of the refrigerator door," I wondered if my initial judgment had been too hasty. Mrs. Daniels went along with the refrigerator door and in fact called the Taurian a "gallumping gourmet. But," she continued, "if you're looking for an intellectual companion, quite frankly this is not the cat for you." This made me almost cross enough to give up the sign for Polar Bear — he is a terrific intellectual companion. However, when Mr. Fairchild said Taurians would "burrow into a blanket whenever the emotional climate became charged with tension," I reversed gears again. If there ever was a cat who hated any kind of climate being charged with tension more than Polar Bear, I have yet to meet him or her. He's really terrible about thunderstorms. Finally Bootsie had her direct advice: "Don't let unpleasant news of other pussy-cats," she said, "get you agitated and unsure of yourself." Frankly, it didn't seem to me that having unpleasant news of other cats would bother Polar Bear at all. What he would mind would be pleasant news of other cats. All in all, my final score for him as a Taurian was only 2 out of a possible 5.

Gemini (May 21 to June 20), the sign of the Twins, came next — one which Mr. Cole defined as a "somewhat masculine sign." At first I felt this sign might well be the one I was looking for — Polar Bear had, after all, been neutered — but Mr. Cole's next words were far from Polar Bear indeed. "The Gemini cat," he said, "will thrive in a houseful of creative people who are inveterate party-givers. He will then adopt your desk as his own and in his most ingratiating manner see to their every desire." Since Polar Bear's party behavior begins with a dawn attack on the caterer, and ends with an Achilles' heel charge on the last one to leave, I could hardly think of a more opposite description. Mrs. Daniels, on the other hand, piqued my interest with a reference to chess. "Your Taurian cat," she said, "will fall asleep while you play chess, while a Gemini cat would be right in there kibitzing, hardly able to contain his excitement, while patting with a paw the next piece you should move." Perfect as such a cat would be for me, I again had to admit it was not Polar Bear. His idea of excitement in a chess game is to knock the pieces off the board — something which, in a game in which you're ahead, would drive even a player in good health to an early grave. Mr. Fairchild said his Gemini cat entered his parties "on the heels of the first arrival and proceeded to stand about with an aristocratic air waiting to be introduced. . . . Eventually she made her departure along with a bunch of new friends and, as she went out of the front door, gave us a 'such-fun-do-hope-we-meet-again-soon' look." This was so far from Polar Bear I didn't even have the heart to think about it. As for Bootsie, she said flatly of Geminis, "You are of a dual nature. You are generous, just, changeful and fickle —

none may trust your love." I considered this, where Polar Bear was concerned, libelous and, combined with the party goings-on, I ended up giving him, for Gemini, a flat zero.

Of Cancer (June 21 to July 22), the Crab sign, Mr. Cole had this to say: "One minute a ball of fun, the next moody," and warned that your guests "might even find her sulking in the corner for no apparent reason, unapproachable, and even you whom she best knows could risk a handful of claw or, worse yet, a faceful of hiss." Upon reflection, thinking about Polar Bear and this assessment, I decided to take the Fifth — and by that I did not mean a 5. Cautiously I moved on to Mrs. Daniels. She called the Cancer a "Fraidy-Cat," and added that they had "a scuttling walk." I had to admit that, although Polar Bear was hardly a fraidy-cat, where things he was afraid of were concerned — things like thunderstorms, firecrackers, too much rain, and the vacuum cleaner — he did indeed scuttle with all four legs bent so low they barely kept his body from touching the floor. Mr. Fairchild told of the Cancerian cat's special look, the "see-how-I'm-suffering-but-far-be-it-for-me-to-complain" look. In extreme emergencies, he noted, "they will use its companion piece, the 'of-course-no-one-understands-me-I'm-just-a-cat' look." Polar Bear, I had to admit, was a master of both of these. Bootsie's advice to Cancer cats was also intriguing. "You must remain open minded," she said, "and allow others to influence you in the right directions." Once again, I liked the idea of trying that one on Polar Bear, but it was really a bit much to tell him to *remain* open-minded when, after all, the only open-mindedness I'd ever seen in him was over something about which he had not yet made up his mind. Nonetheless, Cancer came closer to him than any other sign I had studied so far, so I ended up giving him a 3.

Leo (July 23 to August 22), the sign of the Lion, looked at the start a good bet for Polar Bear — after all, what he looks like, second only to a bear, is a lion, and Henry Cole got the bet off to a good start. "All cats," he said, " 'own' their humans, but your Leo, of all cats, possesses them totally." And Mrs. Daniels added to the idea of this being Polar Bear's sign. "The Leo cat," she stated, "is the most catly of cats, felinity raised to its highest power." Mr. Fairchild, however, had a warning. "He's a big cat," he declared, "who does everything in a big way. Beware, though, of making promises you can't keep. He's also an idealist and if you once slip from the pedestal on which he's placed you, it will be a long time before you're able to reinstate yourself in his good books." If this wasn't right on target, I didn't know what was. But so was Bootsie, whose advice to Leo cats sounded as if it had been written for Polar Bear. "Don't be afraid," she wrote, "of thunder or lightning. Remember, you occasionally make loud, lonely, frightened sounds and frighten people too." There was no question in my mind but that Leo went even beyond Cancer for Polar Bear's possible sign. I gave it a 4.

I approached Virgo (August 23 to September 22), my own sign, with high hopes, not the least of which was that Mr. Fairchild had given the Virgo People's Sun Sign as one of the best suited for Virgo cats' moon sign. I decided to ignore that he had also included in this category Gemini, Leo, Capricorn, and Pisces. In any case, Henry Cole bolstered my hopes further. Moving by the fact that he said Virgo was "the sign of the Virgin, a naturally female sign," I moved right on to something else. "The

6th House of the Zodiac," he pointed out, "symbolizes 'I analyze,' " and if there was ever a cat who analyzed everything more than Polar Bear, I believe you would have to go into analysis yourself to find him or her. Even if I permitted him to chase mice, which of course I did not, I am sure he wouldn't have had to kill them — all he would have had to do would be to analyze them to death. Mr. Cole also went into Virgo's endless critical proclivities as well as their "fussbudgeting" and "worrywarting. While cats are creatures perfect unto themselves," he said, "your Virgo doesn't realize this; the major consequence being that she continually seeks a higher level of faultlessness." Ignoring the "she" here, I took a moment to bask in this praise for both of us. Mrs. Daniels pointed out that Virgo was ruled by the planet Mercury, which governs communication. I basked in this also. Both Polar Bear and I were terrific communicators. In fairness, I should point out that Mrs. Daniels did go into our fussiness and finickiness. "Alas," she wrote, "this is not one of the easiest signs with which to live." But how, I wanted to ask her, could it be otherwise? As I've always told the people I work with, it is never easy to live with someone who is always right.

Nonetheless, it remained for Mr. Fairchild to put the finishing touches on my placing Polar Bear in Virgo. "Your Virgo Cat," he said, "critical and choosy from birth, reserves the apogee of his suspicion for pills and will go to almost any lengths, including biting your finger, in order not to swallow one." That surely was Polar Bear all the way. And, if I needed a finale, I had it from Bootsie. "The pupils of your eyes," she said, "grow larger and larger at the sound of a pigeon." Not even the sight, mind you, just the sound.

There was no question but that I had achieved what I had set out to do — Virgo was Polar Bear's sign. I gave him a 5 on it, and refused even to look at the Libras, Scorpios, Sagittariuses, Capricorns, Aquarians, or Pisceses. Indeed all that was left now was for me to figure out his exact day of birth in Virgo. I know there are people out there who will say I just chose September 2 because that was my birthday, but they will be wrong. By now an expert in astrology, I did it in a way which I am sure would have made even Nostradamus proud. First I figured out that Polar Bear had to be nearer Leo, which was ruled by the Sun, the most powerful planet in the solar system, and one to which I had given a 4, than he was to Libra (September 24 to October 23), and Libra, for heaven's sake, was just one more of those damn signs ruled by a girl — again, the planet Venus, if you please, the planet of Beauty, and Love and Harmony. All right, I didn't mind her coming after Virgo, but sure not *in* it. Anyway I didn't need her, not with that fine Leo before Virgo. And, remember, I didn't ignore the cusps and the ascendants or the trines or anything else either. And it all came out September 2 — 2 A.M. September 2, to be precise.

Of course there will probably be a few of you out there who will want to know, besides the time and the date, the year. I am not going to tell you. Frankly, Polar Bear is just as sensitive about his age as the next man — and if that man happens to be me, I see no reason why I should go around blabbing it all over the place. If you want to write me about it, go ahead — it's a free country. But, I warn you, I am now a famous astrologer and, like Sydney Omarr's, my whereabouts are not public knowledge.

V ∘ *You Ought to Be in Pictures*

One of the most exciting pieces of news a writer can have about a book he has written is that it is going to be made into a movie. When this happened to my first book about Polar Bear, however, I did not get as excited as you might expect.

It is true that I harbored for a moment a passing dream, which I hoped would be well written, about a house in Bel Air and a swimming pool — in fact two swimming pools, one for me and one wired-in, like his balcony, for Polar Bear. But nothing elaborate, mind you, like having Perrier water in our pools or anything like that. In other words, swimming pools or no swimming pools, I kept my feet on the ground.

The reason I could not get more excited and that I kept my feet on the ground is a simple one. This is that, despite having heard that one or more of my books are going to be made into a play or a movie, I have a very poor track record of having it actually happen. Not that I haven't come close, I want you to know, but, at the end, no cigar.

On the very first day after the publication of my very second book, *The Last Resorts,* for example, I entered a friend's party and was quickly ushered to his television set. His set was not only on but was on with the then very popular Sunday night broadcast of none other than the late Walter Winchell — at that time the be-all and end-all of gossip columnists. Mr. Winchell's lead item that night was an announcement from Mr. Irving Berlin that Ethel Merman's next musical, with Mr. Berlin doing the music and lyrics, would be my book. Everybody congratulated me and treated me as if I was sum punkins — an expression you probably don't know but which would be good for you to look up in your dictionary. A word looked up, you know, is a word remembered. I looked it up, as a matter of fact, and it wasn't there. As I told you, dictionaries are written by children.

In any case, the very next morning, I had a telephone call from Mr. Berlin himself. He asked me if I had seen the broadcast, and, when I said that I had, he asked me if I would come to see him. I said of course I would, after which he explained he was in the hospital but that I was to come there anyway.

When I arrived at Mr. Berlin's bedside he shook hands and then looked sharply at me. "Do you," he asked, "have anything against Flo Ziegfeld?" I shook my head. I did not tell him that Mr. Ziegfeld had died — something I later looked up — when I was twelve. "Good," he said. Then came another question. "Do you," he asked, "write dialogue?" This time I nodded my head as sagely as I could. "Good," he said again. "We'll get started tomorrow morning." He paused and looked out the window. "I want to start," he continued, "with 'Alexander's Ragtime Band.' " He paused again and then looked straight at me. "But," he said, "we'll have to hurry — my health is not good. I'm a very ill man, you know. Frankly, I'm at death's door.'

The door was a long time opening — Mr. Berlin was then sixty-one and he did not pass on until forty years later, at the age of one hundred and one. We never, however, went to work on our project. The trouble was that Mr. Berlin had neglected to inform Ms. Merman about his plans before the Winchell show, and that very day Ms. Merman issued a statement that she did not appreciate Mr. Berlin announcing her shows without his having the courtesy to inform her of them in advance, and that therefore she would not do *The Last Resorts*. Mr. Berlin next tried Ms. Mary Martin, but Ms. Martin curtly replied that she was not in the market for Ms. Merman's rejects. Therefore, that was not only the end of Ms. Martin but, as it turned out, Mr. Berlin also.

I do not wish to go into everything that went on from there. Suffice it to say that the Messrs. Howard Lindsay and Russel Crouse took over from Mr. Berlin and, after they finished a "book" of my book, they sent it to Mr. Cole Porter. Mr. Porter, however, replied that he did not want Mr. Berlin's rejects, and that was the end of not only Mr. Cole Porter but also of the Messrs. Lindsay and Crouse. Altogether, *The Last Resorts* was optioned by eleven different producers, including Mr. George Abbott and Mr. Harold Prince, and had eleven different books of it written, including ones by such distinguished dramatists as Jean Kerr and the late John Patrick. Indeed Mr. Porter once told me that he alone had received no fewer than five books of my book. In the end, though, it was never produced. Nonetheless, it was announced so many times that a friend of mine from Texas came all the way from there just to see it. I did not see him, but after he went back to Texas he wrote me that he had liked the show very much. To this day, however, I have never been able to find out what show he did see that he thought was it.

I have had a few other somewhat similar close misses — albeit not so highly publicized ones — with other books I have written being optioned for plays or movie rights. Therefore, understandably, I did not go to the bank on the news about my cat book. Indeed, this time my dream about Bel Air and a swimming pool was, as I said, a very short dream — one which was marred at the beginning by the fact that I knew Polar Bear wouldn't be too crazy about a swimming pool anyway.

The producer of "The Cat Who Came for Christmas" was to be Mr. Pierre Cossette, a man whom I had never met but who was the producer of what, I was told, were the terrific Grammy shows. Although I had never seen a Grammy show, I was also told he would do a terrific job on my cat story. In any case, one of Mr. Cossette's first efforts was to give a press interview in which he announced there would be a nationwide contest to choose the cat who would play Polar Bear — one which, he said, would be the biggest search in Hollywood since the search for Scarlett O'Hara. He also said that not only would there be "kitty kasting kalls" all over the country to find "the proper catidates" — Mr. Cossette is very big on puns — but also that the final contest would be held in Madison Square Garden.

At the prospect of a Scarlett O'Hara search, I was considerably less enthusiastic than Mr. Cossette. I visualized hundreds of cats running all over Madison Square Garden and thousands more outside, and I could see almost endless possibilities of cats fighting, getting hurt, and even getting lost. Mr. Cossette said I simply didn't understand the value of "free pre" — which he explained to me was free publicity. I said that I did, but that what we would undoubtedly get would be "post mort" — which I did not explain. In the end we agreed on an entirely different kind of contest — one by appointment only.

Actually, the more I thought about the whole idea of a contest, the less I thought of it. I have, you see, a thing about contests — one which goes way back in my childhood to my first teenage summer. That summer there was an advertisement in a Boston newspaper about a contest — one which was to see who could make the most words of three letters or more out of the letters in the words "Pierce Arrow." The contest was limited to New England, but it was being run by the national Pierce-Arrow company, maker of the automobile of that name which in those days was a very big thing — bigger, indeed, than the Cadillac or Packard or in fact any competitor.

The first prize was to be a Pierce Arrow — a vehicle whose cost, as I remember, was $2,000 — an astronomical sum for those days. The second prize was a $1,000 ticket on a Pierce Arrow, and the third prize was a $500 ticket. The ad ran in June, as I recall, and all entries had to be in by the end of August. There was nothing for me and my faithful Brookie to do but give up a summer of swimming and sailing and baseball and tennis. Instead, with Brookie beside me, day after day, night after night, I typed line after line of word after word on sheet after sheet. At thirteen, one has incredible persistence, and if

Brookie, at eight, did not have quite as much as I did, he at least tried his best by sticking beside me. I worked from a dozen or more dictionaries and typed and retyped the words, single-spaced, on the same line, way over in the left margin. If I came to a word that was not included in at least two dictionaries, I added a note about it on the same line — over and over again, the same kind of entry, such as "foreign word not in most American dictionaries," or "Australian bird, only in English dictionary, not in American."

Finally, late in August, I finished. I sent in my hard-worked pages. I waited patiently but hopefully. I did not see how anyone could have found any more words unless they had used more foreign dictionaries and had borne down more heavily on foreign words. In any case, sure enough, in early September the paper announced the winners and, even more surely enough, there was my name. I had won, the paper said, third prize.

The whole family, including Brookie, shared in my excitement. And when I received from the company not only a letter but also a check for $500, my happiness was complete. All I had to do, the letter said, was to take the letter and the check down to the nearest Pierce Arrow dealer.

Brookie and I went together, and although at first they did not want to let Brookie into the showroom where all the cars were — Brookie was never very good about tires — I took him in anyway. I found the man apparently in charge and showed him my letter and my check. He looked at them both for some time but then gave them both back to me. "Well?" he asked. I told him if it was OK with him I would like to have the money instead of the check. I told him politely that I had nothing against Pierce Arrows, but I was only thirteen and therefore would have to wait three years just to drive mine out of the showroom — and this, I pointed out helpfully, might be pretty inconvenient for him. If he would just give me $495, I said, I would be happy to call it square. He shook his head. "No," he said, "we can't do that. The check is only good *on* a Pierce Arrow — toward the purchase *of* a Pierce Arrow."

I considered this development for some time. Well, I asked him, how much would he take for my check? "I can't take anything for it," he said. "We don't cash checks." I told him that then, I guess, I would just have to cash it somewhere else — at, say, a bank. Once more he shook his head. "Look at your check," he said. "It's not a cashable check except *for* a Pierce Arrow." By this time I was getting pretty discouraged, and Brookie was getting restless. I did, however, have one last idea. Well, I suggested, if he didn't mind, I would just wait there until the first customer came along to buy a Pierce Arrow and then I would give him my check and the customer could just give me, say, $490 for it. The man shook his head a last time. "You can't do that," he said. "You check is nontransferable. It says so, right on it. Look at it."

The last thing I wanted to do right then was to look at that check again. Instead, I called Brookie over and pointed to the white-walled tire of the nearest brand-new Pierce Arrow. Before the man could do anything, Brookie rose to the occasion. Then, together, we turned on our heel and paw and made our exit.

When I got home I realized that not only had I been had, but I also began to have my doubts about the whole contest. My doubts centered on the first and second prize-winners. If nothing else, I wanted to know how they had gotten more words than I had and, if so, how many more.

Their names were listed in the paper with their addresses. The first prize winner had an address in Portland, Maine; the second, in Providence, Rhode Island. I called information for their telephone numbers. Neither, apparently, had a telephone.

Nonetheless, as I said, at thirteen one is persistent. An older friend of my brother who had a driving license drove me first to Portland. There was no such person at the address — in fact no one at that address or around it had ever heard of such a person. Next we went to the address in Providence. The same situation obtained there. I had, at last, proof. The whole contest had been a fraud. I had really been the winner, but I had won nothing. Later that fall I learned that the company, having already decided to go out of business, had used the contest to get people to buy their last cars in the dealerships.

To say the whole experience soured me on contests is to put it mildly. Once bitten, I was not only twice shy — I was permanently so — and as time went by not in the least shy about it either. To this day, if I see people in line to buy lottery tickets I endeavor to dissuade them. I am not saying lotteries are frauds — they're not — but the odds are astronomical, and the payback, even if you do win, after the state and the federal government and everybody else, including the person who sold the ticket to you, get their cuts is hardly more than fifty percent. Even the worst slot machines pay over sixty percent.

All in all, when Mr. Cossette came up with the idea of a contest to find a cat to play Polar Bear, I did not believe he had any intention of staging a fraud, but at the same time I wanted iron safeguards. In answer to this he reiterated that the contest would be on an appointment-only basis and furthermore he said I could be one of the judges. The other two, he said, would be the director of the movie and himself.

Alas, this too rang a bell — and again not a good one. The only time I have ever been a judge in a national contest was an experience which paled even my Pierce Arrow debacle.

The date was 1972, and the occasion was the Miss U.S.A. Pageant — one which was held, that year, in a hotel in Puerto Rico. At first my selection had seemed a high honor — indeed, the person who informed me of my selection told me it was really a very high honor because, he said, the final show was not only going to be televised live but would be one of the first live national television shows to be carried via satellite and therefore would be seen by over seventy-two million people. Every single one of us connected with the show would be, he said, looking at me sternly, vitally important to the success of the whole thing. And, he concluded, no one would be more so than I, as one of the judges, would be. "In front of seventy-two million people," he said looking me right in the eye, "the last thing we want is a bomb."

As a matter of fact, a bomb was just what we did have. But I am getting ahead of my story. Hardly had I arrived in Puerto Rico when I was greeted by a real greeter type. "I'm Mitch Potter," he said, holding out his hand. "I'm in charge of handling the judges." I raised my left eyebrow at this — I can only raise my left eyebrow because I have very little hair on my right eyebrow, but I do it, if I do say so, very effectively. "You will have complete freedom," Mr. Potter said. "Complete freedom," he repeated. Obviously he had read my eyebrow.

Mr. Potter then explained what our job judging the

girls — I remember he never used the word "women" — would be. We would have to pick Miss U.S.A. from the fifty-one winners of the states' pageants and that then Miss U.S.A. would go on to compete against "girls" from other countries to be Miss Universe. I asked him why Miss Universe — why not Miss World? "Because," he explained patiently, "there already *is* a Miss World contest." He paused. "As a matter of fact," he continued, "there is a Miss Universe contest, a Miss World contest, a Miss America contest, a Mrs. America contest, a Miss Venus contest, a Miss International contest, a Miss Black America contest, a Miss Teen-Age America contest, a Miss Junior Miss contest, a Miss Pre-Teen-Age America contest . . ." I held up my hand. I had heard enough. The thought that one is not as special as one thought one was is never easy to take. "The difference between the Miss America contest and the Miss U.S.A. contest," Mr. Potter explained, "is that the Miss America contest has a talent competition. We don't." Mr. Potter was obviously very proud of this. Pride was apparently a big thing with the Miss U.S.A. Pageant. "Over the years," he continued, "we've had some of the most famous names in the world as judges. Why, we've even had *ambassadors*." I wanted to know what ambassador. He paused a moment, obviously thinking, then brightened. "The ambassador," he said, "from Thailand to Sweden." Oh, I said. At this point he began to look us over critically. "I would also like to say," he said sternly, "that over the years every single one of our judges has entered into the spirit of the thing — with two exceptions. They were two glamour boys from Hollywood who were more interested in chasing the girls than in judging."

I was going to tell him that I supposed there would

always be rotten apples in any barrel — even among Miss U.S.A. judges — but I didn't get a chance, because once again he seemed to be looking at me critically. "For your information," he said, "every three girls have a chaperone who is either with them or knows exactly where each one is at all times. The girls are all on the fourth floor of the hotel — no one is even allowed on that floor except the chaperones. Not even their fathers or their brothers. At the elevator doors they have police."

That very evening, Mr. Potter told us, concluding his not-so-brief briefing, would be our first judging. "It's the Semi-Finals," he said, "Evening Gowns and Swimsuits. I suggest that, as the girls go by, you use abbreviated symbols, like 'O' for outstanding, 'S' for so-so, and 'D' for dog." With that he started to leave us, but before he did I told him I would never use that final symbol — it was an antianimal expression.

The next morning, I went to see a rehearsal for the television show. If you've ever seen one of the many "Miss" shows, you may find it hard to believe they have a rehearsal, but they do. In fact, for three days they do. Then, you may well ask, why isn't it a better show? You may well ask this, but I, as a former TV critic, do not feel that I am the one to give you the answer. Suffice it to say that the rehearsals are, if such is possible, worse than the actual show. In any case, sitting in the rehearsal hall, I was spotted by Herb Landon, the executive director of the pageant. "You're not supposed to be here," he said sternly. "The girls aren't supposed to be looked at by the judges except when they're being judged." He paused. "But," he continued, "as long as you're here you might as well stay, and I want to tell you something. If there is one thing I resent it's the implication that these are hard, tough kids.

We take great pains to see that our girls are good girls. We are really beyond reproach.

"It's all gone now," he went on, warming to his task, "the whole idea of a girl with a great body swinging down the runway. She may not even have a great body — why, we've had Phi Beta Kappas. Our girls meet *kings!* It's a matter of breeding — look at them! They're not hard. They're nice, neat, clean girls from good families. Notice how they're dressed — just for rehearsal! Even if they're wearing shlumpy clothes, they're clean!"

I went next to the swimming pool, where I had been told I would find a man named Sid Sussman, who, my informer informed me, had been responsible for an enormous number of girls getting to the Miss U.S.A. and other national pageants. I found Mr. Sussman sunning himself with a large cigar in his mouth. "I've been called the Vince Lombardi of this racket," he said. "It's a hard thing to live down. I just handle D.C., Maryland, and Virginia now, but I've also handled Pennsylvania and other places. I used to handle Florida, but I took a bath there. I run close to three hundred pageants a year, and I work all year long. I've got a 'farm system' — Miss Teen-Age, Miss Pre-Teen, Miss Junior Miss. You name it, I run it. I'm the creative type. I like to take a kid off the street and make her something."

Make her *what?* I wanted to know. He thought for a moment. "Well," he said, "I had the kid who later was married to Richard Zanuck." Mr. Sussman puffed his cigar. "In my local contests," he said, "I wouldn't presume to tell a judge who to pick. All I do is pick the judges." He smiled. "I don't mind doing a little indicating — the only thing I mind is when someone says a girl is my girl. I resent that. I may be a bachelor, but with eighteen thousand girls a year in my pageants, I'm not hard up for female company. But the fact is, I've got to like my winners. Remember, you pick them for one night. I have to live with them."

Before interviewing the girls, the judges were given biographical sheets about them. On these the girls had entered their lives' ambitions, as well as why they had entered the Miss U.S.A. contest. A surprising number, I noted, had answered both of these questions together — that to be Miss U.S.A. *was* their life's ambition. There was also the question of who do you think is the most important man in the world today. It was very close. The winner was Billy Graham. He had four votes, followed by President Nixon and Bob Hope, who had three each. An extraordinary number of the girls, I learned, had been in dozens of contests. Miss Georgia, for example, had been in seventy-nine. She had been Miss Peach Queen, Miss Rhododendron Queen, Miss Labor Day Queen, and Miss North Carolina Motor Speedway Queen. Miss Minnesota had been Miss Hibbing (Minn.), Miss Iron Range, and Miss City Courts Employees Queen of St. Paul. Miss Kansas, I noted, was Pep Club President. What, I asked, is a pep club? "I work with the cheerleaders," she told us. "I'm responsible for the pep of five hundred girls." Miss Indiana was peppy, too. "I love being a cheerleader," she said. "I've been a cheerleader for six years. It's been practically my whole life."

Just the same, some of the girls had memorable answers to our questions. My favorite was Miss New York, a remarkable young woman named Alberta Phillips, the only black woman in the contest and the one who I thought should have won it — if for no other reason than for the way she answered my question as to how she got into it in the first place. She smiled. "During my interview," she said, "I lied about my color."

The final afternoon I played golf. Coming back to the hotel, I found it surrounded by hundreds of picketers of the Puerto Rican Socialist Party. "¡FUERA YANQUI! ¡FUERA MISS U.S.A.!" their signs read. Their leader, Florencio Merced, explained to the media their objections. "The pageant," he said, "represents a vile utilization of women as sex objects."

That evening, when the show was on the air and just before the winner, Miss Hawaii, was announced, there was a tremendous rumbling sound. Not until later, however, did I learn what it was. We had, indeed, bombed. Or, rather, I should say, we had been bombed. Still another Puerto Rican party, the Independencias, had attempted to knock the show off the air by getting at the electronic equipment on the seventh and top floor of the hotel. Since there were police there, they couldn't get to the seventh floor, so what they did was bomb the sixth floor — the floor where all the judges' rooms were.

I did not, I want you to know, take it personally — there was, after all, no way they could know that I felt about the pageant just the way they did. The bomb actually went off in room 663 — *my* room was 662. When I was finally allowed in there by the police, the room was a shambles of broken glass. The whole porch had been blown off, and with it — nowhere to be seen — were my brand new swimming trunks, which I had put on the porch to dry. Gazing at the wreckage and thinking of the Coronation Ball, which was still to come, I tried, as I always do, to look on the bright side. Swimsuit was, for me, now out — the fact is, I wouldn't have had a chance in Swimsuit anyway. The way I saw it, I would just have to score heavily in Evening Dress and Personality.

Nervous as I was about again being called on to be a judge, I had to admit there were seminal differences between being a judge of an international beauty pageant and being a judge to pick a cat to play Polar Bear in a movie. For one thing, in this contest there would be no Swimsuit competition at all. And this was just as well. Although I have known many cats who liked to swim, Polar Bear is not one of them. Indeed he is very much not one of them — something I indelibly deduced one morning when, as is his wont, he was circling my bathtub and managed to fall in. Unfortunately, despite the nice warm water, he not only completely lost his cool, he also managed his fall directly adjacent to what I shall delicately describe as the lower part of my stomach. Before I could do anything, after several desperate attempts to claw the water, he then proceeded to claw until he reached what to him was shore, but to me was something else. I shall not say more except to say that, despite my quick capsize and masterful rollover, Polar Bear wasn't the only one who lost his cool that morning.

If there would be no Swimsuit competition, neither would there be Evening Dress. All cats in the competition would, like Polar Bear, be dressed alike — in fact, they would all be formally evening dressed, resplendent in their white whiskers and tails. There remained, however, two other important competitions. The first was Personality. Unsatisfactory as this word is for cats, who, after all, have more of this than any "person" I have met, this would indeed be undoubtedly the quality which would be key to the one who would get the part. Nonetheless, side by side with Personality would be the equally crucial one of Talent — the very qualification the Miss U.S.A. Pageant so prided itself on not having, if you'll pardon ending on a preposition, any of.

And, judging — if you'll also pardon that word — from the letters and pictures which poured in, there was certainly no lack of talent among the potential contenders. Before I even got to the matter of Talent, however, as I read the letters I was amazed, to begin with, by how many white cats there were. You don't see that many white cats in people's homes but, make no mistake, there are hundreds, thousands, and, I would guess, even hundreds of thousands of them. Not a few people even offered white female cats for the contest and, admitting this in their letters, wanted to know if the gender of their cat would exclude them. To these I immediately replied that it would not — that Lassie the Dog was, after all, a male and why should not Polar Bear the Cat be female? There would be, I assured one and all, no sexism in any contest of which I was a judge — it would be E.R.A. all the way.

Surprised as I was at the number of white cats, I was even more surprised by the number of these cats who, as their owners expressed, "did things." These "things" seemed indeed almost endless. There were people who had cats who could tell the time of day, who could wake them with a paw on their face, who could tell there was someone at the door before the doorbell rang, who could tell the telephone was going to ring before it rang and who could turn off the answering machine when it annoyed them. There were also people who had cats who could shake hands, who could sit up and beg, who could walk on their hind legs, who could retrieve and who could jump through hoops, and even who could lie down and roll over and pray. There were other cats who could turn on the faucet in the sink, who could use the toilet, who could open closet and kitchen cupboards, who could even open heavy doors by repeatedly jumping up and turning the doorknob, even cats who could open lightweight windows and close heavy ones. There were cats, too, who could play the piano and even pick out tunes, who could read books — or at least picture books — who could watch TV and turn it on as well as off, who could look at themselves in the mirror and even primp, who could type, and not only on a typewriter but also on a word processor. Finally, there were cats who could empty the trash or garbage.

Just the same, the more I read what these cats could do, the more I realized that Polar Bear, too, "did things." In fact he did an awful lot of those very same things those other people's cats did. He couldn't tell time in general, but he could certainly tell when it was time for something he wanted. He, too, woke me with a paw on my face, although when he was particularly hungry, he preferred, depending on his mood, a tail tickle or a full tail swipe. And he too knew when there was someone at the door before the doorbell rang — indeed, he could tell they were coming to my apartment the moment the elevator stopped and they got out.

As for many other things those other cats did, like shaking hands and sitting up and begging and walking on his hind legs and retrieving and jumping through hoops and lying down and rolling and praying — all of these weren't necessarily things he couldn't do, he just wouldn't do them. He could turn on faucets, he could open and close closet doors and cupboards, and, if he couldn't open lightweight windows and close heavy ones, this was again not because he couldn't — he just didn't do windows. Finally, when it came to emptying the trash or the garbage, Polar Bear not only could do that — and regularly did so when he was looking for something he wanted — he also went a step further. He put things in the trash or garbage when they were something he did not want, such as boxes of medicine I had for him, or the nail clippers I used on him or a comb he didn't like. He did this, and in fact he did so much of this, that, when I couldn't find one of those things, the trash basket or the garbage can was one of the first places I looked.

There remained, just the same, one large question. The fact that there were cats who could do, and sometimes did, remarkable things did not mean they would or could do these things on command or on some specific occasion. And, even if they could or would, could or would they perform them on a set — in a totally strange place with dozens of total strangers around and dozens of distractions such as lights, dollies, whipping wires, and even traveling cameras over their heads and zooming in on them? Could or would they, too, perform without their own "person" giving them their commands — without even their own person being there at all and being left with a total stranger trainer?

One thing I did know — Polar Bear would not do those things, not even things he did regularly, when anybody else was around, no matter who was telling him to do them, and that included me. And, as for doing those things on a set with all the distractions and the strangers, I could only advise any movie company which planned on such an operation to take out a catastrophic policy — one which should be carefully written to include not only equipment and people but also the pun.

Not that I ever harbored any illusion of Polar Bear being able to play Polar Bear to begin with. A cat who, after all, didn't even want to be a celebrity when the whole job of becoming one had been handed to him on a platter, and who didn't have to do anything about being one because it was all done for him, certainly would have about as much desire to be a movie star as your average armadillo. Just the same, as I compared what he was doing with his life with what other cats were doing with theirs, I had an uncomfortable feeling. I do not mean that I was in the least dissatisfied with him the way he was. As a matter of fact, my thoughts didn't concern me at all — something which is very unusual for me — they concerned only him. I just wondered if he wasn't missing something that could make his life more interesting. Too much of his life, after all, it seemed to me, was spent napping, and the only time his napping seemed to be interrupted was when he was getting ready for a real sleep.

Therefore, without further ado, and again not with any idea that he could do many or even several of those feats the other cats could do, but merely that he might like to learn at least one of them, I resolved to get down to the job of training him. The only trick he had ever learned to do in all the years I had had him was to walk — or at least stay — on a leash. Surely there had to be something he could learn to do besides that.

My first job, I knew, would be to get some good books on the subject. And, embarking on this, the very first book I came upon had a good piece of news right on the cover. It was called *The Complete Guide to Training Your Cat*, by Ray Berwick, and even above the title was the line "Who says you can't teach an old cat new tricks?"

I didn't want Polar Bear to see that — he is very sensitive about the word "old" — but for me, as a mature teacher, it was as I say very good news. It meant that, when it came to training, you didn't have to start your cat from scratch — or, rather, at kittenhood. The second book I came upon, by Paul and Jo Loeb, also had an encouraging title — *You* CAN *Train Your Cat*, it was called. And, if the capitalized "*CAN*" seemed a little defensive, it was still, I decided, basically positive. The third book I came upon, however, had far more disturbing news, and this news too was, if you please, right in the title. It was a book by Leon Whitney, a veterinarian, and it was called *Training You to Train Your Cat.*

Frankly, I had never realized that I had to be trained before I trained Polar Bear. Ever since my Brush Hill School days, let alone the Army, training has never been my long suit. I've always thought I was very good at training other people, but I have never felt other people were worth a damn training me. But, obviously, this time I would have to bite the bullet. It was really maddening, though. Apparently I would have to be professionally taught how to communicate with an animal I had been communicating with just fine, thank you, for more than ten years. But, for Polar Bear's sake I resolved to do it.

One thing I did not need was anyone telling me what was the best book on the art of communication with an animal. It was one given me many years ago by none other than my longtime friend Doris Day. It was, Doris told me then, her favorite book, and I know that it still is. It is called *Kinship with All Life,* by J. Allen Boone, and it was published as far back as 1954. To me, at this time, faced with the possibility of a movie cat, it was particularly fascinating because it began with a movie dog. The dog was, as a matter of fact, the most famous movie dog of all time — more remarkable even than the various Rin Tin Tins and Lassies which followed him. His name was Strongheart, and he made his first film, *The Silent Call*, as far back as 1921 — two years before the first of the Rin Tin Tin movies and a full seventeen years before the first of the Lassie films.

As compared to the many Rin Tin Tins and Lassies, there was only one Strongheart, but what a dog he was. Originally trained as a military dog and for police work in Germany, he was brought to Hollywood as a three-year-old by the screenwriter Jane Murphin and her husband, Larry Trimble, a director. Up until Strongheart, no animal of any kind had ever been given a leading role in a film, but with his very first film, *The Silent Call*, Strongheart was catapulted into becoming not only Hollywood's top-ranking star but its top box-office attraction of all stars, people stars included. In between a couple of his films, and more or less by chance, Mr. Boone, a writer and film producer — a man who up until the time he met Strongheart knew, as he wrote, "practically nothing about dogs" — was given the job of looking after the dog while the Trimbles were away.

Mr. Boone was also given, he records, just three basic instructions on how he was to treat Strongheart. He was not to "talk down to him," not to use "baby talk" with him, and, most important, not "to say anything to him with my lips that I did not sincerely mean in my heart." With just these three injunctions, Mr. Boone soon realized that Strongheart was not only able to understand human talk but also to read "human thinking." As time went on, however, Mr. Boone also realized that everything in their communication "moved," as he put it, "in only one direction — from me to him." Determined to change this, Mr. Boone embarked on a program which included, among other things, instead of his taking Strongheart for a walk, Strongheart taking him. He would indeed do nothing when they started a walk except just stand there until Strongheart decided where they would go.

Reading this was very encouraging to me because, as I have already mentioned, when I put Polar Bear down with his leash and harness in the Park, I didn't pull him — I let him decide where he wanted to pull me. I wouldn't have admitted to Mr. Boone that the reason I didn't pull him was that it wouldn't do any good, but at least I didn't anyway. The trouble was, of course, Polar Bear never wanted to go anywhere except stay where he was — but still, the point is I really was following Mr. Boone's teaching to the letter even if I couldn't follow it to the extent of Polar Bear going somewhere.

Mr. Boone never, apparently, worked with cats. But, after Strongheart, he did communicate with a wide variety of other creatures. Indeed, toward the end of *Kinship with All Life* he even attempted communication with an army of ants. These ants had invaded his porch, and brandishing both a broom and poisons over their heads, he addressed them as follows:

> "You ants may not be aware of it," I said, "but I am in a position to wipe most of you out of existence within the next few minutes with this poison and this broom. But that doesn't seem to be the right answer. We humans have been killing one another off in matters of this kind for centuries and we are worse off today than we were when it started."
> Then remembering how every living thing likes to be

appreciated I began sending all the complimentary things I could think of in their direction. I told them how much I admired their keen intelligence . . . their zest for living . . . their complete dedication to whatever they happened to be doing at the moment . . . their harmonious action in a common purpose . . . their ability to work together without misunderstandings or the need to be constantly told what to do.

At this juncture Mr. Boone paused to take a look at the ants through his magnifying glass. Since the situation was, as he described it, "worse than ever," he decided to bring his broadcast to a close:

> "That's all I have to say to you ants," I said. "I have honestly done my best in this situation. The rest is up to you fellows. I am speaking to you as a gentleman to a gentleman."

Sure enough, that very night Mr. Boone went out on his porch and there was not an ant in sight:

> Not one! The icebox door was still wide open, with inviting food inside and there was some food on the nearby table. But not an ant in sight . . . those little fellows had actually kept their part of the Gentleman's Agreement. This happened several years ago. Since then I have never been bothered by ants in any manner, at home or abroad. Occasionally a scout ant passes through on his way from outdoors to outdoors and pauses just long enough for us to exchange a friendly, silent greeting with each other.

Finally, in his last chapter Mr. Boone decides that when a fly decends on him instead of shooing it away or grabbing a Flit gun he will make friends with it. He noticed, again with his magnifying glass, that when the fly paraded on his finger, he would begin to rub his legs over his head, causing his head, as Mr. Boone puts it, "to bob briskly up and down in my direction":

> Assuming that this could be his way of expressing appreciation, and not to be outdone in good manners in my own house, especially by a fly, I began bowing just as politely back to him. I was grateful that none of the neighbors could see me through the windows.

A few days after making friends with his fly, Mr. Boone gave him the name Freddie — one which made me a little nervous because that is the name of my peerless editor at Little, Brown, and I was afraid she would think I was making fun of her. I was not, of course — Mr. Boone named the fly. I had nothing to do with it, honest I didn't. In any case, one day while Freddie was standing in the palm of Mr. Boone's hand, getting his wings stroked, Mr. Boone decided to begin, as he puts it, "silently talking across to Freddie as a fellow being just as I had learned to do with Strongheart":

> I would ask the little fellow in my hand a question, and then give careful heed to all freshly-arriving mental impressions. . . .
> Unexpectedly, every question that I sent across to Freddie was followed, through the medium of these returning impressions, by a silent counterquestion. I asked Freddie what he was supposed to be doing in my world; back almost instantly came a demand to know what I really was supposed to be doing in *his* world. I asked him why it was that flies treated us humans so badly; right back came the question: why had we humans always treated flies so badly.

If Mr. Boone could have a "dialogue," as he called it, not only with Strongheart but also with ants and Freddie the Fly, surely I could have one with Polar Bear. After all,

I had been having, if not silent dialogues, at least out-loud dialogues with him for a decade. Just the same, if as a former amateur in this communication business I was now about to turn pro, I realized it was probably high time for me to consult other professionals. Accordingly, following Mr. Boone I decided on Beatrice Lydecker, a woman who once told me she had communicated with more animals than anyone else.

I first met Ms. Lydecker some years ago in California. I did not yet have Polar Bear — or, rather, Polar Bear did not yet have me — but I well remembered Ms. Lydecker told me at the time that, although she first got into communciation with animals by talking with horses, she had also had great success with dogs and cats. One of her first customers, I remembered she had said, was a lady who had two cats, one of whom was always spraying her furniture. The lady wanted to know which one was doing the job and had turned the problem over to Ms. Lydecker. I asked Ms. Lydecker how she had solved it. "I just asked them," she replied. "Right away the guilty one admitted it." I told her I was, if I might use such an expression in animal communciation, dumbfounded. "The one who is doing it *always* admits it," Ms. Lydecker explained. "Animals are very honest if you ask them directly about something."

Frankly, at that time I had had some doubts about this. And, since I had Polar Bear I now had many more. Often I had asked him directly about something he did — such as upsetting the garbage to get something he wanted — not only did he not answer me directly, instead what he did was indirectly, as I have said before, to offer his assistance to search for the alleged perpetrator. In any case, now with my new-found resolution to establish more successful communication with him, I decided to make an appointment with Ms. Lydecker the next time she was in New York.

When Ms. Lydecker arrived, with her assistant, at my apartment, it was of course too much for Polar Bear. He immediately low-tailed it to the bedroom. Embarrassed, I started to go get him but Ms. Lydecker stopped me. "No," she said, "I'll tell you just where he is. It'll save you time." She closed her eyes and went into what I thought was meditation. In a moment she opened her eyes and spoke to me. "I see him near water," she said. Helpfully I suggested the bathroom, but Ms. Lydecker shook her head. "No," she said, "he's near water but not that near." I pointed out that there was only one other room, and that was the bedroom. Perhaps he was there? Ms. Lydecker brightened. "That's where he is," she said. Again I started to go get him, but Ms. Lydecker again stopped me. "No," she said, "I don't need him. I'm going to talk to you about how you communicate with him."

Ms. Lydecker told me she had been communicating with animals since she was a young child. Children, she told me, communicate better than adults with animals because they understand, as she put it, "nonverbal language" and also because they have not yet learned to think of animals as "something different from themselves." At school, she pointed out, the children lose their nonverbal skills when they acquire verbal skills. Ms. Lydecker also clearly believed that women are better at trying to communicate with animals than men because, she told me sternly, "Men close off this kind of thing by their logic and statistical thinking."

This was again bad news for me — trying to train myself

to train Polar Bear and now being told that women and children would be better at it. I took some comfort, though, in the fact that I am actually so rotten at statistics maybe I could be a terrific communicator even if I were just a man. Also, I was basically a subscriber to Ms. Lydecker's belief that one of the reasons most grown-ups have so much trouble with communication with animals is that they interpret everything about animals from what they would feel is their position instead of from the animals' point of view. "When animals go out and start sniffing around," Ms. Lydecker told me, "we usually think they are just going around planning where they're going to the bathroom. They're not doing that at all. What they're doing is reading their daily newspaper."

For a moment I wondered if this was why paper-training with some animals was so difficult. I decided, however, not to explore this further with Ms. Lydecker. One thing I did find she was extremely firm about is that all animals can read our minds. Certainly, knowing Polar Bear, I went along with that. And, for that matter, the corollary to it — that the trouble we have comes from our not having the ability to read *their* minds. Ms. Lydecker clearly believed that the way we should do this is by the use of "visualization," or "mental pictures." She explained that the best way to do this would be for me to take a picture of Polar Bear in the position I wanted him after he had done what I wanted him to do. For example, if I wanted him in what she called the "stay" position, I should photograph him in that position and then memorize that picture until the image was clear in my mind. Then I was to put the picture away and, with practice, I would be able to create that mental picture at will, so that the next time I wanted him to stay somewhere, all I had to do was bring up that picture in my mind while I was telling him to do it.

While I was doing this, Ms. Lydecker went on, what I would really be doing was having ESP with Polar Bear. I'd be conversing with him in his language and, she said, "Chatting with him will seem natural to you."

I could hardly wait for my next real "chat" with Polar Bear. Before she left me, however, Ms. Lydecker used an example from her first love, horses. "If you're trying to teach a horse to go over a jump," she said, "what you do is mentally visualize the horse taking the jump with complete ease."

Curiously, when I came to my next authority for training myself to train Polar Bear, he turned out to be the well-known English psychologist David Greene, author of *Your Incredible Cat*. And, in his section called "How Fast Does Your Cat Learn," there sure enough was jumping training.

Dr. Greene suggested using a child's toy or constructing one's own hoop from a "stiff plastic tube, formed into a circle and held with a wooden peg." Frankly, I'm not good at this sort of thing and I never seem to have things around that everybody else seems to have when they want to work on something — and these certainly included plastic tubes and wooden pegs. But I did my best by taking off a tire from my bicycle and not bothering with a peg at all. When it comes to ingenuity I'm no genius, but I am ingenious.

Nor did I stop there. What I did was put the hoop in the doorway to the kitchen and block the spaces around it and then put Polar Bear's dinner on the other side of it. He went through the hoop like a shot. He did it so well, in fact, that I decided I didn't need any more intermittent steps but was ready for what Dr. Greene called the "final stage" of the I.Q. test. But for this stage, according to Dr. Greene, I had to scratch Polar Bear's supper:

> The final stage of the training consists of holding up the hoop and calling out "Come On!" without showing the cat any food. Just extend your hand as if offering a reward and give the command. The idea is to link this instruction with the desired action so firmly that the words are sufficient to produce an eager leap. . . . The test is completed when the cat jumps through the hoop correctly on at least two out of three occasions. Now rate his IQ using the chart below:

Number of Commands Given	*IQ Rating*
60 +	Below Average
50–60	Slightly Below Average
40–49	Average
30–39	Above Average
29 or Less	Very Intelligent

This time I was not successful. In fact, without his supper on the other side of the hoop, Polar Bear was awful. Frankly, I am not going to give you his final score. All I will say is that as far as his jumping through the hoop, "correctly in at least two out of three occasions," he never did it — in fact, the only time he ever did it was when he felt it was the best way to get away from both me and the hoop altogether. Finally, as far as the number of commands I gave, I lost count at 100. When it came to mastering supposedly the simplest of all tricks Polar Bear was not just below average, he wasn't even on the chart. And, if the truth be known, by the time I finished, Polar Bear was so heartily sick of anything that even looked like a hoop that I think if at this point he had seen a kid with a Hula Hoop you could have scratched one kid as well as his hula.

One thing I did learn from Dr. Greene — this was that it was apparently very important what position you got into before you talked to your cat. For years I had just talked to Polar Bear any old way — close to, head-to-head, from a distance, or even from another room, and I got his "aeiou" 's back fine, too, wherever I was — and I had no trouble interpreting them. But if I was going to turn pro at this talk game, Dr. Greene made it clear that positionally I would have to get down to business. And down to business was just what Dr. Greene had in mind. Above all, he pointed out, I was not to look at Polar Bear's face:

> Instead, while the cat is looking at your face, gradually sink down on your heels so as to come close to his level. . . . Now look slowly away from the cat, before allowing your gaze to return to his face. As you do so, half close your eyes before restoring eye-contact. Then, when you are looking at one another, blink several times. . . . Once your approach has been accepted, the cat may acknowledge this trust by lowering his lids and blinking or by using one of the greeting signals already described.

I found, I am sorry to say, the opposite. Instead of "lowering his lids and blinking," Polar Bear gave me a look which clearly stated that I should do nothing until the men in the white coats arrived and after that I was to stop doing what I was doing and get up and go along quietly with them. But nothing stopped Dr. Greene:

> To get on even better terms, use the head rub by placing your forehead against his and rubbing your head and chin against his head. This is a warm and affectionate greeting · message used between two friendly cats.

Here Dr. Greene was going too far. I yielded to no man alive, and few dead, on how to "get on even better terms" with my cat, and I had no intention of allowing somebody else to tell me how to snuggle and scrubble him. I also wanted it understood that nowhere, despite the disappointments I had had, did I believe that Polar Bear was dumb. Obviously, when it came to training, *I* was the dumbbell. But reluctantly I did have to admit that, under my direction as a trainer, when it came to stacking up as a trickster against those other white cats, Polar Bear didn't have a prayer.

Reaching the end of my tether on this training thing — where patience is concerned I have, it is true, often been accused of having a very short tether — I called a friend of mine, Linda Hanrahan, a fine trainer, and asked her to come over and make a firsthand assessment, not only of me as a trainer but Polar Bear as a possible candidate to play himself in the movies. When she arrived I told her my tale of woe — that the only trick I had ever gotten Polar Bear to do, outside of staying on his leash, was to lie down — and that, frankly, was only when he was already lying down.

When Polar Bear came in Mrs. Hanrahan took one look at him and told him to lie down. Whereupon, amazingly, Polar Bear lay down. After that Mrs. Hanrahan herself sat down. "The first thing you have to do to train a cat," she said, "before they do their first trick, is to trick them into thinking it's not something you want them to do for you, it's something they want you to do for them." I didn't understand this very well, so Mrs. Hanrahan went on. She explained to me that she and her husband, Joe, had no fewer than three trained cats, and that all of them only did what they were supposed to do because of what happened afterward. Tyrone, for example, she said, was a remarkable gray tabby who did extraordinary things. Nonetheless, although he had been doing tricks for years, he still had to be tricked to get him into his carrier even to go for a "shoot," as she called it, and then he only did his work for a reward of special vitamins he liked which came in a tube. Her other two were just the same — Rhedd Butler, a beautiful red, would perform only if at the end she knew she could make a beeline for her favorite fake fur puff; while Sally of the Soaps, as she was known for her soap opera work, would perform only if at the end she got special scratching and brushing.

Mrs. Hanrahan asked me to stay in the living room while she took Polar Bear into the bedroom. "I want to try a couple of things," she said. Lots of luck, I wanted to say, but I did not. Nonetheless in an extraordinarily short time Polar Bear came flying back into the living room, closely followed by Mrs. Hanrahan. "I want to tell you something," Mrs. Hanrahan said, sitting down. "He won't make it." Then, thinking I would be upset — when actually I was very relieved — she added, "Don't worry about it. The hardest thing any trainer has to cope with is the fact that practically everybody who has a cat thinks he or she should be in the movies or on television, and they insist on bringing them over to show Joe and me what they can do. What they can do, in a word, they don't. Their cats can do things at home, but not in a studio." She paused. "The best Hollywood trainer I know, a man who works with lions and tigers and bears and elephants and kangaroos and everything else — and has most of them able to do incredible things — told me that the most difficult animal he's ever had to train was the common house cat."

*　　*　　*

After Mrs. Hanrahan had left, relieved as I was about the whole thing, I was not sure how Polar Bear would feel. I knew he really wouldn't like even the idea of being a movie cat, but I also knew him well enough to know that in that inscrutable little contradictory brain of his he might still be harboring the illusion that he at least ought to be considered for the part, even if in the end, of course, he would turn it down. And so, without further ado, and at least to make me, if not him, feel better about it all, I carefully pointed out to him that if I, the one who had made his career possible, was not even being considered for the part of playing me, why on earth should he, ill qualified as he was, be considered for playing him? I at least had real acting experience. In fact, I had played a memorable rug shepherd in a Brush Hill School Christmas pageant — or at least I had until they brought in a real sheep and Brookie the sheep dog decided to herd it.

I also went a step further. I carefully compiled a list of people, if not cats, who never got to play themselves in movies made about them. Did Charles Lindbergh, I asked him, play Charles Lindbergh? Did Glenn Miller play Glenn Miller, or Monty Stratton play Monty Stratton? He did not know who Monty Stratton was, but the answer was obvious. Of course, none of them did — my friend Jimmy Stewart played all of them. Did Thomas A. Edison play Thomas A. Edison, or Clarence Darrow play Clarence Darrow? Again, of course not — Spencer Tracy played Edison and Darrow. And there were countless other examples I had for him. An actress like Frances Farmer was played by Jessica Lange. A singer like Loretta Lynn was played by Sissy Spacek, and even boxers like Rocky Graziano and Jake LaMotta were played, respectively, by Paul Newman and Robert DeNiro. At least a dozen actresses, I pointed out to him, had played Jacqueline Kennedy, and as for Charlton Heston, a man who after all had played pretty nearly everybody else, when it came down to him being played by somebody after he'd gone, my guess was that their choice would be Ronald Reagan.

Anyway, just when I felt I had all the bases covered with him and the whole thing totally nailed down — so that there would be no misunderstanding between us — an extraordinary thing happened. Hollywood, as they say, called.

I will, as they also say out there, take it from the top. I was doing an article on the late John Huston and, in the course of it, I naturally wanted to interview his children. I had done Anjelica and Tony, but somehow I had missed his director son, Danny. When I called Danny he suggested I come over that very day in the late afternoon because he was casting that day and was going to England that night. He named the place — a loft far over on the West Side of Manhattan.

When I arrived, there were half a hundred actors and actresses. Some I knew well, including Dina Merrill, Teresa Wright, Tammy Grimes, and Katharine Houghton, Katharine Hepburn's niece. Some others I knew, too, as one does with actors and actresses, not by their names but by their faces. All of them, it seemed, were engaged in reading scripts — some were even reading in low voices to each other.

I gave my name to the young man who seemed to be handling it all, chatted briefly with some of those I knew, and then sat down and waited. After some time the door opened and someone called my name. I went in and there, in another room, at the end of a long covered table, sat Danny Huston, a producer friend of mine named Steve

Haft, an associate producer, and a casting director. Behind them were half a dozen other people, and what they were doing, obviously — I learned for the first time — was casting a movie. In front of the table was one stool. Equally obviously, that was where I was supposed to sit, so sit I did. As I did so, however, I decided that since this was not the kind of one-on-one interview with Danny I was after, I would at least start with a joke. My leg was bothering me that day, and I had brought a cane, and so, without further ado, I banged my cane on the floor. "This," I said, "is an outrage. Every single person out there but me has a script — I wasn't even given the courtesy of being given one. I don't even know what part I'm up for. I don't even know whether the damned movie is a comedy or a tragedy. All I know is, whatever it is, I can do it."

Everybody seemed to stir uncomfortably. My jokes have a way of taking a little getting used to — which is one of the problems with them. Two people in the back of those seated even started to come toward me as if there had been a call for a bouncer. Danny, however, stopped them. Instead he looked at me directly. "Do it again," he said. I don't like repeating my jokes. Few of them, when you come right down to it, bear repetition, but if there's one thing I can't stand it's my jokes falling on deaf ears. In any case, assuming Danny was perhaps a little hard of hearing, I said it again, loudly — loudly enough, indeed, to make the two who had started forward believe they were right in the first place. But this time Danny himself rose and, telling the others to take a short break, motioned me to come around the table. For some time we sat together and discussed his remarkable father. I took some notes and afterward took my leave.

I thought no more about the whole thing until I had

finished my article and, several weeks later, was out in California. There Marian called me, very excitedly, from the Fund for Animals' New York office. "Guess what?" she asked. I could tell from her voice it was something good. My first guess was that someone had left the Fund a million dollars. "No, not that," Marian said. My next guess was that they had found a cat to play Polar Bear. "No, not that either," Marian said. "What they've found is the cat to play a part in a new movie. And," she added, "guess what — *you're* the cat."

I told her she must be kidding — at the most, they might want me to try out for some part. "No," Marian said firmly, "you've *got* the part." What part? I wanted to know. "It's a part in the movie *Mr. North*," Marian continued. "You'll be playing an elderly butler." A *mature* butler, I automatically corrected. Marian ignored this. She told me I would have to be in Newport, Rhode Island, a week from Tuesday night — that the movie was based on Thornton Wilder's last novel, called *Theophilus North*, that John Huston would be starring in it, and that Danny would be directing. Marian also said that they had sent over a script, and did I know what my first line would be? I did not. "Well," she said, "you're asleep, and somebody says something about Newport, and you're meant to wake up and bang your cane on the floor and say, 'Newport, damnable place! No lady here ever heard the beginning of a concert, or read the end of a book.' "

For the first time I got the idea of how it all happened. Then what do I do, I asked — by this time as excited as Marian. "You go back to sleep," she said. I didn't like the sound of that, but, in a moment, I was all actor again. How many "sides," I asked her, did I have? Marian didn't even know what "sides" were — good help is *so* hard to get nowadays. All right, never mind, I said. How many lines? "Six," she said, "not counting the one I already gave you."

Well, I wasn't to be Hamlet, but then one had to start somewhere. One thing I now knew — how I got the part. By pure luck, with my joke in front of those people, I had come up with something very much like the first line of the butler. And Danny, who was on his way to England to look for, among other things, an English-born butler, and who, like his father, was always on the lookout for someone who would come cheap, had decided I, with practice, would do. Back in New York, however, I wondered how I would handle the matter with Polar Bear. Here I had maintained that one of the reasons he wouldn't be in the movie was that I wouldn't either, and now here I was, behind his back really, about to tread the boards without him. One idea I had was to take him to Newport with me and show him, firsthand, how he wouldn't like making movies, but this plan dissolved when Marian informed me that we would be staying at a motel.

Polar Bear and I had only once stayed at a motel, and he didn't like it at all. That particular time, when I tried to order his midnight niblets, I knew the jig was up when I not only had to explain what niblets were but also what room service was. Apart from Polar Bear's feelings, however, the idea of where I would be staying was unbelievable. Maybe I was not going to be a star but surely there was some distance between that and staying in a motel. In Newport, of all places — a place where, in the days when I was there, even staying in a hotel was beyond the pale. As for staying in a motel, to think that this was going to happen to someone who in his better days had stayed at The Breakers with the last granddaughter of

Commodore Vanderbilt, and who attended the last private dinner party at Marble House, given by Frederick H. Prince, the last private owner of Marble House and the owner of forty-one railroads — really, it was so unthinkable I decided not to think about it.

All in all, I was glad I had decided not to take Polar Bear with me and subject him too to such humiliation. But very soon, too, I decided something else. This was that, from the time Marian and I arrived, we had a wonderful time. Make no mistake, the smell of the greasepaint and the roar of the crowd is heady stuff. All right, the makeup is, if not smelly, at least itchy and irritating, but for me the roar of the crowd, particularly since it was in reverse — we were shooting outside, and they stopped all traffic — was very exciting. Acting, when you came right down to it, is not just more fun than writing — because anything is — it is also more fun because you're not so damn alone. You're a *team*, I tell you. John Huston was too ill to do his part and had been replaced by Robert Mitchum, but if, for example, Lauren Bacall went up on her lines in my first day's shooting, why, I was there to calm her down. And, if Anjelica Huston came to me for guidance, I was there to give it to her. If Robert Mitchum was having an off day — as a matter of fact he wasn't there any day when I was there — I was there to fill that breach, too.

Within a few hours I even felt capable of trying out a bit of business with Harry Dean Stanton, who, as the Cockney sidekick of the hero, Tony Edwards, was the funniest man in the show. I even refused to take offense when he suggested that I not look at the monitors during the shooting, nor see the rushes at night. "If you do," he said, "it'll throw you off for tomorrow." Frankly, by that time I felt nothing could throw me. I particularly enjoyed the alfresco luncheons with the extras who were bus-loaded down from Boston. Some of them had stories going back to Garbo and Rudolph Valentino. Only at one lunch did I sit alone, and that was at my own insistence. I had to, I explained — I was working on my line.

It was true — I had one line that afternoon. Nonetheless, by then I felt like such a seasoned actor that I was not surprised when Marian came over and asked me if I was willing to do an interview with a camera crew which was shooting a film on the making of the film. When the crew appeared, the interviewer turned out to be a young woman who looked to me to be a child. She told me Mr. Huston, as she called Danny, had suggested me — and, as she mentioned him, sure enough I spotted Danny lying down in the grass and pretending he wasn't there. Immediately I decided to give the young woman, and Danny too, their money's worth.

Her first question was not difficult. "What," she asked, "do you think is the main trouble with Hollywood today?" Looking as pensive as I could, I told her that the trouble with Hollywood today was that the actors didn't learn their craft. At this, the young lady looked up. "Frankly, Mr. Amory, I'm not familiar with your career. How long have you been in the movies?" It was my turn to ask a question. I asked her what time it was. Surprised, she looked at her watch. "It's a quarter of five," she said. Young lady, I told her sternly, I have been in this game since seven o'clock this morning. "Do you," she asked, "like making movies?" It's a living, I told her, but it wasn't all beer and skittles. How would *she* like to be my age and taking orders from a twenty-five-year-old whippersnapper? I pointed over at Danny, but it didn't do much good — she just wasn't able to make the necessary age translation. "Do you," she asked, "plan to make any more pictures?" I nodded sagely. "What kind of movie would you like to make?" she continued. I'd like to make a Western, I told her, with Charlotte Rampling. I did not tell her that I had been in love with Charlotte for years but I had never gotten to meet her because she had stupidly married somebody else and gone to live abroad where it was easier for her, I suppose, than living where she might meet me.

In any case I did tell her that after Charlotte and I had made our Western I intended to buy a home in Bel Air with two swimming pools. "Two!" she exclaimed. Yes, I said firmly, one for me and one for my cat. "Your cat!" she exclaimed again. "I thought cats didn't like water." I told her Polar Bear didn't mind horizontal water, he just didn't like vertical water, and that was why I couldn't take showers anymore; I had to take baths. As for swimming, I pointed out, he wouldn't actually go into his pool, but then neither did most Hollywood people. They just had to have a pool so they could sit around it, talk about their tans and their fans. Polar Bear didn't have a tan, but he would want a pool just the same, so he could talk about his fans.

After I had made two movies, I told her, I intended to go right into politics. "Why?" she asked. Because, I explained to her, if you are going into politics in California, you had to be a movie star first, otherwise you couldn't get in. "Why?" she asked again. "Why" was obviously her favorite word. I patiently explained to her it was because a movie star got to meet so many people and therefore they could best find out what the little people were thinking. I did not mention her, but I pointed over to Danny. There was one of them over there, I told her. Why didn't we go over and find out not only what he was thinking, but also if he was.

Months later, when the movie was out, the mail of course poured in. Well, I'm exaggerating. Perhaps I should say it just came in. No, I'll be more accurate, it trickled in. Actually, there were two letters, and one of them, if the truth be known, didn't think I was very good. But, as I've always said, a star can't judge his performance from fan letters. The other letter said I was terrific. Of course some people said it was from my sister, but people are always saying things like that when you get big. It wasn't from my sister at all — it was from my sister-in-law.

I waited faithfully for William Morris and ICM and all the other big agencies to call me for other pictures. But not a single one of them did — not for a Western or even an Eastern. No one even wanted me to play myself in the movie about Polar Bear. The way I figured it, they had all decided I would now be too high-priced. And so, in desperation, I started trying to figure out who, next to me, would do a good job in the movie about Polar Bear. Eventually I settled on George C. Scott. George C. Scott wasn't me, but then, after all, who was? And he did have possibilities.

Accordingly, the next time I was in Hollywood, I paid a call on George. When he and I get together, we like to play chess. And this time was no exception. Midway through our final game I took the bull by the horns — one of my least favorite expressions — and asked him if they made a movie from *The Cat Who Came for Christmas* would he be willing to play me? I carefully did this, incidentally, when it was my turn. George thought for a moment, looking at me. "You can tell them," he said, "I would be interested." We proceeded with our game. Then, shortly before the end — which George was winning — he looked at me again. "Don't tell them I'd just be interested," he said. "That doesn't mean a damn thing. Tell them I'd be very interested."

I thanked George and, afterward, when I went out to dinner with George and his wife, Trish, and another friend, I was determined to show my appreciation by at least getting the check. We were at The Ginger Man, a restaurant owned by Carroll O'Connor, and when the others were talking and I got the waitress' attention, I told her that I would like to get the check, if that would be all right. "Oh, no sir," she said, "Mr. Scott has already told me he wants the check." That was apparently that. I had, however, another opportunity to talk to her a few minutes later. Listen, I told her, I'm a friend of Mr. O'Connor's and he told me to tell you that I was to get the check. "I'm sorry, sir," she said again, "Mr. O'Connor didn't tell me and I don't know you, and Mr. Scott is a regular customer." I had still another chance — this time I was stern. I want you to know, I told her, lying in my teeth, I'm Carroll O'Connor's chief writer in New York. I wrote *In the Heat of the Night.* "I'm sorry, sir," she said a third time, and once more that was that.

But, before dessert, I had one last chance. This time I spoke to her conspiratorially. The reason I want the check, I whispered to her, and Mr. O'Connor wants me to have it, is because today is Mr. Scott's birthday. "Oh," she whispered back, equally conspiratorially. "I understand." And, sure enough, some time later, she slipped me, unnoticed by George, the check.

As George and the rest of us started to get up, however, the restaurant suddenly darkened and through the door came, glowing with candles, the largest birthday cake I have ever seen. Immediately the entire restaurant not only burst into applause but, standing up, started to sing — looking directly at George — "Happy Birthday to You."

At the third "Happy Birthday" line, when the lights from the cake reached our table, I saw George's face. It was a bright and furious red, and it was glowing straight at me. The man who had refused an Oscar was not a man who liked his birthday celebrated in a public restaurant. He lives in a house high in the wilds of the Malibu hills with an unlisted telephone number and an unlisted address on an unnamed street, with all his neighbors carefully instructed, on pain of execution, not to reveal its location. If somehow you do manage to find the house and have the temerity to ring the bell, you will be greeted at the door not by George and Trish but by two mastiffs who are the size of small dinosaurs.

In any case, as the cake was put down on our table, over the din of the last line of "Happy Birthday" and the clapping of the restaurant guests, I could hear, addressed to me, in George's patented Patton voice, various expressions of fury which ended with "DAMN you, Amory — it's in OCTOBER!"

George had, as usual, a factual point — his birthday was in October, and our dinner was in May. In vain on the way out, I tried to explain to him that I didn't know when his birthday was and that I had tried over and over, but that it was the only way I could get the check. My explanation did no good. I didn't hear from George for almost a year.

And, come to think of it, I haven't heard hide nor hair of a movie called *The Cat Who Came for Christmas*. Which, I might add, to Polar Bear's way of thinking, was the best news he'd had since the book came out.

VI ∘ *Meanwhile, Back at the Ranch, I Read Him His Rights*

When I was a small boy — if a large one — I had a favorite aunt. I pronounced this, of course, sounding the *u*, as befitting the proper Bostonian wife of one's uncle, and not what has been corrupted by the rest of the country into a small bug. Her name was Lucy Creshore, and one of what were then regarded as her peculiarities was that she rescued a large number of stray cats and dogs. A sizable number of these she kept right in her own home with her.

I loved my Aunt Lu, and I loved to go to her house and have, as she called it, "stray play." On one occasion, however, I was not at her home alone. I was there for a large Thanksgiving dinner — which in those days regularly included an extended family — and when at this dinner one of her stray cats ventured toward an older cousin of mine, he kicked it. I first picked up the cat and then I kicked my cousin. I got him a good one, too, right in the shins, and afterward I asked him how he liked it. He didn't, and so I put down the cat and we had a fight.

It was a good fight, too — one in which, anyway, there was no more kicking. I really don't know whether I won or not, but I do know that before dinner he and his sister and his father and mother all left — which I took to be an indication that at least he didn't want to fight anymore.

It was a large family of many aunts and uncles, and I never could keep track of everybody and so, on the way home, I asked my father what relation the boy I fought was to me. "He's your second cousin once removed," I remember my father saying, and he then proceeded to explain what that was. I did not, however, pay too much attention to this, because I was already working on one of my bad jokes — which I didn't say but which was on the order that I was glad I had removed him before dinner.

Unfortunately my cousin was not the only member of the family who did not like Aunt Lu's ménage — or as some called it, her menagerie. They thought her house was a mess and they criticized her for it. This only made me more fond of her, and somehow years later, when my college time came around, this relationship came full cycle. This was because that time coincided with some of the worst years of the New England textile business, in which my father was engaged, and it was my Aunt Lu who paid my way through my first three years of college. In my last year, as president of the *Harvard Crimson*, I made enough money to pay my own way. In such office, however, I learned a hard truth. If you have been president of the *Harvard Crimson* in your senior year at Harvard, there is very little, in after life, for you.

In any case, many years before college Aunt Lu had given me as a Christmas present a book. It was a copy of *Black Beauty*. It had immediately become my favorite book. I learned it practically, and almost literally, by heart — that remarkable story of man's inhumanity to horse. I learned, too, the almost equally remarkable story of its English Quaker author, Anna Sewell. *Black Beauty* was the only book Miss Sewell wrote in her life. She was in her fifties when she wrote it and so ill when she did so that it took her seven years and she had to dictate the last chapters because she was in too much pain to hold a pencil. She sold her book outright for just twenty pounds and, dying within a few months of its publication, never lived to see its incredible success — to become indeed the sixth largest-selling book in the English language.

I was also brought up on the story of how *Black Beauty* first reached the American public. Ten years before its publication in 1868, two trotting horses, Empire State and Ivanhoe, each drawing two men, had raced forty miles over rough roads from Brighton to Worcester for a purse of a thousand dollars. Both horses averaged a speed of more than fifteen miles per hour — and both, after the race, died. They had literally been driven to death.

The next day a letter appeared in the *Boston Daily Advertiser*. It read as follows:

> It seems to me that it is high time for somebody to take hold of this matter in earnest, and see if we cannot do something in Boston as well as others have in New York, to stop this cruelty to animals. . . . I, for one, am ready to contribute both time and money, and if there is any society or person in Boston which whom I can unite or who will unite with me in this matter, I should be glad personally or by letter to be informed.

The letter was signed by a great-great-uncle of mine by the name of George Thorndike Angell. He was also a great-uncle of my Aunt Lu. In any case, as a prominent attorney and well-known philanthropist, he soon had a formidable group of leading citizens who responded to his letter, including not only well-known Boston merchants but also some distinguished literary figures. Even before Angell, Emerson, Thoreau, Dr. Oliver Wendell Holmes, and John Greenleaf Whittier had already spoken out against cruelty to animals. But Angell went further. The American Humane Education Society, which came about after his letter to the paper, was the first of its kind in America, and the first publication of the Society was *Black Beauty*. Called by Angell "the 'Uncle Tom's Cabin' of the Horse," the book soon found its way to some three million American readers and virtually every school library in the country.

The book made such an impression on me that it was a boyhood dream of mine to have, some day, the kind of refuge to which the horse Black Beauty finally comes. And today the Fund for Animals has indeed such a refuge — one which not only bears the title, the Black Beauty Ranch, but also has under its entrance sign another sign. This reads as follows:

I have nothing to fear
And here my story ends.
My troubles are all over
And I am at home.

— Last lines of *Black Beauty*
Anna Sewell

Actually, our Black Beauty Ranch, which is located in Murchison, Texas, in the fine nonprairie verdant grasslands of the eastern part of that state, came about not only from my boyhood dream but also from a rather more practical matter. This was that, after embarking on the rescue of animals, we sorely needed our own place to keep — and from which later to adopt — these animals. In the case, for example, of our rescue of the Grand Canyon burros, we had hoped, after first rounding up and then lifting them by helicopter, to adopt them from corrals right on the canyon's rim. But this had proved impractical for two reasons. The first was that we brought up far too many animals — 577, in fact — to do careful on-site adoptions. The second was that many of the burros were in no shape to be adopted right away and we had to have a place to take them, vet them, and either get them into such shape or continue to keep them.

As time went on we began to rescue not just wild burros but also wild horses and wild goats as well as a wide variety of other animals. Indeed, as I write this, Black Beauty is now home to over 600 animals which range over 605 acres and include everything from racehorses to raccoons, from mules to monkeys, from elephants to foxes, and from llamas to such luminaries as Nim, perhaps the world's most famous "signing" chimpanzee, and Shiloh, the last of the infamous Atlantic City "diving" horses — horses which were made to dive six times a day, seven days a week, into a pool ten feet deep sixty feet below them.

I really don't know what possessed me to take Polar Bear to the ranch. I knew all too well how he would be about any exception to his feelings about traveling, but I also felt that, in this particular instance, I had to take exception to his exception. As is my wont — which I like to reserve to myself because I am not fond of other people's wonts — I rationalized my decision in various ways. Polar Bear had, after all, learned to walk on a leash — or at least stay on a leash while I walked around him — why should he not also be able to learn to walk around the ranch, particularly when it was a walk on which I intended to carry him?

When I am going away I always take care not to pack the night before and let Polar Bear see the suitcase and therefore give him less time to be, as he always is, when he sees it, first cross, then mad, and finally furious. Even if he is going with me I do this, because, unlike some of the more fortunate members of the cat-owned fraternity, I am not at liberty to bring out his carrier and show him he is going, too — for the simple reason that wherever I am going is not going to be where he wants to go, for the even simpler reason that he never wants to go anywhere.

So, as usual, quickly and invariably forgetting something, I packed the very morning of our trip, coaxed Polar Bear with a grip of iron into the carrier, and took off for the airport. To say he was better than on previous trips would not be true. Neither would it be true to say he was worse. He seemed worse, but that was only because I had purposely put out of my mind how bad he had always been before.

What brought it all back was the fine-tuning of his "aeiou" 's. These he started the moment we were in the taxi and worked to full pitch when we entered the airplane. Here, after first telling me with a particularly piercing "aeiou" that he wished to be taken out of the hated carrier so that he could at least die where he pleased, and then, when partly out, or rather half in and half out, he began his truly operatic "aeiou," which meant he wanted to leave the plane entirely. Suffice it to say that he was so bad that the flight attendant actually spent considerable time commiserating with me. "Isn't there anything," she asked, "he likes about flying?" I assured her there was not. In Polar Bear's opinion, I told her firmly, an airplane was nothing more or less than a submarine and, furthermore, it was a submarine which, to his way of thinking, had dangerously oversurfaced.

Once off the plane, with Polar Bear still securely in the carrier, I proceeded by bus to the rental car establishment. I do not like to have someone from the ranch have to come to meet me. Everyone at the ranch is busy, and the drive from Dallas to Murchison is close to two hours, and therefore anyone coming to meet me and taking me back would have at least eight hours of driving.

Our trip was in the summer, and it is hot in the summer in Dallas — albeit less so where we were going. In the automobile, after carefully seeing that all windows were secured, I turned on the air conditioner and let Polar Bear out of his carrier to roam and jump the car at will. He was surprisingly good — much better than he was in the plane — and interested in everything, particularly as the verdure became greener and less the desert kind of plains so many people think of as everywhere in Texas. Soon we were not only in green hills but also in horse and cattle country. Polar Bear knows all about horses from the carriage horses in Central Park, but cattle were something else again. Strange creatures as they were, they seemed, from his point of view I'm sure, to have a most desirable way of life. When they weren't actually eating they were chewing, and when they weren't eating or chewing they were lying down and obviously resting up for more eating and chewing.

The nearest town to the ranch is Athens, Texas. Nearby,

however, are both Paris, Texas, and, of all places, New York, Texas. I have often wished that latter could have been the location of the ranch — there are so many people I would like to write to from that address.

In any case, as I turned down the dirt road leading to the ranch, I felt, as I always do, a growing feeling of excitement. Usually, taking people down this road, I insist upon a game — the first one to see one of our burros gets a dollar. But this time I didn't — even though Polar Bear was so glued to the window I think he would have won easily. At the ranch gate I first stopped, as I always do, to check the Black Beauty sign, and then pulled a little way inside, stopped the engine, and just looked around. There were animals visible everywhere. There, off in the distance, reared the huge head of Conga the elephant. Farther off, a herd of wild mustangs were running. And, closer at hand were all kinds of animals whose troubles, indeed, as the sign on our gate said, were all over and who were at home.

In short order one of the ranch hands drove up in the ranch pickup. With him, running alongside the pickup, was Lady, a mutt husky who is, as we call her, our ranch "foredog." Polar Bear was about to think very little of Lady when she somehow communicated to him that she was a guard dog not of people but of animals. The ranch hand had seen pictures of Polar Bear but he had never seen him in person and so, proudly holding him up, I asked him what he thought of him. "Well," he said, "I never expected him to be so what." I could not make head or tail of this and I took immediate umbrage at what the man said. Polar Bear, after all, is far from a so-what anything, least of all a so-what cat. And then, in a flash, it came to me — it always takes me a while to accustom myself to the Texas accent — his "what," of course, was "white."

After exchanging the rental car for the man's pickup, Polar Bear and I took off for a tour. On the way to our first pasture I kept thinking about that East Texas accent. It really has to be heard to be believed. I am not just talking here of "all" for oil, or "are" for hair, or "arn" for iron, or "ass" for ice — remember, I am still in the "a's" — I am also talking "bard" for buried, "kain't" for can't, "dayum" for damn, "fur" for far, "griyuts" for grits, "hard" for hired, "hep" for help, "lags" for legs, "own and oaf" for on and off, "pap" for pipe, "poly" for poorly, "rass" for rice, "stars" for stairs, "tahm" for time, and "tarred" for tired. As if this wasn't enough, all the time they are convinced they are talking the "Kang's Ainglish," and it is other "paypull" who have turned the language around with "ever what" for whatever, and even "ever whichaways" — which, incidentally, is one of their favorite expressions.

I also thought about a call I had one day from a man at the ranch to my New York office. "Cleveland," he said, "I know how you feel about adopting just one burro and that you always want two of 'em to go together." I told him I did indeed. "Well," he said, "there's this fella here from Hogeye, Arkansas, who wants to adopt just one. But, Cleveland" — the man paused — "he's a real nass fella." Nice, I automatically corrected. "Well," the man went on, "I toad him how you felt, but he says he's got a pony and a goat and he jes wants one. He's in the barn with it rat now and he's already named it. He wants to call it Ben Wheeler."

Ben Wheeler was the name of the nearest town to the

ranch, "Pop. 477," as the sign reads. I still hesitated. "Cleveland," the man said again, "I tell you he's a *real* nass fella." I gave up correcting and agreed. There was a long pause. Finally the man spoke again. "Cleveland," he said, "is there a paper in New York called the *New York Times*?" I told the man there was indeed a paper in New York by that name, and they sure would be disappointed that he hadn't heard of them. But I was curious why he wanted to know about it. "Because," the man went on, "this fella says he rats for it, and he wants to rat about the ranch for it." I was very excited. I told the man to be sure to be nass to him — I said it exactly as he said it this time, so there would be no mistake. "Of course I'll be nass to him," the man said. "I told him I was really busy, but if he wanted to follow me around and ask questions that'd be just fine." There was another long pause. "Cleveland," the man said, "tell me something. What would a fella from Hogeye, Arkansas, be doin' rattin' for the *New York Times*?" This time I was firm. I told him never mind what he was doing, just be nass.

The long and short of that story is that the following Christmas Eve the best story that was ever written about the Black Beauty Ranch appeared in the *New York Times*. The writer was Roy Reed, one of the *Times'* most distinguished writers, and a man who now indeed lives in Hogeye, Arkansas. That very afternoon, through directory assistance, I found his telephone number. The woman who answered the phone was, I presumed, Mrs. Reed. In any case, I endeavored to tell her, in the best Texas accent I could muster, that I aimed to talk to Mr. Ben Wheeler. "I'm sorry," she replied, "Mr. Wheeler cannot be disturbed right now. He's eating his Christmas dinner." She then asked me if I wanted to speak to her husband. Before her husband came on the line, however, I had the chance to tell her not only what I thought of her husband's article but also that I knew that Mr. Wheeler had found a wonderful home.

On the way too I thought of another memorable visitor to our ranch, one etched in all our memories. He is the distinguished prizefighter, the Reverend George Foreman, a man who has a church not far away. After touring the entire ranch he asked the man who took him if he could adopt some burros. The man agreed and asked if he would like to pick out his choices. But he did not want to do that. "No," he said, "I'd like you to pick them. I'd like you to pick the four burros on the whole ranch who you think have the least chance of ever getting adopted."

The man did so, well knowing that those burros, too, like Mr. Reed's, would have the right kind of home.

I have one animal I always visit first when I go to the ranch. This is a very special burro named Friendly. When we arrived at the main burro pasture, I got out of the pickup, first putting up the window to see that Polar Bear didn't follow me. Before I spotted Friendly in the pasture, however, she spotted me and came not running — burros rarely run — but trotting, which for a burro is full speed for anything but flight. As Friendly came close and I reached to pat her I looked over to the pickup and saw that Polar Bear was not only looking but scratching to get out. Immediately I went back and picked him up and carried him out to meet what I was sure was the first burro he had ever met. Friendly is tough on animals her size or larger but with something smaller, particularly one as small as Polar Bear, she is a perfect lady — so much so that in this case Polar Bear was not even jealous. And while Friendly plowed her head into my stomach and Polar Bear began exploring her neck with his paw I thought, as I always do, how much this burro had meant to our first major rescue.

Friendly had come up in a sling under the helicopter in the very first batch of burros we rescued in the Grand Canyon. I was in the corral when she was lifted up over the rim and delicately dropped to the ground. I was also one of the crew who untied her. Friendly did not, as all the other burros had done, trot immediately and rapidly away from us — instead she just stood and looked at us in that contemplative and philosophical way I was soon to learn was her trademark. Whatever had happened to her — the roundup, being tied in a sling, being picked up and fastened to a roaring helicopter overhead, being carried seven thousand feet up in the air, and then finally being let down among all of us and hundreds of onlookers — it had all been sudden and uncomfortable and ridiculous and even crazy, and she surely thought that was what we must all be. But she also realized, I felt then and still feel, that no one had really hurt her, and therefore we were not all bad. That first night, after dusk, I had gone out to the corral again. For the first time I walked through what had been, only a few hours ago, those "wild" burros, and I was looking for her. Behind me, sitting on the fence, I heard some of the cowboys who had taken part in the rescue laughing at me. I turned to look at them and suddenly I saw what they were laughing at. All the time I had been looking for Friendly there, in the dark behind me, quietly plodding along and knowing full well, I am sure, how funny it was, was Friendly.

We had already publicly said that wild burros would make good pets — better pets, indeed, we had claimed,

from the point of view of temperament, than horses —
and we had also said that, rather than get your kid a pony,
get him or her a burro. We said that because we needed
to get homes for our burros, but at the same time we
didn't really know just how good they would be, and we
certainly hadn't had it proved to us. The burro who proved
it was Friendly. That was why, then and there, in those
first moments at the corral when she stood and looked at
us and had not trotted away, I had given her her name.
In a way I felt Friendly was responsible not only for the
successful Grand Canyon rescue and adoption program
but also for the much larger later rescues at the Naval
Weapons Center at China Lake and Death Valley —
more than five thousand burros in all.

I did not see whether Polar Bear would become jealous
when, still holding him, I gave Friendly the kind of all-
out bearhug, if in this case a one-armed one, I was used
to giving her. I did remember, though, as I was doing this,
what had happened on another occasion when she, not
Polar Bear, was watching me hug another burro.

It had happened more than ten years before. Friendly,
you see, at the time of the Grand Canyon rescue, was
pregnant. Later, at the ranch, she had her baby, which
we named Friendly Two — and always spelled it that way.
The first time I ever saw her baby she had trotted over
with her from a distance in the pasture. That time, when
she had started to put her head into my stomach, she had
suddenly stopped, moved back, and instead — with some
pride — pushed her baby toward me. I had hugged and
hugged and gushed and gushed over the baby until, suddenly, even more quickly than she had stopped before,
she pushed in, pushed her baby away, and pushed her
own head back into my stomach. It was just as if she was

saying that she wanted to show me her baby, and had wanted me to hug her, but enough was enough. I was never to forget that she was Friendly One and her baby was Friendly Two.

This time, though, it was Polar Bear's turn to decide that my hugging of Friendly One had gone on quite long enough, thank you very much. In fact he squirmed so meaningfully that I had to stop patting Friendly and let him give me a push in the stomach, Friendly not withstanding.

It was time to move on anyway, because there were many other burros to whom I wanted to give personal attention. One in particular was one of those rare cases in which a burro, after an adoption, had come back to us. Adoption policies at the Fund for Animals are strict. Our contract reads that any animal may be taken back by us if "in the subjective judgement of the Fund the animal is not properly cared for, watered, fed, looked after, etc. even including the word 'happy.' " Ed Walsh, the Fund's peerless New York lawyer, without whom there would be no Fund, said that what I wanted wasn't very legal, but I told him to put it in anyway for the good of my soul. Ed complained that my wanting it and the good of my soul didn't make it any more legal, but Ed doesn't understand Episcopal souls very well. Frankly, I don't think he thinks Episcopal souls are completely legal anyway. In any case, this particular burro was returned to us because he was, his former adopters said, "too wild," and that they "couldn't do anything with him." He arrived back at the ranch at 2:00 one afternoon, and by that evening he was not only eating out of a ranch hand's hand, he was also nuzzling all visitors, even total strangers.

After the burros came the mules. There are dozens of

these at the ranch, and one of the reasons we have so much affection for them is that our more difficult rescues could not have been made without them. When, for example, burros had to be driven down from the high ground to which they regularly repaired when being chased, the cowboys mounted mules, who are both craftier and more surefooted in difficult high-ground open situations.

There was justice in this, of course, because the reason a mule is smarter than a horse is that its mother was a burro. If the father was a burro and the mother was a horse, the result is a hinny. The ranch people maintain that a hinny is even smarter than a mule for the very reason that the father is a burro, but, as I have many times told them, they might very well get away with saying something like that in Texas but I had to live in New York. As we looked at the mules, however, I had to admit they were extraordinary animals. My personal favorite is Ghostly — an all-white fellow who has such a remarkable combination of smartness and gentleness that he has won the hearts of all of us, and even did Polar Bear's when I tried a picture of a white mule and a white cat together. It wasn't easy with one arm around Polar Bear and the other on Ghostly, and the picture didn't come out. But then my pictures rarely do since they stopped making Brownies. I was terrific with a Brownie.

After the mules we went looking for horses. There are so many different kinds of horses on the ranch that it is hard to pick either stars or favorites. All in all though I think Polar Bear's favorite was a small, stunted, lovable little guy who was perhaps the most awful starvation case we had ever encountered. He was rescued on a Thanksgiving

Day, so we named him Pilgrim. On the day when he was found he could hardly move at all but was desperately trying to inch his way toward what would have been his Thanksgiving dinner — the bark of a tree. At first trusting no one, he now seems to trust everyone, and Polar Bear was no exception. As I stood with Polar Bear in my arms, Pilgrim came forward and started what I knew to be a friendly whinny, to which Polar Bear first responded with at least one of his tentative "aeiou" 's and then, to my surprise, reached out a definitely friendly paw.

Our next horse stop was with a white horse named Cody. I did not let Polar Bear near him because, of all the stories on the ranch of man's inhumanity to horse, his is perhaps the most outrageous. His former owner, an Atlanta doctor, became so angry that he would not come to him as he would to a boy who looked after him that one day, in a fit of anger, he shot the horse in the knee. Not satisfied with this, he then rigged a block and tackle with weights and left Cody shackled with no medical attention for ten days. A group of Atlanta women took the doctor to court but, although the prosecution was successful, they were unable to gain custody of Cody. Nonetheless they persevered to the end, and after first buying Cody at an auction — which would have led to a slaughterhouse fate — next raised the money to have him transported to Black Beauty Ranch.

The first time I saw Cody trying to hobble around on an all but useless front leg I was certain he was in such severe pain that he should be put down. The vet, however, asked me to defer such a decision until that afternoon. And, that afternoon, the next time I saw Cody he was in one of the pastures, far off from where he had been before. If he had been in as much pain as I thought, the vet pointed out to me, why would he have hobbled all that way? I had no answer, but I was still worried that, with wild mustangs around, when it came to grain-feeding time he would not have a chance. A ranch hand answered that by having me watch him at feeding time. Cody not only got his share, but, with ears laid back and teeth bared at any horse who tried to take any food from him, even the wildest of the wild mustangs soon saw there was little percentage in trying to get Cody's share. Needless to say, when I brought Polar Bear to see Cody, I too kept our distance. The way Cody swings that head of his, I have learned, the only way to approach him is to keep someone he sees regularly between you and him.

Only one of my favorites was missing — Whitey, the horse we almost got. Whitey became the symbol of countrywide carriage-horse abuse when, a few summers ago, he staggered for a moment on New York City's Sixty-second Street, then, literally delirious from the heat, he suddenly fell over on his side. There he would have died had it not been for the quick reaction and expert first aid administered by a registered nurse and two visiting Californian veterinary students. Although New York City carriage horses are supposed to be off the streets when the temperature reaches 90° — one of the few victories the Fund for Animals had then achieved for these animals — a woman who went to see Whitey noted that this was the same horse who, six weeks before, she had seen collapse from the heat and had observed being first kicked and then whipped to his feet by his driver.

Led by the New York radio commentator Barry Gray, the Whitey case created a furor — one which, although Whitey's owner refused the Fund for Animals' offer to buy him, did at least lead to Whitey's being removed from the city entirely. It also led to tough new carriage-horse legislation which bars the carriage horses from operating in traffic during rush hours and basically confines them to Central Park. Remarkably, the New York City Council passed this bill 31 to 3, and although vetoed by Mayor Ed Koch, it became law when the council overrode the mayor's veto 28 to 4 — the first time a mayor's veto had been overridden in twenty years. Just why Mayor Koch saw fit to veto the measure is still a mystery. The only explanation would seem to be that he apparently turned the same blind eye toward the misery of the carriage horses with which he watched the incredible corruption within his administration — something which led to his later well-deserved defeat at the polls.

Our last horse engagement was to visit the far pastures — the domain of the Fund's wild horses. For no animals has the Fund for Animals fought harder than for these. I personally had high hopes for the wild horses when President Reagan first came into office. He had, after all, once made the stirring statement that "the best thing for the inside of a man is the outside of a horse." President Reagan's feelings, however, were apparently limited to Republican horses. Although fewer than seventy thousand wild horses ever grazed our public lands — yours, by the way, and mine — in comparison with some four and a half million cattle and sheep, all of course grazed by the ranchers at ridiculously low fees — nonetheless, the western ranchers and their toadying politicians had their way.

Roundup after roundup was authorized by Congress, and the Bureau of Land Management in the 1980s alone was voted millions upon millions of extra dollars to do their brutal work. This work, incidentally, they almost never did themselves, but instead ladled out to cronies.

On one of their feedlots in Nevada, when I asked the man who ran the place if I could see his cripples, he replied, "Oh, you wouldn't want to see them — and you sure wouldn't want them. Some can't even walk and some have their eyes out." That man, by the way, ran his infamous corral with no veterinarian and received ten thousand dollars a day.

When it came to the Bureau of Land Management's adoption policies, these were almost as cruel as their roundups and holding pens. Although under the Wild Horse and Free-Roaming Burro Act they were not supposed to adopt out more than four horses to a person, by the use of phony fee-waivers and "powers of attorney" they would often give out as many as a thousand horses to one person. And, although the act specifically said the horses were not to go to slaughter, they gave away, as our lawsuits proved, hundreds of animals knowing full well they would.

Here it should be noted that wild horses are not "broken" at Black Beauty — the word is never used. What they are is "gentled." Nor, during this process, are they ever approached by truck or even on horseback, because that is how they were originally driven and captured. They are approached only on foot. After the personal approach comes the personal delivery of some grain — just dropped and left. Then, a day or so later, an apple or a carrot is presented, this time by hand. Finally, when this has gone on for several days, there comes the first and very gentle pat. From that time on, the ranch hands maintain, a child could do the rest. And in the case of my granddaughter Zoe, age twelve, a child did.

*   *   *

By this time I felt Polar Bear was up to meeting the largest of the ranch's lodgers — the elephants. As we approached Conga, and Conga approached us, I held Polar Bear back a little — not so much to add to his apprehension but so that I could sneak a backward glance at his eyes. These, I was glad to see, contained, along with their usual travel-weary owlishness, a by now practiced, if not totally resigned, agreement to look over whatever manner of monster I was next placing on his menu. Conga, I must say, mountainous as she must have seemed to Polar Bear, was at her gentle giant best. Holding Polar Bear as I was, with a fence between him and Conga, even as Conga's trunk came over the fence toward him, he was far more fascinated than he was frightened. And, I am sure, what he found most fascinating about elephants was that they seemed to have tails at both ends.

Actually Conga is friendly to all residents and visitors, both people and animals, and even welcomes one and all to her pasture — albeit she does not want anyone but regulars to sit on her fence. As for her neighbors in the next pasture, before we had a companion elephant for her, she took such a shine to one particular burro that every evening she would take some hay over and, dumping it close by, first put her trunk over the fence and hug the burro and then, moving away, would proceed to do the one trick she knew, kneeling on one front knee, with one back leg extended.

At the ranch we do not encourage ex-performing animals to "do their thing," but in this case we had made an exception. We had also noticed that the old saw that elephants are afraid of small animals does not hold in Conga's case. She is not in the least afraid of field mice, and dogs as well as cats go in and out of her pasture with impunity. Knowing all this, I was certain, as I held Polar Bear reasonably close to her, that she would not alarm him. And she did not. I did have the feeling, though, that Polar Bear thought there was entirely too much of her, but since he feels that way about virtually every animal larger than himself, I did not let it worry me. Normally, when I am on one of my regular ranch visits without Polar Bear, I go right under the fence and under Conga, too, and pat her everywhere including under her stomach. I also reach right into her mouth and pat her tongue — she loves that. On this visit, however, I drew the line at both of these intimacies. Just the same, after putting Polar Bear back in the pickup, I gave Conga some special pats specially edited for Polar Bear's benefit.

In short order Conga's companion, Nora, arrived. Nora, in comparison to Conga's fourteen, is a six-year-old African, and I was sure she would appeal to Polar Bear. For one thing, she is less than a third of Conga's size. But if I had assumed the meeting would be easy, I certainly assumed wrong. I should have realized that Nora is a very young elephant, and Polar Bear, bad as he is with new adults, is even worse with new children. Elephant children, I soon learned, were no exception. Nora didn't make things any easier either because, among other things, she is a lot faster with her trunk than Conga. In any case, Nora expected the kind of food we generally bring around — apples, oranges, bananas, watermelon, sweet potatoes, and such — and, seeing Polar Bear, seemed to make the immediate decision that he was something between a banana and a sweet potato. She made a very sudden and very rapid trunk reach toward him. Immediately and bravely out flew Polar Bear's paw. It was touch and go there for a second but, looking back without the benefit of Instant Replay, I had to give Polar Bear the round, and I was proud of him.

Both elephants came to us in all-too-typical ways. Conga came from a roadside zoo in Florida where, about to be replaced by a younger elephant who knew more tricks, she faced either being sent, in zoo parlance, "down," or, literally, being put down, or killed. Nora, on the other hand, came to us from a circus — one which was successfully prosecuted for cruelty by a long-time friend of the Fund, Bettijane Mackall, who then sent Nora to us. As we stood with Conga and Nora I was, as always, brought back to my first relationship with elephants in such places as Kenya, Tanzania, and Mozambique. Even before the days of the mass poaching, among the Fund's earliest gifts to other societies were Africa-bound infrared equipment and other sophisticated antipoaching weaponry. Today, after the cruel carnage, and despite the far too long deferred ban on the ivory trade, we still are far from sanguine about what continues to go on. Dick Lambert, for example, husband of Florence Lambert, one of the Fund's most stalwart elephant supporters, became so incensed at governmental corruption that, after offering to give his own airplane for antipoaching work, he eventually took back his gift. "We weren't satisfied," Mrs. Lambert says, "that the governments were doing enough."

Nor are all of the elephants' troubles confined to Africa. If anyone thinks so, perhaps he or she should pause for a moment, as I did there at the ranch, and think of an incident which occurred at the San Diego Zoo — one which, at least up to that time, had long been considered one of this country's most respected. It began when

Dunda, an African elephant like Conga and Nora, was transferred from her long-time "home" at the zoo itself and taken to the zoo's Wild Animal Park, where she was to go into a "breeding program." Here, lonely and frightened, Dunda, according to the zoo, swung her trunk at a keeper, although this was never proved. Afterward, the head elephant keeper, Alan Roocroft, ordered what he called a "disciplinary session." What happened at this session — which did not become public for months — was that, a full day later, after her alleged trunk-swinging, Dunda was stretched out on the floor with a block and tackle and, while Mr. Roocroft yelled voice commands, other keepers, positioned on each side of her head, alternately beat her at varying intervals for two days with ax handles.

Just how the zoo was able to cover up this story would seem incredible unless one was familiar with both the zoo and its highly organized publicity network. Even Dunda herself, her head a mass of welts and bruises, was hidden. Finally, however, primarily because of two zoo elephant keepers, Steve Friedlund and Lisa Landres, the story did break. And, when it broke, it broke in all particulars, including the fact that Dunda was a gentle elephant and never had done the trunk-swinging of which she was accused. From then on the hero of the story was Dan McCorquodale, a remarkable California state senator and chairman of the Senate's Natural Resources and Wildlife Committee. Despite opposition from not only the San Diego Zoo but also from virtually every zoo in the state, he demanded and chaired a hearing on "the Dunda case."

The zoo brought out witness after witness, from their board members to their curators and from their veterinarians to Joan Embry, all of whom had a vested interest in the coverup, and all of whom, it seemed, made three claims — that the beating had not been severe; that severe discipline was necessary in the handling of elephants; and that the Dunda case was an isolated incident. None of these claims was substantiated, and as for the beating of Dunda being an isolated incident, it was soon apparent that such beatings at the zoo were routine, if for no other reason than that they made it easier for the elephants to perform tricks. One of Mr. Roocroft's favorites, we learned, was to conclude a Wild Animal Park tour by having the visitors seeing him lying down on the ground on his back and having an elephant stand over him with one foot just over his face.

I was to be the first speaker on Dunda's side. But before I even testified, I was subjected to much pressure not to do so, including being called by the chairman of the board of the zoo. Then, literally just before I was introduced, Mr. Roocroft himself came over to me and said that he was "authorized" to offer me the zoo's "best bull elephant." This, he said, he would personally take, at the zoo's expense, to our Black Beauty Ranch and, "no matter how long it took," would breed him to Conga and that we could have the baby. I was so flabbergasted that for some time I didn't even answer, but when I did, I did so in a voice which I hoped would be heard by Senator McCorquodale. I told Mr. Roocroft that the Fund for Animals had never been in favor of breeding animals but that now, knowing him, I was not sure we were in favor of breeding people.

Fortunately, we had witnesses on our side who were far better able to keep their tempers than I was, and, not long after the hearing, despite the opposition, Senator McCorquodale's bill to ban the beating of elephants passed the California legislature by a wide margin.

After the elephants we headed back to the ranch house and supper. Here Polar Bear was to visit the animal I wanted him to meet most of all, one of the ranch's most loved creatures — a cat. By no means young in age, she is, in point of residence, the oldest animal on the ranch, because she was already there when we bought the place. Her name is Peg and, if Lady is the foredog of the ranch, then Peg is assuredly the forecat — if, for no other reason, than that she has only three legs. Her fourth, her right front, is off at the shoulder — lost, we were told, to a leghold trap on neighboring property.

From the moment Polar Bear and Peg met there was an understanding between them I had never seen with Polar Bear and any other animal. Perhaps it was the fact that, after a day spent with so many others, he was at last face-to-face with one of his own kind. Or perhaps it was that he seemed immediately to recognize Peg's infirmity and not only respected it but felt he would not be offered the kind of challenge he might have expected from barging into another cat's domain. In any case, it was extraordinary. Almost immediately Polar Bear leaped up on the sofa and went into his Buddha meditation pose — gazing directly at Peg, who was seated across the way. Then, slowly, Peg arose, looked around for a moment, and then hopped over toward Polar Bear. Just before she leaped toward him she turned a little sideways and so landed beside him. As Polar Bear turned to look at her, she too turned to look at him, but neither look from either one of them betrayed even the slightest hint of the typical hostile cat stare.

And, not immediately but in good cat time, Polar Bear slowly turned over on his side and reached out with all four paws. So did Peg — albeit with just three. In a moment all seven paws were actually touching each other's stomachs and in that position first Polar Bear, who had, after all, had a very long day, closed his eyes and then Peg closed hers and both were fast asleep.

For some time I just sat and looked at Polar Bear and Peg together — particularly at Peg. To me, Peg has long been the living symbol of the cruelty of the fur business. No animal, with the exception of the ape, the raccoon, and the otter, uses his or her frontal extremities more deftly than the cat. To go through the rest of a life without the use of a front paw — in Peg's case, a whole front leg — was tragic enough, but at least Peg was just one animal. When one thought from her to the literally millions of other animals whose only escape from the awful leghold was to gnaw off their own leg, one could easily realize that trapping was one of the worst of all man's inhumanities to animals.

My own fight against the fur trade went back even before I founded the Fund for Animals. I remember particularly an exhibit I had at the New York World's Fair in 1965. We had live animals behind glass in various showing rooms. The most popular of these had been the final room, called The Den, which featured a beautiful model in a cloth coat together with her three friends — a German shepherd, a coyote, and a wolf. Barbara Walters came out from the Today show and interviewed me. "Cleveland," she said, "do you really think you're going to stop the women of American from wearing furs?" I told her I didn't know, but that I was sure as hell going to try and that particularly I was going to try to make them relate the fur on their back to the cruelty involved. I remember well Barbara's surprise, and I did not blame her — at that time it seemed so far off. Today, however, it does not seem so.

Not just in this country but all over the world the fur industry is under attack. My particular favorite antifur slogan is that of the Friends of Animals: "Get the Feeling of Fur — Slam Your Hand in a Car Door." I am also partial, however, to my own way of handling someone wearing a fur coat. This is to walk behind them and say to someone beside me, in a loud voice, "It's just what I always told you — it makes her look so fat." I like to do this so much I do it even when there is no one beside me — I just pretend there is.

For years the furriers have countered antifur arguments with truly extraordinary logic, as witnessed in the following quotation from *Fur Age Weekly:*

> The first tool, as anthropologists use the term, was not the first stone to be hurled or the first stick to be wielded. Lesser anthropoids can do that. The first precision tool requiring nimble fingers was probably a bone needle used to sew hides together. . . . Thus it is not unreasonable to assert that the fur industry is largely responsible for the extraordinary adroitness and coordination of the human hand — particularly that crucial, uniquely human device, the fully opposable thumb. The ability to stitch rabbit pelts together ultimately became the ability to assemble transistor radios, perform delicate surgery and play the music of Chopin.

Furriers also have a remarkable ability to distance themselves and their business from the cruelty. When, for instance, as far back as 1972 I showed a Fund for Animals trapping film on Walter Cronkite's Evening News, two of the country's leading furriers told me personally it was the first time they had ever actually seen animals in traps. Furriers still do not admit traps are cruel, but at the same time they do their best to convince the public that they trap very few furs but instead ranch almost everything. The reality, of course, is far different. Actually an enormous amount of all furs, even mink, are trapped, and only chinchilla is totally ranched. In any case, make no mistake, fur ranches can be almost as gruesome as traps. I shall never forget one experience I had with a ranch in Idaho — one of, of all animals, beavers. It was supposed to be a "model" beaver ranch, but whatever it was, it had gone bankrupt. The receivers turned out to be Teresa Kloos and Alexia Reynolds, two extremely humane young women, who, when advised to have the beavers killed, refused to do so. Instead they contacted the Fund for Animals.

The first time I saw the beavers I couldn't believe it. If this was a "model" ranch — their only water was their own urine — I wondered what a bad ranch was like. Nonetheless, we went to work. We took out advertisements asking for people who wanted to adopt a beaver — or, rather, two beavers — and in short order, in a state which at that time had been almost totally "trapped-out," as they call it, of beaver, we soon had hundreds of applicants. Many Idahoans, it seemed, had sorely missed that wonderful animal and had either ponds or a river on their property. The "expert" wildlife biologists we spoke to told us that our beavers, who had been more than three generations in the ranch, would not survive three days in the wild, but thankfully this proved almost totally false. Out of 905 beavers we lost less than half a dozen — through road kills or other accidents — and most became almost as highly regarded by their owners as the owners' own pets.

As for myself, to this day I keep — facing the desk in my office — a picture of Blackie, as I called the first beaver we placed. He is a beautiful animal, with a silvery shine in his black fur, and his eyes seem to be looking at me just the way they did when I pushed him toward his first pond. There is a special glint in those eyes — one which I've always taken as a last quick "thank you." To this day when I see a woman — or, for that matter, a man — in a beaver coat, I am disgusted.

I also keep on my desk a letter from a fur rancher, albeit a pretty impersonal one, since it was addressed, "To All Anti-Fur People." Nonetheless I found it fascinating. "God," the man had written, "was the first furrier. This was because," he later continued, "God told Adam and Eve to clothe themselves in skins." And therefore, the man concluded, what he was doing was, "following in God's Footsteps and doing God's Work."

My answer to that man was that I did not believe many furriers would go to heaven, but that if by chance he should be one of the few, I felt entitled to hope that, when he got there, God would turn out to be a very large, and very cross, beaver.

Actually, strained as through the years have been my relations with furriers, they are no more so than my relations with hunters. The reason is simple. Hunters have never seemed to understand what I have tried to do for them. As far back as 1963, for example, on the Today show I announced the formation of a new club — one to be called the "Hunt the Hunters Hunt Club." All the club ever tried to do was to define the word "conservation" for the hunters the way they have always defined it for the animals. We were shooting them, in other words, for their own good. But from the beginning the hunters made no effort to understand this, even though we made clear we never used words like "shooting" or "killing." Instead we used the hunters' own words — words with which they would feel comfortable — "culling," "trimming," "harvesting," or just "taking." We wanted them to understand that if we didn't take them, in no time at all there would be too many of them. They would be crowding the woods, and the fields and the roads, and they would be breeding like flies.

All we really asked of the hunter, when you came right down to it, was for him to take the long-term view of the whole thing and not the selfish short-term view. In the end we both wanted, after all, the same thing — we both wanted a stronger herd. We even asked them directly if they had ever seen a hunter out there in the middle of the winter, starving in the woods. It was not a pretty sight.

The hardest criticism we had to take was that the "Hunt the Hunters Hunt Club" had no season on hunters. Nothing could have been further from the truth. The club's very second rule forbade members to take hunters — and I quote — "within city limits, in parked cars or in their dating season." And the third rule clearly stated that, after harvesting their hunter, members were not to — and I quote again — "drape him over the automobile or mount him when they got home." Mounting the cap or jacket, we felt, was in better taste.

The next hardest criticism we had to take from the hunters was their claim that we were out to exterminate them. This was unfair, and really was, we felt, hitting below the belt because, as we made clear from the beginning, when the hunters' numbers fell below a certain level we had another whole program to deal with that — we would breed our own hunters. We called this program "Hunters Unlimited." It is true that not many of our members had experience with hunters' children, but from the ones they did know they were certain that, with a little practice, they could do as well. Naturally, though, we wanted to breed the kind of hunters who would jump about and flush properly and make sporty game. We were certainly entitled to that — after all, it was our money which was paying for the whole program.

An extraordinary number of people wrote me after the broadcast asking to become members of the club, which I found very gratifying. And, more than a quarter of a century later, the syndicated columnist Roger Simon wrote a column which to my mind highly qualifies him to be at least an honorary member. Mr. Simon's work was occasioned by the Fund for Animals' challenge to the so-called "hunter harassment" laws — which some state legislatures, pressed by the NRA and other hunter advocacy groups, had passed despite the fact that the law's constitutionality was widely questioned. Mr. Simon wrote, in part, as follows:

> We all know that many odd things are legal in this country. You can burn the American flag. You can march around wearing sheets and burning crosses. You can exhibit dirty pictures at government expense.
>
> You can also shoot an arrow into a deer's eyeball. That's legal. It is *illegal* to speak the words: "I don't think you should shoot that arrow into a deer's eyeball."
>
> Five people were arrested in Maryland for doing this

last weekend. . . . Forest and Wildlife Supervisor Joshua Sandt, who supervises the state deer herds, defended the hunters. "I think the biggest problem people have is that they tend to believe that animals think and feel the same way we do," Sandt said. "First off, they don't think and, second, their nerve endings are not the same as ours."

Well, first off, Joshua Sandt couldn't be any dumber if you cut off his head. And second, if Sandt really believed that animals "don't think" and have different "nerve endings" then I guess it would be OK if people went out and shot arrows into dogs and cats, too.

The next morning at the ranch we were up betimes. This is an expression I not only wish more young people knew the meaning of but also made more use of — particularly since so many of them, at least in the morning, are chronic somniacs. Polar Bear, I am glad to say, is always up betimes. He was so even when I first knew him and now, in his more mature years, continues to be. I was particularly glad he was so that morning, because it was to be a very special morning for him — one in which he would meet, if he would pardon the expression, a fellow animal celebrity, one who is indeed one of the world's best-known animals.

He is a chimpanzee, and his name is Nim. Born in 1973 at the Institute for Primate Studies in Oklahoma, he was, at the age of two weeks, at the direction of Dr. Herbert Terrace, a psychologist at Columbia University, taken from his mother and brought to New York City. Here, at the home of one of Dr. Terrace's students, Stephanie LaFarge, Nim would not only live in a house with a human family, he would also sleep in a crib at night and, in the daytime, wear clothes, sit in a high chair, eat at the family table, and be trained to use the toilet.

Just like any other baby, Nim was bottled and burped, diapered and rocked, tickled and played with, and, in turn, just like any other baby he smiled and laughed, yelled and cried. From the beginning, however, from his very first giggles, all the humans around Nim talked to him in sign language, the language of the deaf. And, in the very same way a baby begins to understand words, Nim began to understand signs.

One day, still in the very early life of Nim, something happened which related very strongly to the fact he was about to meet Polar Bear. One of his teachers, ever on the lookout for something which would excite Nim, brought with her to his "class" one day something in a carrier. Peeking through the hole Nim saw that inside was a white cat. Nim was very excited. "Open me," he signed, pointing to the box. "There's a cat in the box," the teacher signed back to him. Nim of course knew that, but seeing the teacher would not immediately open the carrier he began a whole variety of other signs, including "Open cat," "Cat hug," and "Cat me."

Eventually Nim, squealing with delight, was allowed gently to play with and hug the cat. There was only one problem — whenever the teacher held the cat Nim got jealous. At first the teacher did not know whether he was jealous of her because she held the cat or of the cat because that was what Nim wanted to hold. Nonetheless the visit went well, and at the end of it Nim had very gently hugged and kissed the cat good-bye.

At the end of almost four years of schooling Nim had become the most famous of all the "signing" chimps. He had appeared on the covers of numerous magazines and had had two books written about him. But Nim was once again separated from those he knew and loved and was returned to Oklahoma. Then, from there, Nim was sent to a New York laboratory. Here was a chimpanzee who had not only already done more than his share of service to humanity — more than a score of his student teachers had either written theses about him or had otherwise bettered their careers through their work with him — and yet that apparently wasn't enough. He would now undergo experimentation.

This was totally unacceptable to us, and we resolved to go all-out for Nim. Many other like-minded societies joined us and, finally, threatened with what would surely be a highly publicized lawsuit, the University of Oklahoma agreed to remove Nim from the New York laboratory and take him back once more to the place where he was born. While Nim was there, he would once again be under the care of his first owner, Dr. William Lemmon.

I knew that Dr. Lemmon had had many large offers for Nim — from well-known zoos all the way to circuses — but I also knew that I had one thing in my favor. This was that Dr. Lemmon was no admirer of circuses and not even one of most zoos. Finally, after I had an all-day session with him in Oklahoma, Dr. Lemmon agreed to let us have Nim under one condition — that the Black Beauty Ranch would indeed be his permanent home. It was my turn to make a condition. I told Dr. Lemmon that Black Beauty was like the Ark — we wanted two of a kind, and he would have to find us the right companion for Nim.

Dr. Lemmon met his condition well. He came up with an ex-circus chimp named Sally, one who was over breeding age and who was as even in temperament as Nim was uneven. The day she arrived at the ranch to join Nim was a memorable one. If it wasn't love at first sight, it was certainly love after first bite. And, from the very beginning,

Sally proved that even at Nim's worst she was able, if not to charm him, at least to calm him.

As we approached the porch of Nim and Sally's house, both of them had, from far off, their eyes glued on Polar Bear. And, as we got closer, I could see that this would not be the all-too-often situation that it is with strangers approaching — of a visitor poking at chimps. This would be the opposite — the chimps wanted to poke at the visitors. I did not want this, however. I knew that Nim had a terrific memory for almost everything that had happened in his childhood and, while I wondered whether he could recall, back in his past, that first white cat, I took no chances on any gentle touch. Fortunately, I did not have to worry. Nim immediately grabbed his tire and started showing off and, after waiting for Sally to calm him down, I cautiously moved forward with Polar Bear. As we came closer I noticed Polar Bear's eyes moving back and forth, following Nim as he rode the tire.

Suddenly Nim rode over to us and gave his sign for "toothbrush." Obediently Polar Bear and I went for his toothbrush and paste. I handed them to him, but still there was apparently something missing — he was making a sign with which I was unfamiliar. Suddenly I remembered. Nim wanted his mirror. I went and got it and handed it to him and, while Polar Bear watched in amazement, Nim first held up the mirror, then brushed his teeth, and finally and very politely offered to do the same for Polar Bear. Fortunately, though, Polar Bear pleaded a previous engagement. Even I have a very difficult time brushing Polar Bear's teeth, and he wasn't about to stand still for the job being done by a chimpanzee.

I had wondered if, when Polar Bear and Nim were face-to-face, Nim might not have a go at his old signs of "Me cat'' and ''Me hug,'' etc., but he did not. I know some of Nim's sign language, and others at the ranch know much more than I do, but none of us are inclined to make a big thing of it. Actually most of the time Nim understands so much of human language that signs are not even necessary. Usually I will ask Nim something such as if he thinks it's going to rain. He will immediately look up and around at the sky and then either nod or shake his head as the case may be. Signs in such instances do seem superfluous. And, if there is one thing all of us at the ranch want for Nim, it is that he have no more pressure in his life. If he wants to sign, he signs. If he doesn't, he doesn't — and that's that.

Close contact with Nim, who, although I wouldn't say it in Polar Bear's presence, is undoubtedly the smartest animal I have ever known, always makes me think of just how close he came to being just one more laboratory animal. This was vividly brought home to me at the time of Polar Bear's visit, because at that time, I was working on an ''Op-Ed'' article for the *New York Times* in which I addressed two laboratory cat experiments which I found particularly reprehensible.

The first of these occurred at Louisiana State University. Here, under an eight-year two-million-dollar Department of Defense contract, cats first had parts of their skulls removed, then, put in vises, were shot in the head. The experimenters' purpose, they said, was ''to find a way to return brain-wounded soldiers to active duty. Basic training for an Army infantryman costs $9,000,'' they stated. ''If our research allows only an additional 170 men to return to duty . . . it will have paid for itself.''

The second experiment I wrote about occurred at the

University of Oregon. There, under a seventeen-year million-and-a-half-dollar grant, psychologists surgically rotated the eyes of kittens, implanted electrodes in their brains and forced them to jump onto a block in a pan of water to test their equilibrium. This experiment had resulted in one of the country's most famous laboratory "break-ins" — and the subsequent indictment of one of the animals' "liberators." During the trial not only were the experimenters unable to cite a single case in which their experiments had benefited humans but, in the end, the cruelty the kittens had endured was too much for Judge Edwin Allen, who presided at the trial. The testimony he had heard, he said from the bench, had been "disturbing to me as a citizen of this state, as a citizen of this city and as a graduate of the University of Oregon."

I concluded my article by stating that a judge was just what was needed — a judge first, and then a jury — and that the experimenters had been both long enough. When, however, the *Times* came to print letters in answer to my article, they chose two highly critical ones from the opposite ends of the country — one from Stanford and one from Harvard. The Stanford letter was from Thomas Hamm, Jr., director of Stanford's Division of Laboratory Animal Medicine, a man who spoke at length of the "elaborate protocols in place" to protect Stanford's laboratory animals. He did not, however, mention that all but a few of Stanford's sixty thousand laboratory animals spent their entire lives underground — under, in fact, a parking lot. Nor did he mention that when the Fund's California coordinator, Virginia Handley, complained that Stanford's dogs were never exercised, he replied, "There's no scientific evidence that dogs need exercise. We did try putting them on a treadmill but they didn't want to stay on it."

The second letter, from my own university of Harvard, was in its own way even more remarkable. It was written by Dr. David Hubel, a man who said I was threatening the search for cures to "all the diseases that blight human life and happiness." Like Mr. Hamm, Dr. Hubel failed to mention several matters, chief among which was the fact that, on taking on a new job in 1989, he had written a letter to some thousands of doctors and members of his society — one which began as follows:

> If I accomplish nothing else as President of the Society of Neuroscience I want to try to mobilize the doctors of this country to fight the Animal Rights Movement. If even a minor fraction of our doctors would say one sentence to each patient ("Don't forget that without research on animals we wouldn't have been able to treat your disease, and such research is being seriously threatened by the Animal Rights Movement"), the result might be impressive. If posters could be put on the walls of waiting rooms, and pamphlets on the tables in hospitals and in offices, it could make a huge difference. One small phrase or statement at the bottom of the doctor's bill or prescription form would help.

From such a man I could hardly expect sympathy to my laboratory cruelty charges. Nonetheless, Dr. Hubel's evident paranoia about "animal rights" struck close to home. Although I have a book in my office entitled *Animal Rights*, written by the English humanitarian Henry Salt as far back as 1892, the fact remains that the Fund for Animals played a major role in the phrase's more recent currency. Indeed, through the good offices of Mr. and Mrs. Edward Ney, we were in the very early days of the Fund presented by the Young and Rubicam advertising agency with a slogan: "Animals Have Rights, Too." This, which we promptly put on our T-shirts and bumper stickers, almost immediately achieved wide popularity. Early on, however, I was asked what we meant by it and, frankly, I was not sure — it hadn't, after all, been my idea. Nonetheless I attempted three short paragraphs, as follows:

> The right to freedom from fear, pain and suffering — whether in the name of science or sport, fashion or food, exhibition or service.
>
> The right, if they are wild, to roam free, unharried by hunters, trappers or slaughterers. If they are domestic, not to be abandoned in the city streets, by a country road or in a cruel and inhumane pound.
>
> And finally the right, at the end, to a decent death — not by a club, by a trap, by harpoon, cruel poison or mass extermination chamber.

Looking back on those lines, I think they still express what I feel today. But there are many times when the Fund is fighting battles for animals when I frankly find the phrase "animal rights" difficult — as, for instance, when we were fighting the timber companies in the Northwest for killing bears because they ate the sap in what the timber companies regarded as their trees. In fact, during this fight I realized that, to the timber company people, the mere mention of "animal rights" conjured up bears marching down the main street toward the Capitol and then marching in to take seats and raising their paws to vote. Nor have I always been happy about the way the phrase is sometimes construed by its more far-out adherents. In the matter of bears again, for example, when Sean O'Gara of the Fund for Animals reviewed a remarkable movie, *The Bear,* he was immediately brought to task by an animal rightist who wrote *The Animals' Agenda* magazine that he was "infuriated" by the "numerous injuries" to animals in the film. The man then went on to enumerate these — that "dogs were muzzled and tethered," "horses are saddled and ridden," and "bears eat real fish." The latter was his only concession. He was not, he said, "suggesting that bears should not eat fish," but that "the injury to the fish is not simulated."

Candidly, I was at a loss to answer that one — and left it to Mr. O'Gara. I was not, however, at a loss when, not long before Polar Bear's visit, a group of animal rights leaders came to the ranch one evening for dinner. Nervously I explained to the chef that our guests would be "vegans." The chef looked midway between blank and concerned, so I went on quickly to explain that veganism was beyond vegetarianism — that vegans did not eat milk, butter, eggs, or cheese, or indeed any dairy products. I told him not to worry, though, about it, because our guests said they would bring fake hamburgers and fake hot dogs with them. By this time I was sure the chef was beginning to believe in the idea of five loaves and two little fishes. I didn't, however, have the heart to tell him that wouldn't work either, because fish, too, was out.

We were all sitting around enjoying our meal at different tables in the main ranch dining room when, looking across at the chef, I saw him obviously biting, for the first time in his life, into a fake hamburger. I looked over at him and attempted to ask, as quietly as possible, how he liked it. Unfortunately at that moment, as so often happens in such situations, all other conversations suddenly appeared to die at once. The chef looked up after his mouthful. "Cleveland," he said, "do you want the truth?" I told him I always wanted the truth. He considered this for a moment and, then, after a quick look at the rest of his hamburger, looked up straight at me. "Cleveland," he said, "it just barely beats eatin' nuthin'." To the animal rights activists' credit, however, there was immediate laughter.

On Polar Bear's last afternoon at the ranch there were still dozens of different animals for him to meet. I started with a particular group who would normally run free in the ranch's wildlife area but who in this case were either too lame or abused to do so. These were several rabbits. To me rabbits are the animals God forgot. Indeed they seem to spend their entire lives in fear and stress. As pets — and they can, with understanding, make great pets — they all too often end up being dumped out not only after Easter, but also at other times of the year. In the laboratories they undergo truly awful experiments, not in the least of which is the infamous Draize test on their naked eyes for, of all purposes, cosmetic testing. And, in the wild, they simply lack the weaponry to be anything but easy prey to a seemingly endless array of foes.

Polar Bear was very good about the rabbits — and not just because they were, aside from Peg, the first animals he had met that were his size. They were also the first who were obviously more nervous about him than he was of them. It made me think of some day taking him to Simpsonville, South Carolina, where we have a whole rabbit sanctuary — the only one I know of in the country. It is run by a woman named Caroline Gilbert, who not only feels the way I do about rabbits but knows at least ten times more about them than I. She has hundreds of rabbits — everything from ex-pet rabbits to ex-greyhound-training rabbits to ex-laboratory rabbits. Her two favorites are Benny and Abbit-Rabbit. She discovered Benny at a rabbit show trying to defend himself against three men's efforts to remove him from his cage while a large group of spectators giggled at the "mean" rabbit. Abbit-Rabbit, on the other hand, was sold as a pet at a flea market to a mother with eleven children. A week later the mother called Animal Control because Abbit "wouldn't play anymore," but instead just lay on his side. She wanted to know if she could, as she put it, "trade this one in and get another."

Next on the agenda came a visit with the ranch's most recent arrivals. These were animals who had survived a nine-day period during which they were neither fed nor watered, and they had come to us, after a successful prosecution by Mitchell Fox and the Progressive Animal Welfare Society, all the way from the state of Washington. Polar Bear's favorite among these was, much to my surprise, a llama. He made our fourth llama, and we named him — after having already used up Lloyd, Llewellyn, and Llewis — LLD. If we get any more, please remember we are in the market for more "ll" names. I personally ran out with LLD.

Polar Bear, I knew, had never seen such an animal before, and I had never seen him show so much curiosity toward anything new. But his strong "aeiou" 's were unmistakably favorable. Accordingly, for his meeting with the llamas, I chose a face-to-face encounter rather than one at ground level. For, contrary to what we have been led to believe about llamas, ours do not spit. Once in a while, however, when they do not wish to get in or out of a truck or something like that, they can not only kick like a mule but, in some instances, can behave even more stubbornly. Nonetheless, at their best our llamas are the kissiest of all the animals at the ranch, and I was not in the least surprised when two of them came over and decided to kiss Polar Bear at once. But, partial as he obviously was to them, this seemed to him a bit much, and, after first flashing out his warning paw, he next ducked his head into my jacket. He was not about to let even new friends take such double liberties, no matter with how many *l*'s they were spelled.

There was still another group of animals to visit — our wild goats. As we approached their pasture I knew that Polar Bear had never seen a goat before. This was because, before we reached them, he heard them and pricked up his ears in that special way I have learned he greets a sound he has never heard before. Coyotes have their musical howls, burros their wonderful brays, horses and mules their infinitely variable whinnies and snorts, but, among all animals' sounds the "baa" of the goat is, if not the most musical, certainly the most incessant. By the time we reached them — and they were approaching us as rapidly as we them — their chorus was such that Polar Bear decided to join in and at least give them — or me, I wasn't sure which — one of the strangest "aeiou" 's I have ever heard from him. Afterward, though, he shrank back and, while still peering to some extent, also managed to continue to bury himself in my jacket. This was understandable. Goats are a herd animal. They rarely travel alone — and in Polar Bear's opinion there were, in the first place, too many of them and, in the second, they were too close at hand. Polar Bear likes better-mannered creatures who know enough to keep their distance until they are properly introduced.

Our goats are San Clemente Island goats — a rare breed of Spanish Andalusians whose problems began in earnest when, during World War II, the late President Roosevelt, in a burst of typical pro-Navyism, gave San Clemente Island outright, and apparently in perpetuity, to the Navy. The Navy immediately put the island to use as a shelling target not only from ships at sea but also for field trials of new weapons from the air — something they continued to do after the war. How the goats had been able to survive forty years of this is a mystery, and the terrain of the island, with its rugged and craggy protective cliffs, only partially explains it. More important was the goats' uncanny ability to find and take immediate cover once attacked. This prowess, we would soon learn firsthand, matched that of experienced troops in battle.

In all, during the Fund's rescue of more than five thousand of these animals, we were at war with the U.S. Navy, in court and on the island, for more than six years. To me, looking back at it, there were three particularly memorable incidents. The first began in the halls of the Pentagon itself. Here, with Dana Cole, our California lawyer, I made my way toward the office of Vice Admiral Tom Hughes, Chief of Naval Logistics and apparently also Admiral of the Goats. Among the offices we passed was that of Secretary of Defense Caspar Weinberger. He was a man who had preceded me by a couple of years as president of the *Harvard Crimson* and also one whom, through his assistant Benjamin Welles, we had long been trying to reach to get him to intercede for us in favor of the goats. Along the whole incredible corridor was oil painting after oil painting, apparently depicting famous sea battles, which pictured one ship after another blowing up other ships. All of these, I presumed, were enemy ships.

Finally we turned into the admiral's conference room. Here there was a full complement of captains, lieutenants, ensigns, and civilian personnel. Shortly thereafter Admiral Hughes appeared, introduced himself, shook hands, and sat down. First he lit his pipe and then, without preamble, rose and went to the large map of San Clemente Island on the wall. From here things began to go from bad to worse when the admiral, as well as his point man on the map, brought up the question of the endangered flora and fauna on the island. Whenever the admiral said anything, all the others at the table nodded and said, almost in unison, "Aye, aye." Finally the admiral went over and sat down. "You see, Mr. Amory," he said, "our hands are tied. We have to get rid of the goats. It's the Endangered Species *Law*."

I had been good so far, but bringing up the Endangered Species Act was too much. No one had fought harder for this act than the Fund for Animals, and for it to be used now against us, and on such flimsy grounds, was truly infuriating. I pointed out that, as I understood it, there were exactly three endangered species of fauna on the island and that, as I also understood it, two were birds and one was a lizard. I told the admiral that I was prepared to admit that an occasional goat might occasionally step on an occasional lizard, but I would certainly like him to name an instance of a goat eating a bird. I also asked him if his gunners, when they shelled the island, took care to avoid both the birds and the lizard.

There was a long silence. Finally I could stand it no longer. I looked first at the admiral and then at the others. Dana remembers that I called them a bunch of murderers, but I think I phrased it much better than that. I did, however, mention for the benefit of the Annapolis men present that what they were shooting was their own mascot. In any case, the result was predictable.

As we left the Pentagon, Dana suggested that, having failed with the Navy brass, we should now take our case to the media — which had been consistently favorable to us and the goats. We started with the ABC network. On the way I told Dana what I proposed to say — that I now knew why the Navy had botched the rescue of our hostages in Iran. "How?" Dana asked. It was because, I said, they evidently thought they were going over to shoot them — they didn't know they would have to rescue them.

"If you say that on the air," Dana said to me slowly, "you will have to get yourself another lawyer." Don't worry, I told him. And, as I look back, I really think I intended not to say it. But, when we reached the network, all the effort we had put into the goats somehow got the better — or worst — of me. "What do you think of the Navy turning you down?" the interviewer asked. I know now, I said firmly, why the Navy had botched the rescue of our hostages. They thought they were going over to shoot them — they didn't know they would have to rescue them.

"That's great," the reporter said enthusiastically. "We're going to lead the news with it." With that he went away, and I looked at Dana. He refused even to look at me.

It was almost time for the Evening News, and for some moments we just sat there waiting to see it. Suddenly, just before airtime, the reporter reappeared. "Here," he said, "look at this." He showed us a news clip. The clip said that Secretary Weinberger had overruled his admirals about the goats and that the Fund for Animals would be allowed to rescue them after all. "We're going to lead with this," the reporter said excitedly.

At first I too was so excited that I couldn't think of anything but our victory. But then, suddenly, I remembered what I had previously said. I asked the reporter if it would be possible not to use it. "I don't know," he said, disappearing again. "You'd better," Dana said, "hope hard."

Mercifully, they did not use what I had said. In any case, the second most memorable incident — the rescue itself — was shaping up in California. Our first job was how to take care of all the media who wanted to be in helicopters to take pictures of the country's first major helicopter "netgun" rescue. What Mel Cain, our peerless pilot, and New Zealanders Bill Hales and Graham Jacobs, inventors of the netgun, did that day on that island — with a dozen news helicopters buzzing around them — was truly extraordinary. The very first goat was run down on an up-run path — Mel always insists on either an up or level run, not a down one in which a goat captured in the net could hurt himself — and that first goat was beautifully and accurately netgunned. While Bill jumped to the ground to tie the goat's legs, remove the net, and put the animal in the sling, Mel made a quick circle. Then, when he returned, Bill quickly hooked the sling to a ring under the helicopter, and the goat was then flown back to the corral, where it was gently landed and untied. The whole operation had taken less than four minutes. In all that day more than sixty goats were rescued, some from very difficult terrain.

The third and final memorable incident of the rescue occurred when, later, we were allowed to enter the hitherto totally forbidden unexploded-shell area. Here I was alone with Donna Gregory, the Fund's corral boss, one morning down at the very end of the island. We had a truck there which we were using as a holding corral and were awaiting Mel and Bill's first morning run. All of a sudden, bouncing along the rough dirt road toward us we saw a Navy jeep with two naval officers sitting in front. As they turned up the hill toward us at full speed, I didn't know what we had done wrong, but I told Donna it sure looked as if we would shortly be headed for the brig.

Finally the officers arrived and jumped out of the jeep. "Mr. Amory," the senior officer said excitedly. I "aye, aye'd," "sir'd," and all but saluted him. "Mr. Amory," the officer went on, "have you or Miss Gregory seen any suspicious-looking ships in this area?" Ships? I automatically queried. "Yes," he said, "we've had reports of a Russian ship in this vicinity, and we wondered if you'd seen anything like that." No, I said quickly, adding, "No, sir." "All right," he said, "but keep your eyes open. And if you see anything at all, take your truck and drive right to the command post." With that both officers jumped back into their jeep and took off without another word.

It was all Donna and I could do to keep from laughing before they were out of earshot. Here we were, on a U.S. Navy–owned island, far out in the Pacific — an island bristling with every kind of radar and detective device known in modern warfare. And yet our entire national security apparently depended upon whether or not Donna, who wears thick glasses, and I, who on a good day might be able to see a hundred yards, saw a Russian ship. It gave one pause, all right — in fact, as I looked at Donna, I could see it gave us both pause.

One enduring dividend which came to us from the goat rescue was a whole new California shelter. In looking around for a place near San Diego from which to do our goat adoptions, we happened upon the Animal Trust Sanctuary in Ramona and its formidable founder, Patricia Nelson. Ms. Nelson not only insisted on us adopting our goats from her shelter but, upon her retirement, gave it to us — lock, stock, and barrel. To run this, we installed an eighteen-year Navy civilian executive named Chuck Traisi, a man who from the beginning was so outspoken against the Navy's shooting the goats that he first joined us in taking part in the rescue and then, refusing to wait two years for his pension from the Navy, joined the Fund itself. With his remarkable wife, Cindy, he now not only directs what has become one of the country's finest wild-life rehabilitation centers but also operates something which is particularly dear to my heart — a cattery which even Polar Bear would find difficult to criticize.

On Polar Bear's last night at the ranch he participated in what has come to be a regular ritual — the feeding of every animal a special good-night treat. This takes the form of, per animal, at least two large slices of freshly baked protein bread, a delicacy which is kindly donated by a local baker from their supply of miscut or damaged loaves. I have taken a fair amount of kidding about this — that I feed my animals on bread and water — but the fact is, it is actually the animals' very favorite food, outranking hay or oats or any other grain or anything else, and it even ranks so with Conga and Nora as well as Nim and Sally.

The way the horses and burros, the mules and the goats, the llamas and all the others gather for their daily, or rather nightly, bread is simple. The pickup is driven from pasture to pasture, and the animals, well knowing it is coming, gather on the double from whatever distance they are when they first hear its familiar sound. And, as they come up to the truck, they do so in surprisingly good order because they know from experience that even the bossiest will get no more than his or her share and that no one, not even the most timid, will go without. Seeing this on a beautiful, warm starry Texas night is, to me, the most memorable part of a trip to the ranch, and it has proved so to almost all our visitors. When, for example, the Fund's national director, Wayne Pacelle, saw it for the first time, he told me there and then it was the best sight he had ever seen in his life. Since it was pitch dark that night and he, out of Yale, had at that time just turned twenty-three, it was not exactly an observation on which a Harvard man of more reasonable years would want to go to the bank, but still it was nice to hear.

The animals are fed from the back of the truck, and the night Polar Bear was there, when our feeder got out to climb in the back, so did we. I have always been a bit skeptical about the theory that cats can see in the dark as well as in the daytime — if, for no other reason, because when Polar Bear flies in from the balcony, headed for the bed, some nights when the lights are out, he often bumps into either something fairly substantial he knows perfectly well is there, such as a piece of furniture, or me. In any case, on that particular night — which was a dark one — I had reason to wonder just how he would feel about all those open-mouthed animals within biting range, and I took therefore extra pains to shield him. But I soon saw I had little to worry about. He had by then become, at large animals close at hand, an old hand.

One thing Polar Bear did do, though, was to keep looking up at the man doing the feeding and, when the man looked down at him, he immediately looked at me. "I know what he wants," the man said. "He wants some, too." I told the man, a bit patronizingly I admit, that of course he didn't — cats didn't like bread. With that, the man immediately broke a piece of bread into cat-sized pieces and put the pieces into one hand. No, I told him again. Don't. It's no use. I know Polar Bear. He won't touch it.

The man was very stubborn, though, and, ignoring me, he offered the bread to Polar Bear anyway. And what did Polar Bear do? Guess.

You're right — and furthermore he did it with the mouth of a huge mustang also reaching for it. The thing is, Polar Bear is very stubborn too. It's not enough that he won't do what I want him to do — he won't even not do what I tell people he won't do, even when it's something he doesn't do all the time.

VII ∘ *Romance à la Cat Blanche*

When I first arrived in New York, after the publication of *The Proper Bostonians,* I stayed on Forty-fourth Street at the then Old Royalton Hotel, long the residence of two of my favorite authors, Dorothy Parker and Robert Benchley. I hasten to add that it is not that I felt that after the publication of my book continued residence in Boston would be dangerous, it was rather that I felt living in New York would be more broadening and something everybody in Boston sooner or later needs, even though they might not care, in Boston, to admit the fact. In New York I also frequented, right across the same street, the Algonquin Hotel, which had in the lobby the first of a long succession of cats — each of them, appropriately, named Hamlet.

The Algonquin dining room was of course celebrated for its famed Round Table, to which well-known authors repaired for well-known lunches. I was in no way eminent enough to be eligible for regular membership in that august group. However, I was occasionally invited on a sort of trial basis by two formidable curmudgeons of the day, George S. Kaufman and Alexander Woollcott. There I was privileged not only to absorb the rudiments of New York's idea of curmudgeonry but also to hear, firsthand and fresh off the table, some of my favorite stories. Two of these were about none other than Miss Parker herself.

The first of these concerned the fact that Miss Parker had on one occasion a man in her room and, in those more circumspect social times, was promptly taken to task for this by being called by the desk clerk. "Miss Parker," the clerk began, coming immediately to the point, "do you have a gentleman in your room?" Miss Parker also came immediately to the point. "I don't know," she replied. "I'll ask him."

The second story occurred when Miss Parker visited, on Long Island, the home of the publishing mogul of the day, Mr. Herbert Bayard Swope. Since Miss Parker did not drive, she took the train and was met at the station by Mr. Swope. As they approached the Swope house Miss Parker saw that on the house's spacious veranda there was obviously a party in progress — the ladies were in evening dress and the gentlemen in tuxedos. Furthermore, as Miss Parker and Mr. Swope mounted the long stairway, they could see that many of the ladies and gentlemen seemed to be doing a very odd thing — with their hands behind their backs they were bending over tubs of water. In these tubs, although Miss Parker could not yet see them, were apples — which these participants were intending to bite.

Finally, Miss Parker and Mr. Swope were close enough

to take a good look at what was going on. It was obviously something that Miss Parker had never seen before, and for some time she surveyed the scene in silence. Then her curiosity got the better of her. "Herbert," she asked, "what are they doing?" "It's the new craze, Dorothy," explained Mr. Swope. "It's called 'Ducking for Apples.' " This time Miss Parker's silence was very brief. "Herbert," she said firmly, "there, but for a typographical error, goes the story of my life."

I had made my transition from Boston to New York as gently as possible — out of deference to an unnecessarily dangerous shock to my system — and, in keeping with this effort, my next favorite regular haunt, second only to the Royalton and the Algonquin, became the Harvard Club of New York. Again, in keeping with my careful transition from Boston, this was also located on Forty-fourth Street. Here, too, as at the Algonquin, there was also a resident cat, and I liked that. But there was one thing about the Harvard Club I cordially disliked. This was that its walls were adorned with a wide variety of animals' heads. These heads are still there, and though as the years have passed I have learned to live with them, I am more and more concerned about what appears to me their growing resemblance to those of some of the more elderly members.

Fortunately my favorite room in the Harvard Club of those days had no heads. It was, however, concerned with hair. It was the barbershop, and it offered not New York–priced but rather Boston-priced haircuts. These, at least in my case, were ministered under the fine Italian hand of a barber named Louis Butrico, and with him I soon struck up a close friendship. Mr. Butrico was very complimentary about *The Proper Bostonians*, and, like most new authors, I basked in his approval. That is I did until, as our friendship firmed, I could not help being aware that the compliments, nice as they were, were as nothing compared to those Mr. Butrico bestowed upon another Harvard author. This author was none other than Mr. John Gunther, who was not only a very large man but an enormously successful one, and the author of a dozen or more best-sellers, at least two of which, autographed, Mr. Butrico kept right on his barber table. Again and again I was forced to hear not only the sales figures for Mr. Gunther's books but also the number of printings through which apparently all his editions went. Finally, unable any longer to stand for it — or rather sit for it — I resolved on a plan of action.

This action entailed my arrival for my next haircut armed with two copies of a *Reader's Digest* article I had recently written. As I climbed into the barber chair I did not show these to Mr. Butrico but instead hid them under the newspaper on my lap. When Mr. Butrico started, as I knew he would, on Mr. Gunther and indeed took time off from my hair to show me still another copy of an autographed book, I quietly but firmly put my game plan into full gear. First, apparently graciously, I took the Gunther book and opened it to the autograph, read it, and shut it. Then I looked up to Mr. Butrico. Does Mr. Gunther, I asked him, write just in English? Mr. Butrico looked surprised for only a moment, then added that he thought he did. Oh, I said meaningfully. And then, with some ado, I pulled out the first of my *Reader's Digest* magazines and opened it to my article. The edition was in Italian.

Mr. Butrico whistled. "Wow!" he said, grabbing the

magazine and holding it in front of him in wonderment. "I didn't know you could write in Italian." I smiled modestly and said I hoped it was OK — my Italian was not, I was afraid, what I would like it to be. But Mr. Butrico, by now reading, would not permit such modesty. "It's terrific," he said. "It's perfect." I sighed in apparent relief and then, after a suitable interval, asked him if he would like me to sign it for him. He was very pleased and, after I had done this, I again reached under my newspaper and fired my second barrel. Italian was hard enough for me, I said, but this one was *really* tough. With that I handed him another edition of the magazine, this one with my same article in Japanese. This time Mr. Butrico was so amazed he was not even able to whistle. He just looked and looked at it and then finally, in pure wonder, at me. I'll sign this, too, I told him, if you'd like to have it. And this time, with no ado at all, I did.

I never did find out what Mr. Butrico told Mr. Gunther the next time he came in for a haircut, but I do know that from that time on I heard considerably less about Mr. Gunther, and I had reason to believe that Mr. Gunther heard a good deal more about me. I am only sorry, however, that Mr. Butrico had retired long before the publication of *The Cat Who Came for Christmas*. For, had he not done so I would have had, for the first time in my life, a score or more books in different languages to show him. And not the least of these would have been the Japanese edition — one which to me was the most remarkable because among the few things we have which the Japanese do not have — and as a matter of fact do not even make — not the least of them is Christmas. My book in Japanese is called, simply, *New York Cat Story*.

*   *   *

From the publication of my book abroad I learned not only many things about cats in different countries but also just how large in almost every country is the literature of the cat. My favorite example of this was a letter from an American author, Gloria Johnson, of Virginia, who sent me a book called *A Cat's Guide to Shakespeare*. At first when she sent it to me, I wasn't sure whether it was a book for people who wanted to be guided through Shakespeare through the eyes of a cat or indeed whether it was a book about Shakespeare for cats. On opening it, however, I found it was neither. It was an art book containing drawings of cats illustrating various Shakespeare quotations, my favorite being a cat's quote from *Julius Caesar:* "I am indeed, sir, a surgeon to old shoes." Polar Bear, I should point out, is surgeon not only to old shoes but also to new shoes. Whenever he finds a pair of mine he likes, he whips them into biting shape in no time at all.

Among the things I learned from foreign cat books was that cat literature had its beginnings in fables which exist in the folklore of almost every country. These are particularly prevalent not only in the Scandinavian countries as well as Germany and Switzerland but are almost equally so in countries as diverse as Ireland and Russia and even Arab countries. I also learned that, while most of these fables are humorous, and the cat almost invariably the villain, the primary purpose of the fables, from Aesop to La Fontaine, was to demonstrate a moral precept. To me, to have chosen the cat, villain or hero, for such a task would seem an exercise in futility. Indeed, I am indebted to Jack Smith of the *Los Angeles Times* for what would seem to me to be a fairly definitive statement on this ticklish point: "I can honestly say," Mr. Smith writes, "that I never knew a moral cat."

I take, however, some umbrage at this. Polar Bear has a kind of morality which I firmly believe is in many ways more honest than mine. The New England conscience, I have often said, does not stop you from doing what you shouldn't — it just stops you from enjoying it. Polar Bear's conscience, on the other hand, not only doesn't stop him from doing what he shouldn't, it also doesn't stop him from enjoying it thoroughly.

Examples of this will shortly and in good time be painfully addressed in the matter of his breakup of not one but two romances of mine. Meanwhile I shall continue in the more important matter we were discussing — which, as I recall, was cat literature. On this subject it is clearly French literature which deserves first credit for having promoted the cat to something beyond a creature in fable. And this is, of course, as it should be, if for no other reason it was the French poet and novelist Théophile Gautier who reduced all international promotion of the cat to nationalistic dimensions. "Only a Frenchman," he wrote, "could understand the fine and subtle qualities of the cat."

A veritable host of French authors did their best to prove M. Gautier correct, including Montaigne, Chateaubriand, Balzac, Baudelaire, Zola, Cocteau, and Colette, as well as Alexandre Dumas, both *père* and *fils*. Of all of these Colette was easily the most prolific, perhaps because of her often-expressed belief that, as she put it, "by associating with the cat one only risks becoming richer."

Close on the heels of France, however, in the literature of the cat is England. Here the most celebrated feline is undoubtedly Lewis Carroll's familiar Cheshire — the cat who, at one time, is "a grin without a cat," and, at another, a cat to whom Alice finds no use speaking, " 'till its ears have come or at least one of them."

My own favorite character in *Alice in Wonderland*, though, is not the Cheshire Cat but the Executioner — the man who, ordered to cut off the Cheshire's head, argues in typical British fashion. "You couldn't," he said, "cut off a head unless there was a body to cut it off from: that he had never had to do such a thing before, and he wasn't going to begin at *his* time of life."

But Carroll was by no means the prime British satirist of the cat. That honor belongs to the late Scottish writer H. H. Munro, better known as Saki. Born in Burma, the son of a British army officer, Saki was sent at the age of two to live in England with two English aunts whose strictness and lack of understanding would become the basis for so many of his satires. In these Saki did not overlook cats, and in his short story "Tobermory," he produced one of the all-time cat classics.

This is the story of a man who discovers he could teach animals human language and after working with, as Saki puts it, "thousands of animals," finally decides to confine his work to cats — animals who, as Saki again puts it, "have assimilated themselves so marvelously with our civilization while retaining all their highly-developed feral instincts." Specifically, the man narrows his search for his perfect student to Tobermory, a cat he locates in the home of Lady Blemly, to whose houseparty we are introduced at the beginning of the story.

Right away, we know Tobermory is up to no good because his "favorite promenade," Saki tells us, is a "narrow ornamental balustrade," which runs not only "in front of most of the bedroom windows," but also from which Tobermory could "watch the pigeons" — something which immediately brought Polar Bear to mind — as well as watching "heaven knew what else besides." In any case, at the afternoon tea which begins the house-party, the very first question Tobermory is asked, after the host, Sir Wilfred, goes to fetch him, is if he will have some milk. To this Tobermory answers, "I don't mind if I do." But to the second question — what does he think of human intelligence? — Tobermory has no answer. "It is obvious," Saki wrote, "that boring questions lay outside his scheme of things." But Tobermory has a question of his own. "Of whose intelligence in particular?" he asks. "Oh, well, mine for instance," says a guest, with what Saki describes as "a feeble laugh." "You put me in an embarrassing position," continues Tobermory, who then proceeds, without any embarrassment at all, "When your inclusion in this house party was suggested, Sir Wilfred protested that you were the most brainless woman of his acquaintance, and that there was a wide distinction between hospitality and care of the feeble-minded." Tobermory then proceeds with other observations and character assessments which, in the end, result not only in the end of the houseparty but also, sadly, the end of Tobermory.

Saki, one of the greatest satirists of all things English was, at the age of forty-six, killed in action fighting for Britain on the Western Front in World War I. But even before his time the cat had been used as a vehicle for satire by many authors in other countries. Japan, for one example, produced a master of satire who used a cat as the protagonist of his most famous work. The author, Soseki Natsume, a lecturer at the Imperial University, wrote his book entitled *I Am a Cat* in 1905. But it is still widely read today and its author is generally recognized, as the introduction by his translator reads, as "the best writer of prose to have emerged during the century since contact with the outside world was re-established in 1868."

The story concerns a nameless stray kitten who wins a place in the home of, as the book jacket describes the man, a "dyspeptic schoolteacher of many enthusiasms but mediocre ability." From kittenhood the cat grows to cathood and proceeds to give us his comments on the shortcomings of Japanese middle-class life, in which pretenses of the schoolteacher and his friends are almost invariably belittled by the cat in comparison with the cat's own friends, the "sleek and powerful Rickshaw Blackie" and the "elegant Miss Tortoiseshell."

This book too had made at times a disquieting impression on me because, as anyone who has ever been owned by a cat knows, what we want most to know about our cats is what they think about us. And more than once I felt the nameless cat's stern assessment of the schoolteacher as coming far too close for comfort to what well might be Polar Bear's assessment of me. I could even, in my darker moments, visualize that someday, after I had gone to my just reward, a book would come out by Polar Bear about me — or one by a writer using Polar Bear as the protagonist and me as some ridiculous kind of antagonist — only without so much as a mention of my patience, my fortitude, or my steadfast self-abnegation. I could even see a title — *Master Dearest*.

In any case, in *I Am a Cat* the schoolteacher's first words to his wife are, according to the cat, "I am a scholar and must therefore study. I have no time to fuss over you. Please understand this clearly." Later, after seeing the teacher fall asleep over a book every evening, the cat has the first of his many reflections. "Teachers have it easy. If you are born a human, it is best to become a teacher. And if it is possible to sleep this much and still be a teacher, why even a cat could teach." When the schoolteacher begins to fancy himself as an artist, and starts to paint his cat, the cat does his best to be a good model and stay still but finally has to go and relieve himself. At this his master shouts, "You fool!" and then threatens him — which again moves the cat to contemplation. "He had," he tells us of his master, "a fixed habit of saying 'you fool' whenever he curses anyone. He cannot help it since he knows no other swearwords." As for his master's threats, these move him to still more reflection:

> The prime fact is that all humans are puffed up by their extreme self-satisfaction with their own brute power. Unless some creature more powerful than people arrives on Earth to bully them there is just no knowing what dire lengths their fool presumptions will eventually carry them.

The cat even sneaks an occasional look in his master's diary, and indeed favors us with an excerpt from this, one concerning a stroll his master took with a friend:

> At Ikenohata, geishas in formal spring kimono were playing battledore and shuttlecock in front of a house of assignation. Their clothes beautiful; but their faces extremely plain. It occurs to me that they resemble the cat at home.

This of course provokes the cat to return to his favorite subject:

> I don't see why he should single me out as an example of plain features. If I went to a barber and had my face shaved I wouldn't look much different from a human. But there you are, humans are conceited and that's the trouble with them.

Still a third cat satire which, to my mind, belongs right up there with "Tobermory" and *I Am a Cat* is one written by P. G. Wodehouse, a British author who later became an American citizen. In my formative writing days I was so enamored of Mr. Wodehouse's "Jeeves" stories and other sallies at the British nobility that my schoolboy writing efforts owed much to him — so much so, in fact, that more than one came perilously close to plagiarism.

Years later, when Mr. Wodehouse became a friend of mine as well as an ardent supporter of animal causes, he gave me a book of his short stories. In this was included a tale which I believe was the only one he ever wrote about a cat.

It is called "The Story of Webster," and it opens with a group of typical Wodehouse characters discussing the shortcomings of cats — always, apparently, a popular subject with the English landed dog gentry. This discussion boils down, as one gentleman puts it, to the cat's "insufferable air of superiority":

> Cats as a class have never completely gotten over the snottiness caused by the fact that in ancient Egypt they were worshipped as gods. This makes them too prone to set themselves up as critics and censors of the frail beings whose lot they share. They stare rebukingly. They view with concern. And, on a sensitive man, this often has the worst effects, inducing an inferiority complex of the gravest kind.

An example of such cat gravity is shortly visited upon a young gentleman named Lancelot, one who, brought up by his uncle Theodore, a man described by Mr. Wodehouse as "the saintly Dean of Bolsover," had decided much against his uncle's will — and in fact severely placing in jeopardy his inheritance from his uncle's actual will — to enter the Bohemian life and become an artist. And at the time this story opens, Mr. Wodehouse tells us, "his prospects seem bright":

> He was painting the portrait of Brenda, only daughter of Mr. and Mrs. B. B. Carberry-Pirbright, of 11 Maxton Square, South Kensington, which meant thirty pounds in his sock on delivery. He had learned to cook eggs and bacon. He had practically mastered the ukulele. And, in addition, he was engaged to be married to a fearless young *vers libre* poetess of the name of Gladys Bingley, better known as The Sweet Singer of Garbridge Mews, Fulham — a charming girl who looked like a penwiper.

But into this idyll rain, of course, must fall — which it does when Uncle Theodore is "offered the vacant bishopric of Bongo-Bongo in West Africa." But to take on the post, he must part with his faithful cat, Webster, whose tender care he decides to entrust to Lancelot.

From the very first moments of Webster's arrival everything goes awry. Webster immediately engages in washing himself, rotating his left leg rigidly in the air. Upon seeing this, Lancelot is reminded of something one of his nurses apparently once told him — that if you creep up on a cat when its leg is in the air and give it a pull, and at the same time make a wish, in thirty days that wish will come true. This, unfortunately, Lancelot attempts to prove.

Webster immediately lowers his leg, turns, and instead of his leg raises his eyebrow. "Webster, it is true," Mr. Wodehouse tells us, "had not actually raised his eyebrow. But this Lancelot felt was simply because he hadn't any." In any case, from that first altercation everything Lancelot does is, if not in Webster's eyes hopeless, at least something which needs immediate improvement. When, for example, Gladys arrives to meet Webster for the first time, Lancelot begs her before the meeting to remove ink spots from her nose. When a friend lights a cigar Lancelot has to remind him that Webster does not like cigar smoke. As for Lancelot himself, no longer can he go about, when there is no company, in carpet slippers or sit down to dinner without dressing. He even has to explain to his friends that he is sure they have heard of a person being henpecked — well, he is catpecked.

Nor, alas, can he now even consider marrying Gladys. Webster has found her wanting, and in her place has chosen Brenda Carberry-Pirbright — a lady Webster has found eminently suitable by the fact that when she comes to see Lancelot he sticks his tail up, utters a cordial gargle, and rubs his head against her leg.

Lancelot, by now practically on his way to the altar — actually to one of Mrs. Carberry-Pirbright's "intimate little teas" — is stopped only by the appearance of Gladys and the delivery of her ultimatum. "If," she tells him, "by 7:30 on the dot you have not presented yourself at Six-A Garbridge Mews, ready to take me out to dinner at the Ham and Beef, I shall know what to think and shall act accordingly."

After Gladys has gone Lancelot rushes for a drink and, in his haste, spills it — something which Webster not only sees but, "in his eyes was that expression of quiet rebuke." At first Lancelot looks away but then, looking back, he beholds, in Mr. Wodehouse's words, "a spectacle of a kind to stun a stronger man than Lancelot Mulliner":

> Webster sat crouched on the floor beside the widening pool of whisky. But it was not horror and disgust that had caused him to crouch. He was crouched because, crouching, he could get nearer to the stuff and obtain crisper

action. His tongue was moving in and out like a piston.

And then, abruptly, for one fleeting instant, he stopped lapping and glanced up at Lancelot, and across his face there flitted a quick smile — so genial, so intimate, so full of jovial camaraderie, that the young man found himself automatically smiling back and not only smiling but winking. And in answer to that wink Webster winked too.

After this, when Lancelot has, as Mr. Wodehouse describes it, the "goods on Webster," we are assured of a happy ending, one in which Brenda Carberry-Pirbright will no longer be in the picture and Lancelot and Gladys are free not only to go off into the sunset but also, and in good time, to march down the aisle.

Here I feel I must point out that what my friend Mr. Wodehouse was engaged in writing — about Webster's campaign to break up Lancelot's romance — was fiction. What happened to me was far from fiction — it was nonfiction, in fact. And furthermore it happened, as I have said, not once but twice. Indeed, in my considered opinion, looking back over these several years when it all took place, Polar Bear was in both instances not only the alleged perpetrator but the actual guilty party — the first time indirectly, the second time directly.

The first instance began in California. Those of you with long memories may recall an earlier chapter in this book in which some of you may still harbor the feeling that I was unduly harsh in my assessment of certain California girls — in particular in the case of one who wrote me criticizing the name I had chosen for Polar Bear. You might even go so far as to accuse me of a certain bitterness. If so, such, I assure you, is far from the case. The only question, as in all such matters, is what did I know and when did I know it — and when I did, did I do the right thing? I did indeed, and on this score I am as pure as the driven snow. I was not then, and am not now, in the least bitter about the whole experience. It was, after all, a learning experience for the girl, and as for myself I was, like Mr. Wodehouse's Lancelot — a name with which, incidentally, I found myself identifying — saved in the nick of time.

It is true that years ago at about the time I got Polar Bear I myself was, if you can believe it, somewhat smitten with a California girl. I know it is going to be hard for many of my readers to believe this, but there it is. It all began, as such matters of the heart with curmudgeonly bachelors are wont to do, innocently enough. And for the most part it continued that way. It is not that curmudgeons don't have hearts — we do — but our heads, of course, come first. This is indeed the very essence of curmudgeonry, and is why curmudgeons do not, for example, fall "head over heels in love" or any of that sort of nonsense. No curmudgeon worthy of the name ever allowed his head to be on any comparable level with his heels, let alone his heart.

What did happen, and really all that happened, was that I happened to make the acquaintance of, as I believe I've already said, this California girl. She was also, I shall have to admit, so beautiful that she attracted not just California men, which is not hard to do, but also men from other states, other countries, and, I would guess, from a close-up look at some of them, other planets. As for her own looks, she had long black hair, big brown darty eyes, and a figure which would stop a clock — something which is particularly dangerous in California since out there people are, as you know, already three hours behind.

I shall shortly address this subject further — the matter of the time, of course, not the girl's figure — this is, after all, a family book. Meanwhile I wish to state here and now that what I did, and I might add all I did, on meeting this girl was immediately and totally unselfishly set myself to the task of protecting her from all the unseemly attentions she was getting from those forementioned men. Indeed, as I immediately pointed out to her on our very first meeting, these attentions were not attentions at all but rather intentions — and, to boot, they were intentions of an extremely doubtful nature.

But this was by no means all I had to do. Indeed I had to do something almost equally important. This was because, being a very observant person, I had immediately observed that this girl, besides being beautiful, was also both fun and funny and that, while this added considerably to her charm, it did not make my task any easier since, like so many California girls, she had never been taught when not to be funny. Thus, at this very same first meeting, I was forced to part — really long before I normally do such a thing — with one of my most cherished pieces of wisdom for the edification of the fairer sex. This is, simply, that there is, at crucial times, nothing that ruins romance like a sense of humor in a woman.

There was still another formidable obstacle to my objective. This was that she was, again like most California girls, heavily "into" — in that awful California word — all areas of the Women's Movement. Now, no one is a greater admirer than I of the strides this movement has made, for women, but this girl carried the movement into an area for which no self-respecting curmudgeon could for a moment sit still. What she did, if you can believe it, was to carry the movement into the field of romance. I first noticed this when she told me she didn't want to be called a girl — which of course I handled by saying I had no intention of not doing so but that if she wanted to call me a boy it would be fine with me. The second thing I noticed was the way she drew back when, out of pure affection one evening, I had patted her on the head. She said she didn't like to be patted on the head. I told her that she would simply have to get used to it, at least when we were standing up. She was shorter than I and, frankly, from that position I couldn't see any other place to pat her.

But the third and to me most diabolical thing that she did in carrying the Women's Movement into the field of romance was to treat the men in her life, if you please, the way men treat women. She loved them, mind you, and then left them. Thus it soon became all too painfully clear to me that I had not only the task of protecting her from other men — not to mention controlling, at crucial times, her sense of humor — I had also to put my shoulder to the wheel doing something for which, whether she knew it or not, she had an almost equally desperate need — to secure, in a word, her liberation from liberation.

It was not going to be easy, and my first problem was a lack of communication. I do not mean this phrase in the nauseatingly irritating way people supposedly in love use it — again, like humor, particularly at the wrong times — I mean lack of communication in the actual sense of the phrase and, in particular, telephone communication. I have already mentioned the time problem with California. You call before your lunch and they haven't yet arrived at their offices. Then when you do get there and get your message they call you and *you* are out to lunch. When you call them back they, of course, are out to lunch and then they call you back but by then you are gone for the day. This is bad enough for communication among people with regular business hours, but in the case of this girl I was faced with something else again. The girl was at that time working, but here I hasten to say I use the word "work" in the loosest California sense. It has been my observation that the only time California girls are working is when they are working out. In any case, what this girl did at least Monday through Thursday was to arrive at her office shortly before noon, get her mail, and go to lunch, and if she got back by 2:30 in the after-noon — which was, for her, a hard day — she left at 4:00. On Fridays she left before lunch and for good.

Telephone communication with such a girl was, from the East, obviously impossible during the week. That left only weekends. Business people faced with this sort of problem have, I understand, at least a reasonable chance of reaching each other over the weekends, but with California girls you can forget weekends. California girls are never home weekends save in the case of terminal illness. Whether they are est-ing or Rolfing, tennising or skiing, swimming or surfing, snorkeling or white-water rafting, backpacking or hang gliding — and this girl was into all of these — you cannot reach them except in their auto-mobile, where they spend approximately half their lives and which is of course why cellular phones were invented. I could, and usually did, leave a message on her answering machine Friday, but since she never came back until the wee hours Sunday morning by the time she called me, if indeed she did, my hours — which, incidentally, she never learned — were even wee-er. In fact, it would be Monday morning.

In short, I had to give up telephone communication entirely. Instead I did my best to stay in touch with her by mail. At least I had the benefit of a distinctive name. And, make no mistake, I needed it. I was with her once when she was opening her mail, and in it I happened to see a postcard from a man named Michael, protesting undying love. "I don't see," she said, "why men don't put in their last names. I know three Michaels." Nonetheless, as I say, I was luckier and, in one of my first letters, I was so curious as to how she could have possibly managed to get a job I asked her to send me a copy of her résumé. The résumé was hard to believe, even by California girl standards. Under colleges she had listed eleven. I later learned she listed every college she had attended, all right — but on dates.

I had never before in my entire life met a girl who had as many dates, and by this I do not mean dates per week, I mean dates per twenty-four hours. She had luncheon dates, cocktail dates, dinner dates, late dates, and, I presume, late late dates. As a matter of fact, the very first time I had what might be classified as a date with her I asked her when she had started having dates. She thought for some time — which was, in itself, unusual — and then said she couldn't remember. I suggested age twelve. "Oh, no," she said, "I was very dorky then." I had no idea what that meant — California girls have a language all their own — but since by that time she couldn't remember what she said — California girls also have both incredibly short attention spans and really no memories at all — I never did find out. "By the time I started going out," she said, "I always seemed to date older men."

I would have liked, at this point, just to bask in the first real sign of good sense I had ever noticed in her. Instead

I realized it was a golden opportunity to educate her on the virtues not only of older men in comparison with younger men but also particularly of older eastern men in comparison with California men of any age. California men, I pointed out to her, are not even interested in how their girls look — they are only interested in how *they* look. And frankly, I confided to her, they not only spend just as much time in front of mirrors as their girls do but, on average, more. The trouble was, I had talked at some length about this and I had lost her. She was thinking of something else. "My problem was," she said, "that my only real crushes were on unavailable men — like married teachers."

My brief period of optimism about her good sense about older men abruptly shattered, I went back to asking her about her colleges. I asked her why she dropped out of so many. "I did it," she said, "to get away from unfinished business. I mean, of course," she added, smiling, "unfinished exams and term papers and things like that." I ignored this, and asked her how long her average relationship had been. I knew that if I was going to give her the benefit of my advice I would first have to make her see the error of her ways until, of course, she had met me. But she just didn't seem to get the idea at all. "My average relationship," she said, "was six weeks — except when it involved travel. I love to travel. I've been to just about every country except India. I would love to go to India. Have you ever been to India?" I told her sternly that I had, but that she was changing the subject. At this she wanted to know what the subject was. Men and women, I told her — I even used the word "women" instead of "girls." "Men and women," she said, "are two very different things. They are alien nations. Putting them together is like putting dogs and cats together. I am a cat, you know. I love cats."

This was another good piece of news for me, and indeed I was later to meet her two cats. But I realized that if she had decided that men and women didn't belong together it was very important for me to find out why. It had nothing to do with me personally, I told myself. I was really doing it just for her and, one day when we were looking at her cats, I asked her to continue with her analysis of the whole men and women thing. "Men are like wild canids," she went on — she loved animal examples — "they're always nipping at women's heels and they love it best when we're running from them. When we're standing still they have absolutely no interest in us."

On another occasion I asked her point-blank how she broke off her relations with men. "Different ways," she said earnestly. "Usually I tell them I have no interest in romance beyond a certain point." She paused. "Another way is I ask them to please stop sending me poems. I tell them I have boxes full of poems and I don't have anyplace to put any more." I told her she could count on me on that score — I didn't write poems — but again she wasn't listening. "The real trouble is," she said, "men are more romantic than women — at least they are at the beginning. What they really do is go into a herd of us and cut out one of us. But they are certainly not as romantic at the end, when they always get so bitter." She threw up her hands. "That's why," she said, "I can't take them seriously and why I make jokes."

I knew she was a writer and I asked her sternly if, in her writing, she wrote jokes. "Oh, no," she said, "I just talk jokes." Once more I reminded her there was nothing that ruined romance more than a sense of humor in women. I knew I had said it before, but with California girls you have to say things at least three times to have even the hope of their remembering them.

Despite all the time I was taking, all my unselfish efforts, trying to give her the rudiments of respectability, I always seemed to be stymied by one seemingly unconquerable obstacle. In every conversation, just when I had her concentration, and had repeated what I had said at least three times, she would always, wherever we were, get a phone call. And I do not mean just one call — I mean phone call after phone call — she apparently let everyone she knew, at least all those of the male persuasion, know where she was at all times. Finally one day, when we were at the swimming pool at the Beverly Hills Hotel, and she literally had three calls in succession, I could stand it no longer. I admit I was not in the best of moods. I was well aware of two things: that the number of times one is paged over the loudspeaker at the Beverly Hills Hotel swimming pool is as accurate a measure of the size of one's celebrity as exists west of the Rockies, and I was also aware that on that particular day I had not had so much as one measly call. In any case, then and there I decided that, if I was going to make any real progress with my work with that girl I would have to get her as far away from California as possible. I considered Antarctica but finally narrowed my plan down to my apartment in New York. And so, casually, when she came back from her third phone call I broached the subject. How would she like to come to New York for a visit? "New York?" she said. "I hate New York." I reminded her that, hate New York or not, she had said she liked to travel and, I added pointedly, only in New York would she get to see Polar Bear. Whether it was this argument which prevailed on her, or whether she decided on the basis of what I am sure was a motley crew of other men she knew in New York, I do not know. I do know that, after a period of deep thought — which was difficult for her — she agreed to accept my invitation.

I prepared for her visit with mixed emotions. I was excited to have my eastern friends meet her but I did not want to give any of them the wrong impression. I therefore instructed her that it was extremely important, before she met anybody else, that she come to dinner quietly with me, where we could not only discuss her general education without interruption, but also her deportment with anybody else who might know me.

I did, it is true, take the liberty of having one of those New York services prepare a special dinner. But this, I hasten to add, was not for any reason except that my culinary skills, slow but excellent as Polar Bear finds them, are simply not up to very special dinners. I just thought it would be easier, with Polar Bear and all, to have the dinner all prepared and in the oven, ready to serve. I also wanted it to be a candlelight dinner. But this again was, I assure you, for no other reason except that my view over Central Park outside is much better with candlelight inside than it is with electric light.

Finally the day, or rather the night, came. And, late as always, she arrived. So, almost at the same moment, did Polar Bear. She even knelt to pat him just as I had long envisioned she would. But then, out of the blue — indeed the very first sentence she had uttered since she had come in — came the bombshell. "Oh," she said, patting away, "he's so fat!" And then, as if this weren't enough, she compounded the felony. "He's much too fat," she said.

Even Polar Bear did not believe it. To his way of thinking she had, on far too short an acquaintance, made far too personal a remark. He pulled away and instead of his usual "aeiou" he uttered just the very last part of it — what seemed to me a clear "ow." He had been hurt.

As for myself, knowing her, I believed what she had said, all right, but that did not make it any better. It is true that in those days, not too long after the rescue, when he had been so thin, Polar Bear had been putting on some weight. And, as I made clear in my first book, dieting was far from his long suit. But for me, who had worked so hard on his diet — even if he hadn't — her remarks were simply infuriating. I would not have expected her to know a good old-fashioned word like "portly" — as the good old-fashioned men's stores called their large-size sections — but I did expect something besides what she had said. I think, for example, if she had said something on the order of "He certainly is a large cat," or "He's getting a little heavy, isn't he?" I could have stood it. Indeed I would undoubtedly have put it down to the fact that California girls regard being thin as the most important thing in life next to their next date or the community property statute. But to say what she had, and not once but twice, it was just too much.

Frankly, from that moment on all my good intentions toward her seemed to disappear. We did indeed eat the candlelight dinner, and afterward we sat on the balcony with Polar Bear across on his. But even with her at last safe in my apartment, without the possibility of her getting a phone call and with plenty of time for the kind of consciousness-raising session that would be really meaningful — as California girls who have so little of it like to say — I did not even start on her improvement. The fact is, I had completely and irreparably lost my heart for the job. In a word, I gave up.

And, a short time after her New York visit, without the benefit of being in my custody, the California girl did just what, sooner or later, I knew she would do — she married beneath me. I mean, of course, she married beneath her. The man she chose was, of all things, a California entertainment lawyer — which, as I read it, is a contradiction not just in two terms but in three. And her marriage soon went awry, as I knew any marriage she would make except with me would.

However, to hold Polar Bear even indirectly responsible for the whole story is not quite fair. For one thing, it had for some reason the effect of inducing me to more manful efforts about his diet. For another thing the story, as it turned out for the girl, is not that sad. Now happily divorced, a sadder perhaps but certainly wiser woman, she is now a distinguished screenwriter. As for myself, if I am at times a sadder but a wiser curmudgeon, I did at least have the grace, after a suitable period of mourning, to resume if not her instruction — which I saw was hopeless — at least our friendship.

As for the occasional gossip I occasionally run into that I had been in love with that girl, nothing could be further from the truth. In the first place, curmudgeons do not fall in love with California girls. In the second place, I know people say that love is blind but if so, looking back on it all, compared to me a bat was a Seeing Eye dog. I kept my eyes open every single step of the way. All I ever tried to do was to give that California girl — one who, as ultimately was so amply proved, sorely needed it — the benefit of my wise, free counsel. And, I would like to point out, even continuing this work after the fact has not been easy. Let me give you a final example. The last time I saw the California girl we were at the Beverly Hills Polo

Lounge, and my friend Debbie Sunshine, the pianist, began playing one of my favorites, "It's So Nice to Have a Man Around the House." I was humming happily when, all of a sudden, the California girl looked up. "Damn," she said, "I hate that song. I'll bet it was written by some damn man."

Immediately I sprang into action. I told her I had hoped she had learned, after all we had been through, not to say things like that and that the song was undoubtedly written by a good old-fashioned girl and that, furthermore, I would be only too happy to take her up on her bet. We had some argument about this, including my use of the word "girl," but we finally agreed that if the song was written by a woman she would have to mend her evil ways and spend a whole weekend with me. If, however, the song was written by a man, I would have to spend a whole weekend writing anything she wanted for her.

The wager settled, we immediately repaired to Ms. Sunshine and explained our problem. Dutifully Ms. Sunshine rummaged around in her sheet music. Unfortunately she could not find "It's So Nice to Have a Man Around the House." The next morning, however, driven to the airport by two actor friends of mine, Ty Harmon and Leslee Ross, I again explained my problem, and Ty, who is a very knowledgeable fellow about show business — in between jobs he drives for a company called "Diaper to the Stars" — sent me, the next day, a fax. It was brief:

> Sorry. "It's So Nice To Have A Man Around The House" was written by Jack Elliott and Harold Spina.

Not one man, but two! Really, there was no end to the rotten luck I've had with that California girl. I should have considered the odds against me for the simple reason that the vast majority of romantic songs are written by men, because we are obviously more romantic than women. Nonetheless, I decided, after careful consideration of the whole thing, to make the best of my loss. I just wouldn't tell her. I knew she wouldn't bother to look it up, and it was at least an even bet she would forget it. Which would give me a chance, at some future time when the statute of limitations had run out, to point out to her how much people lose who don't remember things. And in the end it would be just one more valuable lesson she had learned from me.

If Polar Bear was indirectly responsible for what had happened in the California matter, for what happened in the second instance when romance reared its ugly head he was, as I have said, directly responsible. And this instance happened with a woman who was as different from the California girl as chalk is from cheese — which is an expression none of you young people have probably ever heard, until now, but now you have.

A tall blonde girl with blue eyes and a lovely smile, she was from Boston and had there learned, either at her mother's knee or in a good Boston school, never in the presence of boys to demonstrate even the possibility that she had as much intelligence, judgment, or humor as they did — as a result of which, of course, she was extremely popular. She was, in fact, an Old Flame of mine. Indeed, we had for some time gone together, although that phrase, along with such later editions as "going steady," or that awful modern "significant other" were at that time happily unknown. All in all, she was eminently suitable — in all senses of the word — as the California girl was not, and was the kind of girl you could without qualm or advance warning take home to your mother — of whom nowadays there seem to be a precious few. Indeed we might well have married had it not been that somehow, for some ridiculous reason she had, just like the California girl, married someone else — a mistake which I was sure, particularly when we ran across each other, she had sorely regretted.

In the fullness of time, however, this Boston girl had, as the California girl later had, a divorce. Since I had also been divorced, this meant that there was now no reason why we should not see each other. And, to make a short story long, when she wrote me she would soon be making a business trip to New York, I was very pleased about it, particularly since it all happened after that California girl had made her extremely poor choice and I was still worried about her. This woman, I sensed with my usual foresight, could easily turn out to be what the doctor ordered to get over any scars the California girl had left on me. And in fact, even before she arrived, I could visualize her sobbing on my shoulder about how she ever could have made such a mistake as not to marry me.

As in the case of the California girl, I had decided on a candlelight dinner. But, as the service and I bustled about in our preparation, I suddenly realized that I had overlooked one important detail in our scenario. And this detail was, of course, Polar Bear. Right away he knew something was up and when Polar Bear knows something is up, his first reaction is to go down. Indeed, he goes into his Buddha meditation pose. This is, of course, to enable him to think exactly how he is going to handle it, and since he does not know what the *it* is going to be, this can entail on his part a very long think. I have observed this enough to know that basically what he is planning is one of two possible courses of action. With the California girl he had obviously decided on a frontal assault and an immediate appearance. On the other hand he could just as well have decided on the exact opposite — a rearguard action and no appearance at all. In this case I had no idea which he would do.

Actually, when the woman arrived she didn't mention Polar Bear and we were indeed already eating our dinner before the subject came up. Then suddenly she looked around. "Where," she asked, "is Polar Bear?" I made one of my typically lame explanations — I don't really remember which one — that I was sure he was in the other room, that he had been poorly lately, or that he had just been to the vet. Whatever I said, right after it she announced blithely — or at least as blithely as Boston women are likely to get — that she was very glad he wasn't around.

At this, of course, I took immediate offense. Instead of saying anything, though, I just looked at her. As I have previously mentioned, I have only one eyebrow that I can raise. But still my one-shot is, if I do say so, very effective. Nonetheless, she just ignored it. "You know," she went on, "you never had cats when I knew you — you always had dogs." She paused meaningfully — Boston women do pause very meaningfully. But for this pause I had a knowing answer, which, as I remember, was a wise nod. She too nodded, in answer to my nod. "Anyway," she continued, and once again blithely, "I'm so glad he's not around because I'm allergic to cats."

For a long moment I said nothing. I had, of course, totally forgotten that in the days when we were going together I not only did indeed have dogs, but also did not have a cat. Now however I was torn. If I spoke my mind I would not only be forgetting my Boston manners, and with, after all, a Boston guest, I would also be kissing good-bye — to use in this connection an unfortunate phrase — another candlelight dinner. If, on the other hand, I politely said something like "Oh, that's too bad," I would be completely untrue to everything I believed — or, rather didn't believe — about being allergic.

My dilemma was solved by the immediate appearance of Polar Bear. Polar Bear is, in his way, the exact opposite of those good old-fashioned children — who, as few of you may recall, in the good old days were supposed to be seen and not heard. Polar Bear likes not to be seen but to be able to hear everything. In this case, he had obviously chosen a nearby hiding place and when he left it, he did so extremely rapidly, as if he couldn't wait a single other minute to meet her — to him up to that time, remember, a total stranger. He first slid to a stop, then made a beeline for her ankles. These he started, tail up and in his most affectionate way, rubbing back and forth.

At this the woman seemed to move as fast as he had. She jumped out of her chair, stopping only to pull a Kleenex out of her purse, and then, standing, looking down at Polar Bear, alternately sneezing and wheezing, gasping and coughing.

This time I was on the very horns of the dilemma. I could do nothing or I could do what had to be done. What I did, of course, as all who know me would know I would, was what had to be done. Scooping Polar Bear up from his unseemly ankle ogling I carried him to the bedroom and deposited him on the bed, after which — and after a brief attempt to explain to him that what I was doing was for his own good — I then left, closing the bedroom door behind me, and went back to see if my guest had expired.

She had not. But what she had done was to retire to a nearby chair. In this, although her gasping and coughing had stopped, she continued wheezing and sneezing and had even added some weeping.

My whole action of taking Polar Bear to the bedroom had taken less than a minute, but in that minute I had done a lot of thinking. Again, I could do nothing or I could speak my piece about allergies. I did the latter. But I should like to make clear that I did this not because I realized that whether I did it or not my candlelight romance was undoubtedly, at least for that evening, over and done with. I did it because, if there is one thing that makes my blood boil — and, being a curmudgeon, there are at least a dozen of these things a day that do — it is people saying they are allergic to cats, and then going to some doctor and having him tell them to "get rid" of the cat and finally taking the cat to the shelter, where of course it will be "put down" — when, instead of all this, there are many alternatives.

I realized that this was not going to be any walk in the park handling this woman in this matter, but I was bound and determined to give it the old college try. Since she was in no condition to talk I at least had on my side my favorite kind of audience — not only a captive one but one which would not be interrupting. I told her that in my life I had had every kind of allergy known to man, and certainly every kind known to woman. I told her that, even as a small child, I had hay fever, asthma, eczema, and hives, and I had in fact been allergic to so many things that they gave up testing me for them. I was, I continued, still probably allergic to most of the things to which I had been allergic then. But if there was one thing I had learned about allergies, it was that if one does not give in to them, one will in time either outgrow them or so immunize oneself to them that it amounts to the same thing.

I waited a suitable interval for all this to sink in. I then went on to state sternly that most of the time doctors tell people to get rid of their cats either because they don't like cats or because it is easier than getting to the bottom of the patient's other allergies. I told her that during my worst allergies, I had once been put for several months in a cabin with air conditioning — a rarity in those days — and existed on just six kinds of food. I didn't expect doctors to do that nowadays, but if they had the gumption to test their patients and find out exactly to what they were allergic, and inoculate them for that, they might well find out that all this handled the cat problem too. And, even if it did not, such doctors should be reminded that a patient can be specifically inoculated against cat allergies. I further said that while I would not recommend that someone who said he or she was allergic to cats actually sleep with one in the bed — at least until he or she had been for some time in another room situation with the cat — in time even that would be possible and would indeed speed up self-immunization.

Finally, after one more suitable interval, I reached my peroration. I asked her point-blank if she realized how often cat allergy had proved to be entirely mental. And, I added firmly, she should not overlook that patients were not the only ones who had this mental allergy to cats — so did some doctors. Indeed, in my opinion, patients often caught this from their doctors — and for this, I added even more firmly, there was apparently no inoculation.

Of course, nobody likes to be told anything physical is mental — particularly not people from Boston. And this woman was, Boston or no Boston, no exception to this. When at last her wheezing, as well as her weeping, had subsided enough so she could talk, she spoke firmly. "With me," she said, "it's not mental. I can't even go into a room where a cat has been." At this I moved in for the kill. As politely as I could, and with as little sarcasm as possible, I pointed out that she had just been in such a room — one, in fact, in which a cat spent most of his life and indeed in which he had still been, and not far from her, at the time she started eating dinner. Yet only when he came out to her and she had seen him did she have her attack. If that did not prove, once and for all, how large was the mental element of it, I would like to know what did.

I could have gone on, of course, but I did not. I really don't enjoy arguing with people who don't know enough about the subject, or don't know the facts or are always bringing up facts I don't know. And the woman was, after all, temporarily incapacitated and I did not want in any manner to seem to be taking advantage of her. I had to remember that she was my guest and, as her wheezing and sneezing had now come to a full stop, it did occur to me that I might well have too soon written off our possible romance. In any case, courteous as always, I gave her my arm and we went back to the dinner table. Over the dinner and even more so over the wine we talked about old times. Aside from the allergy episode the woman could not have been more charming, and as the evening wine on — I mean wore on — I suggested we walk out on the balcony.

We did so, and since it was a lovely summer evening the scene was clearly set for what it was supposed to be from the beginning. I had, in fact, just started to put my arm around her when suddenly she pulled back and once more proceeded to wheeze and sneeze, gasp and cough.

An alert reader with the layout of my apartment balcony in mind will of course immediately surmise what had happened. There will be some — albeit I hope not many — who will put it down to my lack of romantic appeal. But the majority will know that just at the moment when I was about to take the woman in my arms, and I was headed east and she west, Polar Bear made a flying leap out of the bedroom window onto his part of the balcony. The woman had not only seen him over my shoulder, she also had no way of knowing he could not, because of the wire, come all the way to her. One thing was certain — I had learned firsthand that, at crucial times, a sense of humor in a woman is not nearly as ruinous as a full-bore allergy attack.

A lesser man might, at this juncture, have given up. I am not, however, a lesser man, I am a morer man. There and then I conceived a plan which would have a twofold purpose. The first would be to prove to someone with an apparently severe cat allergy that there were not only other remedies than to "get rid" of the cat, there were literally dozens of others. The second would be — and I hasten to emphasize that this would only be second — that I would not be cheated out of a well-deserved romance. When I can do a good deed and at the same time get what I want, I feel all of my powers moving in harmonious cooperation.

I moved, as I always do when I have a battle plan, rapidly. As soon as her allergy attack had subsided and we were walking to the door, I told her I knew she was going to be in New York for three days and that if she would just come back for another night before she left — I suggested her last night, which would give me two whole days — I would not only deallergize my entire apartment,

I would deallergize Polar Bear, too. Surprised as she was that either or both of these were possible, she was also, like most Boston women, game, and she agreed. I next suggested, inveterate bettor that I am, a bet. At this, game though she was, she was also practical, and she wanted to know what the bet would be. I knew she was in advertising, so I said that if she had, during the evening in question, as much as one allergy attack, she would win and I would agree, at her direction, to work on as much as a full page of any ad or other piece of writing she wanted done. If, on the other hand, she did not have any such allergy attack, I would win. "What?" she asked, as I opened the door. Guess, I said, shutting it.

After she had gone I let Polar Bear out of the bedroom and, as I did so, I looked at the room carefully. I already knew enough about what I had to do to deallergize the living room without taking on the bedroom as well. The bedroom, bed or no bed, was out. Deallergizing the bed alone would, I was sure, be more than a two-day deal and, for all I knew, would involve a brand new bed. I certainly did not want to lose that particular bet on, of all things, a bed. I would do just the living room — and that would be that.

Frankly, at first I did not know exactly how much of a job I had ahead of me, but when I set myself to something my middle name is determination. I also made the decision that whatever it was I had to do it would be better not to try to do it all myself. I would, after all, be directing the whole operation and I needed to keep a clear head and not tie myself up with trivial details. Thus, early the next morning I called a couple of chess-playing friends of mine who are on the husky side — which is very rare for chess players — and told them to come over immediately. I mentioned casually that while we were playing chess there might be a little furniture to be moved, so they might want to wear old clothes.

While I waited for them, I decided to do some research on the subject. Even though I felt I knew practically everything there was to know about allergies I didn't see what harm refreshing my knowledge would do. In good time I found, in *Cats* magazine, a fine article by Barbara Kolenda entitled "Coping with Allergy to Cats." This I thought could be just what I needed, but I was worried about Ms. Kolenda's use of the word "coping." It sounded a little on the slow side and I had to move fast. Anyway, Ms. Kolenda advised four steps, and I immediately plunged into her "Step One." "The first thing you have to do," she said, "is to make your bedroom off limits to your cat." Frankly, I had trouble with this right away because if someone is allergic to one's cat I couldn't imagine not wanting to solve the problem enough to be able to have the cat on one's bed. That, in my opinion, is where cats belong. Nonetheless I did see what Ms. Kolenda was driving at — it was, after all, why I had already removed the bedroom from my list of what to do. And, when I came to her "Step Two," I believed I had struck, if I did say so in this connection, pay dirt:

> Perhaps the most useful thing you can do (second only from banning the cat from your bedroom) is to acquire something called a HEPA (High Efficiency Particulate Air) filter. These filters were originally developed for use in the space program and can clean the tiniest particles, including dander, dust and pollen out of the air.

The idea that I, a man who for all my abilities has not yet been able to master either a word processor or, for that matter, a memory typewriter, was going to go really high-tech — the space program, mind you — was heady stuff, and I resolved to get a HEPA posthaste. Furthermore, Ms. Kolenda had other good news about what I was sure would soon be my very own HEPA:

> A good one is capable of exchanging the air in an average room several times an hour, with each pass removing more and more allergens. These filters generally come with one or more prefilters for removing things like fur. . . .

That was really thrilling, and I resolved there and then to get myself a giant one of those babies. In my mind's eye I immediately conjured up giving a party with some damn woman waltzing in with either a whole fur coat or maybe just a fur hat or fur cape — *whoosh,* my giant filtered HEPA would suck it right off her and whisk it away. I even visualized getting a giant shredder for it. I could see myself standing there, watching it all, and with the woman standing there frantic, I would just quietly explain that I was very sorry, ma'am, but I was allergic to fur.

All in all, by the time my chess friends came in and we started to work on the living room I was in high spirits. It was hard work, but as I sat there directing them from the chessboard, I was very proud of them. They didn't miss a thing — the sofa, the stuffed chairs, the curtains, the rugs, and even the books. And what we couldn't totally deallergize with vacuuming — something, all the instructions said, which had to be done several times — we just moved. The way we — or rather, they — did this was to go down the hall and persuade a friend of mine to take "a few things," as I put it, into her apartment. It is true that as the few things grew into a lot of things she got a little worried, and finally when the sofa came and she didn't even have room to get to her door, she demanded to know what it was all about. Just spring cleaning, I told her cheerfully. She did not, however, let this pass. "Spring cleaning!" she exclaimed, "In August?" Oh, I said, so it is. How time flies.

Even after all this, and after sending one of my friends out to search for a HEPA — on a rental basis, of course — I still had two more steps of my own. And "Step Three" was far from my favorite. It was the problem of deallergizing Polar Bear himself. My best advice here came from a pamphlet put out by the Associated Humane Society. It was entitled "Being Homeless Is Nothing to Sneeze at!" The section in question sounded easy:

> Now we come to de-allergizing your pet. Comb and brush your pet well. Bathe in a good quality, watered-down tearless protein shampoo for pets — available in any pet store. Bathe twice and rinse VERY WELL. Next towel off excess water while the pet is in the tub or sink. Then pour over it, saturating the coat totally, a solution of one part fabric softener — like Downy — and four parts water. Work it into the coat and DO NOT rinse off.

Whoever wrote those instructions, one thing I knew — they did not know Polar Bear. Remember, the last bath I had given him was the day after I had rescued him and although he had a few baths at the vet in the years that had since elapsed, he had not had one from me. Nonetheless Polar Bear, once bitten, is not only twice shy, he is forever shy, and on top of this he has a memory which would shame an elephant. The last I saw of him was a full hour from when I first started running the tub. How on earth he knew this was not going to be just another bath for me, but one for him, I had no idea. Perhaps all the movement of furniture and vacuuming and dusting in the living room, none of which he liked, had made him suspicious. Whether it had or not, this time he did not do just one of his minor disappearances — he majored in this one. And, as I say, it took me a full hour to find him — indeed the only reason I did so in that time was that my chess-playing friends, after dusting the books, had not put them back too carefully. So, sure enough, between two of my favorite books, *John Brown's Body* and *Comfort Found in Good Old Books*, I located first the end of Polar Bear's tail and then, behind those books, the rest of him.

The finding of him, however, turned out to be the easy part. When I had to put him down in the tub in the "watered-down tearless protein shampoo for pets" and tried to keep him there, I immediately had not only my hands full but my chest and one of my legs as well. And since I knew full well by that time that this was not going to be just a bath for him but rather one for both of us, I only wished I had dressed — or rather undressed — for the occasion. All in all, by the time I came to the second part of our ablution, the "pour over it" part — in which I assumed the "it" was him — I was in need of absolution, if not from him at least from a Higher Source. We were not only head-to-head, we were toe-to-toe. His meows had become hisses and his eyes were blazing. As for the "solution of one part fabric softener to four parts of water," by then, I assure you, with him spitting foam I was in no mood for splitting hairs or for measuring. Finally, when I came to the last injunction — "work it into the coat and DO NOT rinse off" — capitals or no capitals, I decided, I had had it even if he still hadn't, and I had not the slightest intention of obeying the instruction to "bathe twice."

Once would do nicely, thank you, I decided, if I was going to be in any kind of shape to answer the bell for the big evening.

By the time I finished, one thing was certain. The whole idea of the bath, as I understood it, was to keep Polar Bear's dander down. But however well this may have worked, there was no mistaking that he now had the rest of his dander up. Before I let him out of the tub he was as near to total fury as I had ever seen him. But even in his rage I knew he was thinking of what he could do when he got out which would irritate me the most. What he chose was leaping from the tub and darting immediately for the bedroom. Here he jumped up on the bed and started rolling around — all the time watching me, since I had followed him, to get what he was sure would be a very bad reaction to what he was doing. But I know him too well to give him any such satisfaction. I simply ignored him, and I had a good excuse for this. I could not rest on laurels. With all I had done so far, in the deallergizing of the room and of him, there was still another job for which I had to prepare. And this was, or rather would be, the deallergizing, upon arrival, of the woman herself.

I learned what I had to do about this not from instruction books but from a chance meeting I had the morning after my first date with the Boston woman. The meeting occurred at the New York Athletic Club and was with a friend of mine, a distinguished magazine consultant named John Henderson. Mr. Henderson asked me what I was up to, and I told him if what he meant was what was uppermost in my mind that day, it was, frankly, a bet. I then related to him the whole stern story and told him, in no uncertain terms, that I was under the gun. "Do you really want to win your bet?" he asked me. I told him I did indeed. "Well," he said, "you've as good as won."

Mr. Henderson then parted with the story that he, too, was extremely allergic to cats and that sometime before, calling upon a friend of his, Pamela McRae, a rising young director at the Metropolitan Opera and a woman who had two cats, he had been severely smitten — and in more ways than one. "I was not only terribly embarrassed," he said, "I had to leave the apartment. I literally couldn't breathe."

Why, I wanted to know, did he think I was going to win my bet? "Because," he said, "I got over it — completely." Ms. McRae, I wanted to know, or the allergy? "The allergy," he said firmly. I told him I was all ears. "It's too complicated for you," he said. "Call Maryann."

I knew Maryann Lane was a telephone operator at the New York Athletic Club and I also knew she was a very charming woman who lived in Peekskill, New York, with nine cats and four dogs. I called her in the evening. Talking with her, I found out that not only had she once been allergic to cats, despite now having nine of them, but that so had her daughter Laura. Together with her daughter, she said, she had visited doctor after doctor. "We went," she said, "to Mount Sinai, to Ear and Nose, and literally dozens of private doctors. Every single one of them told Laura and me to get rid of our cats." Finally someone — she couldn't remember who — told her to go to the head of the pulmonary department of New York's Phelps Memorial Hospital.

This time, however, the advice was different. "Don't worry about getting rid of your cats," the doctor told them. "You don't have to. It's not them, it's you." He paused. "I'm going to take care of you." With that he handed

Maryann and Laura two bottles. The first was something called Proventil, the second Vanceril. Both were inhalants. The doctor instructed them to take two puffs of Proventil before they entered a house or apartment in which there were cats and to take two puffs of Vanceril when they were inside such a house or apartment when they sensed an allergy attack coming on.

Maryann and Laura did what they were told. And sure enough, not only do they rarely have to take the inhalants, but they have never, after taking them, had a severe allergy attack. Afterward, not surprisingly, both have become imbued with close to missionary zeal in their desire to get other people to try it. "I've had other people you know besides Mr. Henderson try it," Maryann told me. "Frank, who used to be the head doorman here at the club, and dozens and dozens of other people. I used to tell people that both inhalants are made by Schering and are available at most drugstores, and all they have to do is get their doctors to prescribe them. Now I don't even do that. I just tell people to call the Fund for Animals."

I next told Maryann and Laura, with some editing, the story of my bet and asked them if they were positive I would win. "Absolutely," Maryann said, "if you can make that woman take the medicine." I told her that I could make anything that walks take medicine — except Polar Bear.

Once I had the inhalants in my hand, my idea was that I would alert the doorman in my apartment building to buzz me on the buzzer when the Boston woman arrived, and I would then meet her in the hallway to see that, before entering the apartment, she took two puffs of Inhalant No. 1. I was prepared to do this, and indeed the dinner was in the oven when, all of a sudden, my doorbell rang. I refused to open it. You can't come in, I shouted. Stay there and get way back from the door, and I'll come out. Quickly I opened the door and saw, to my surprise, standing by the elevator, not my Boston woman but a messenger. He was understandably concerned. Nonetheless, he handed me a special-delivery envelope. Opening this, after he had hurriedly made his departure, I saw it was from Lia Albo, the Fund for Animals' chief rescuer. Her message, carefully typed out, was brief. It read as follows:

Chinese Herbal Remedy for Cat Allergies:
   ¼ ounce Korean ginseng
   ¼ ounce white jelly fungus
   ¼ ounce wei-shan

Boil above in *ceramic* pot with 3 to 4 cups of water until it's down to 2 to 3 cups.

Strain and drink.

Can drink hot or cold — can add sugar to taste

Drink daily.

For a moment I must admit it sounded intriguing but, alas, it had arrived too late for my purposes — particularly the part about "drink daily." Clearly it was something I would have had to have started earlier. Also, game though my Boston friend was, I didn't think she would be overjoyed at eating the "white jelly fungus." Nonetheless I was extremely curious to know if it was really Lia Albo's own remedy. I went back in the apartment and called her. "No," she said, "it's really not mine." Well then, I asked, whose was it? There was a long pause. Finally Lia spoke. "If you're going to put it in your book," she said, "why don't you just say it's from Lia's possible new boyfriend's sister's ex-boyfriend."

It was as good as done, I told her. With that I went back to my wait for my dinner guest. This time the doorman did his job and buzzed me on the buzzer and I was standing in the hallway by the elevator when the Boston woman came up. I told her she couldn't go in yet — she had to inhale a little inhalant first. She was surprised, but she was a good sport about it, and took two puffs of Inhalant No. 1 right away. I next presented her with Inhalant No. 2. She was getting a little antsy at this point but felt better when I told her she didn't have to take Inhalant No. 2 right then, but she had to keep it with her and had to take two puffs of it if she sensed an allergy attack coming on.

At last I opened the apartment door and with some ceremony ushered her in. She couldn't believe all the changes I had made. I not only spent a good deal of time showing off the deallergized furniture but also went to some lengths to make her breathe deeply as we stood together near the HEPA, drinking in the de-particulated air. It was, I told her, if I did say so, direct from the Space Center. A little exaggeration, I always feel, is a man's privilege when dealing with a dinner date.

Even the appearance of Polar Bear, pinch-faced as he still was from his bath, didn't for a moment shake my confidence. Nor did it, I was glad to see, shake hers. When, however, I saw her start to lean down and pat him, I insisted that before she did so she take two puffs of Inhalant No. 2. After that, when I went into the kitchen to get our first course, I didn't even bother to look over and watch them. My bet, I was sure, was all but in the bag.

I should have looked. For, all of a sudden, as I put the first course on the table, I heard all too clearly the telltale sounds of the beginning of a wheeze and a sneeze. For a moment I couldn't believe it. The table was between us and I couldn't see either my guest or Polar Bear. I just listened, stunned. And then, along with the wheeze and sneeze, there was not only a gasp, there was also an unmistakably coughed "AEIOU."

Before I even turned to look, I realized I did not need to do so. The sounds were not coming from my Boston friend, they were coming from Polar Bear. She had not pulled back from him, he had pulled back from her. She was no longer allergic to him. But he, even deallergized as he was and breathing in that rarefied air, was now allergic to her.

As I looked at him wheezing and sneezing, I could not believe it. And, curiously, neither could he. But one thing he did believe was who was to blame. And who or what do you think this was? My Boston friend? The deallergized apartment? His deallergization? Even his bath? Wrong, on all counts. Clearly, as usual, he blamed me.

For some time I looked at him and he looked at me. Then, without a word, as I had three nights before, I leaned down, picked him up, took him to the bedroom and shut the door.

By the time I returned, both my Boston friend and I knew that the die was cast and whatever chance we might have had for romance had gone up in, if not smoke, at least de-particulated air. Polar Bear, like Mr. Wodehouse's Webster, albeit in a different way, had called the tune. Both of us being from Boston, however, we did not waste the dinner. And, as we sat enjoying it, I was even emboldened to bring up the question of the bet. It seemed to me, I said, that, looking at the fact from all angles, I had not really lost. She smiled. "Let's call it," she said, "a draw." A draw, I replied almost automatically, is like kissing your sister.

Later that evening, after she had gone and Polar Bear and I lay in the bed, I was glad to see that his wheezing and sneezing had stopped. I also talked to him at length. He has a short attention span, but for once he did his best, before he went to sleep, at least to see, even if he did not understand, how concerned I was. As for me, I did not go to sleep for some time. Instead I went over in my mind everything that had happened, step by step. I like to do this after any controversy I have with anybody because I like to find out where the other person went wrong. And I particularly like to do this in, if I do say so, the very rare cases I've had in my life of unrequited love. I realize this is another expression that probably none of you young people have ever heard of because, as far as I can see, you always get requited love. But never mind — the point is that, as I thought about the whole thing, suddenly I brightened. Into my mind came a picture of the kind of allergy case I had just been through, of a man visiting doctor after doctor and asking them what to do about someone who loves his cat and wouldn't consider giving him up even though his cat was allergic to his girl. By this time I really was dreaming, and in the dream it was all happening to me. And, as I say, I was going from doctor to doctor to doctor. I was just hoping one of them would give me the only answer — get rid of the girl. But do you know what? Not even in my dream would a single damn one of them do that.

Actually, underneath all the romance — which is always at best a doubtful proposition — there was undeniable reality. At about the time of the breakup of my ill-fated amatory advances toward the Boston woman, one which you will recall fell hard on the heels of one of my extraordinarily rare lapses of judgment in the matter of the California girl — well, as I say, after these Polar Bear did, as some cats do, develop some allergies of his own. Unlike most cats who do this, however, and therefore have to go to the vet's for their shots — in his case the shots came to him. This came about through the fact that, with my usual conning artistry I was able to persuade his vet, Susan Thompson, to make, in his case, house calls. But even with all my artistry I was able to do this only upon giving her my solemn promise that I would not tell anyone that she did so. I agreed with alacrity since I knew, wonderful as Dr. Thompson is with animals, she is inclined to be on the forgetful side about her animals' people — specifically, among other things, what they do — and in my case she had neglected to mention that my promise was just not to tell people. It did not anywhere include anything about not writing about it.

On the surface the arrangement of her coming to him instead of the other way around looked like good news for both Polar Bear and me — Polar Bear because he would not have to make his very least favorite journey, to the vet's, and me because I did not have to suffer the slings and arrows of trying to get him into his carrier to begin with, and then the trip and all the rest of it. But under the surface it was not that good news for either of us. For Polar Bear there remained the stark fact that he still had to have, willy-nilly, his shot, and for me, as will in good time shortly be revealed to you, the whole thing had dire consequences.

In truth Polar Bear loves Dr. Thompson, but the fact

that she is a vet precludes him from any demonstration or even indication of this — otherwise he'd have to turn in his union card as a cat. Moreover, being as forgetful as he is about people, he did not realize on her first appearance that she was a vet. But the moment he realized that her appearance in the apartment did not mean she was just one more woman who was coming to see him but was instead someone who was going to give him a shot, all love was lost and she became an enemy. And this change came about not by any means in the fullness of time but on her very second visit. From then on, of course, he would disappear and I would have to locate him and carry him to her. During this endeavor he invariably put on an act which reached the height of his well-developed feline thespian operatics — he accompanied his piteous "aeiou" 's with caterwauling wails. In between, as I carried him to his doom, he was all but saying to my face how could I have possibly sunk so low as to turn him over to such a fiend incarnate for torture specifically outlawed by the Geneva Convention.

And all this, mind you, over a shot which was over and done with in a matter of a few seconds, which did not really hurt him at all and indeed was of such little consequence that afterward he not only didn't bother disappearing again but also shortly became, union card or no union card, positively affectionate toward Dr. Thompson.

Not so, however, toward me. In his curious little twisted mind he never even gave me the benefit of afterward deciding that the whole thing wasn't, after all, that big a deal. To me he was completely unforgiving. But, far worse than this from my point of view was the fact that, as Dr. Thompson began coming regularly, he began to harbor the darkest of suspicions toward any woman who came to my apartment for any reason whatsoever. He made indeed only one exception to this, and that was Marian. I firmly believe that the only reason Marian got off his hook is that Marian is such a softy with cats that not only will she not cut her cat's toenails, she will not even allow anyone else to do so. I do not know whether this intelligence had traveled the cat grapevine or whether Polar Bear made the judgment on his own. I do know, however, that some way, somehow, he knew for certain that Marian would never stoop to such indignity as inflicting a shot on him.

But, as I say, Marian was his sole exception. Any other person of the female persuasion who so much as darkened my door was to Polar Bear, when it came to the possibility of getting a shot in the posterior, a possible perpetrator. And to say that this has not considerably darkened for me the possibilities of any further romantic interludes would, simply, not be stating the truth. And, if you think I'm exaggerating, I am not, because another tragedy too is involved here. This is the fact that most of the women who come to my apartment do so not to see me but, hard as it is for me to bear, to see Polar Bear. And when, instead of seeing him the way they had imagined they would and having the opportunity to pat and play with him, all they see is, first, a disappearance act and, second, a reluctant drag-out, I can assure you it is a long hard road from there to even the possibility of a candlelight dinner. Indeed I think I can state without fear of contradiction that, under similar circumstances, Casanova himself might well have considered becoming a monk.

○ *L'Envoi*

Some of you with good memories may recall that earlier in this book I stated that two curmudgeons under one roof — even if one is a person curmudgeon and the other a cat curmudgeon — was one curmudgeon too many. After all these years with Polar Bear, however, who is, if not a black-belt curmudgeon such as myself, at least a white-belt one, I now believe that I should have allowed, in my flat statement, some room for the possibility of a rounded exception. Clearly Polar Bear and I have proved that it is possible for two curmudgeons under one roof to get along famously — in at least most senses of the word — as long as one of us is occasionally willing to give in to the other. I am not saying which one of us does this more than the other — I do, after all, still have my pride — but I will just leave it that one of us does. But please, realize that I mentioned the word "occasionally."

I also believe, however, that when you have two curmudgeons under one roof you have, basically, two problems. And here I am speaking not just of Polar Bear and myself but rather about the whole broad field of person and cat curmudgeonry. In any case, the first problem is that it is very important which came first — the person curmudgeon or the cat curmudgeon. In my considered opinion, it is the cat curmudgeon who should come first, and then he can teach the person curmudgeon the finer points of the trade. If the person curmudgeon comes first, I believe this would be very difficult. This is because, as close observation of Polar Bear has forced me to conclude, cats can teach but they cannot learn.

The second problem concerns the age-old problem of — well, age. You cannot, for example, expect an old curmudgeon cat to teach a baby boy to be a curmudgeon any more than you should expect a young curmudgeon kitten to teach a grumpy old grandfather curmudgeon. Neither, conversely, can you expect your baby boy to teach your old curmudgeon cat or your grumpy old grandfather to teach your kitten. It just wouldn't work. What you are looking for here, in short, is a proper age balance between a cat's age and a person's age. In this connection you have probably heard that one year of a cat's life is like seven years of a person's life. Well, if so, you have heard wrong. Many cats, for example, live to be fifteen — how many people live to be one hundred and five? Some cats even live to be twenty — how many people live to be one hundred and forty? I am, of course, excepting those people whom you see on those irritating commercials eating yogurt and dancing up and down some mountain.

Frankly, I think the reason they say they're that age is that it's the only way they get to see television, which apparently otherwise they never get to see at all.

Anyway, to put you straight on the whole matter of a cat's age in comparison to a person's age I wish you to look at the following chart, one put out by the Gaines Research Center people. I've gone to a good deal of trouble to get this for you so I want you to look at it carefully:

Cat's Age	Person's Age
6 months	10 years
8 months	13 years
12 months	15 years
2 years	24 years
4 years	32 years
6 years	40 years
8 years	48 years
10 years	56 years
12 years	64 years
14 years	72 years
16 years	80 years
18 years	88 years
20 years	96 years
21 years	100 years

Now please don't get wandering off the track here on me and worrying about your own cat's age in comparison to your age. I want you to keep your mind on what we're talking about and look at the chart strictly from the point of view of person and cat curmudgeonry. Let us say, for example, that ten is the youngest age a cat can really become a recognized curmudgeon and fifty-six the youngest for any person. Again, please look at the chart and, translating the figures, you will see what I am talking about. Actually I became a curmudgeon at forty-nine but, as I told you before, I had damned good reason to hurry it along and I am, of course, if I do say so, precocious. But, even giving Polar Bear the benefit of cat precocity, he could not have become a curmudgeon until he was nine, at which time he was a mature cat and I, at fifty-two, was still a young man. But since he is now — as again I said earlier we don't know exactly how old he was when he was rescued — between twelve and fourteen, and I am now between sixty-four and seventy-two, give or take, as I am inclined to, a few years off, right now as I write this means we are reaching our curmudgeonly peak together and undoubtedly will continue to stay at this peak.

I figure indeed that when he is between sixteen and eighteen and I am between eighty and eighty-eight, we might even be said to have reached the Pike's Peak of person and cat curmudgeonry. On the other hand if, for example, you had a cat curmudgeon of twenty and a person curmudgeon of, let's say, just beyond seventy, you would have trouble, the same way you would if you had a person curmudgeon of ninety and a cat curmudgeon of eight. I know at this point some of you may be getting a little confused, but if you are go back and look at the chart again, and then read these two paragraphs again, it will soon become clear, and you will have learned a lot.

Of course there remains no question in my mind but that I have been a very good mentor for Polar Bear in all his curmudgeonly development and it is extremely gratifying to me that more and more I see him taking the same sort of umbrage I do at the very same totally infuriating modern idiocies. If he doesn't have the range of these which I do — because of his lack of travel — it does not mean that I do not believe that if he had my range he would not get just as mad as I do about such matters as hotel windows which don't open, airplane seats which are designed by one-armed people about four feet tall, and waiters, clerks, telephone operators, and taxi drivers who are all apparently from countries with which, at the time one runs into them, we are still at war.

I base all this on the unassailable fact that Polar Bear gets just as mad as I do about shoddy workmanship, slip-shod service, defective cans and medicine bottles and even soda bottles which take an engineer to open, not to mention the disappearance of good old-fashioned heavy cream and cereal boxes which cost twice as much as they ought to and, when you finally do manage to get them open, you find are half-full. Indeed at certain modern outrages he is even less tolerant than I, and here I will include late-night or early-morning telephone calls as well as those endless and extra-loud television commercials, particularly those with cats in them who have not only not learned their craft but are not nearly as handsome as he is. He even shares my fury at sports announcers with their everlasting praise of sports figures who "stay within themselves." What do they think Polar Bear and I do, for heaven's sakes? Stay without ourselves?

The bald truth is that, frankly, it would take two curmudgeons working together even to begin to cope with all these things. And doing this in tandem has over the years brought us even closer together. I also believe that in these last years I have detected unmistakable signs that in certain ways Polar Bear has made a real effort to emulate me. This is very flattering, of course, and although I do wish he would concentrate less on my few faults and more on my many noble traits, I realize that I have got to take the bad with the good and that no man, as my friend Noël Coward once said, is a hero to his valet. I do not mean to suggest for a moment that Polar Bear is a valet. But I do wish he was. Valets are, after all, just one more example of good old-fashioned people who have very inconsiderately up and vanished. Many's the morning I could use one, and Polar Bear could, too. Frankly, he doesn't pick up anything, not even his toys. I'm really *his* valet — something which, for a mature, busy biographer, is really an absurd thing to have to be. Did Boswell, after all, go around picking up after Dr. Johnson?

What I do wish to suggest, on the other hand, is that when two curmudgeons have such a close personal relationship it is very difficult for either one to be a hero to the other. An example of this is the matter of our ailments. It is, after all, a fact of life that as one grows more mature one also grows in better judgment, superior mental ability, and in all-around good old-fashioned common sense. But it is also a fact of life that, unfortunately, all this increase in these mental areas is often accompanied by a decrease in the physical areas.

I, for example, have developed arthritis of the hip, and in no time at all Polar Bear developed arthritis of the hip also. And while I of course suffer mine in silence, he does not. When he wants, for example, to be lifted to the bedroom window so that he can jump out and see what the pigeons are doing, does he, as I would, manfully hoist himself up there without a word of complaint or a thought of asking for help? Not at all. He goes to the window, looks first up and then to me, "aeiou"'s his little head off, and just stands there until I go over and do the job for him. And this, mind you, when I have caught him when he is in a real hurry doing it himself with no trouble at all. And on top of this, and as if that weren't enough, he has the unmitigated gall — my gall, as I've said before, is always mitigated — to believe that his pain is the equal of mine. Time and time again I have pointed out to him how absurd it is for him to claim that in his little leg, hardly the size of my little finger, he could possibly have as much pain as I have in my leg. Frankly, the only possible reason I can imagine for him even thinking such a thing is probably that, when you come right down to it, it is all in his little mind — which is, again when you come right down to it, about the size of a tenth of mine.

I do not for a moment mean to put down Polar Bear's mentality, and if I seem to do this, I do so, of course, only in comparison to mine. Polar Bear is, and always has been from the day I rescued him, one very smart cat. He is also, in case I have not made this clear, one very beautiful cat. And, finally, he is one very lovable cat — if not toward everybody, at least toward me. Which to me at least proves that he is, besides being smart and beautiful and lovable, a cat with excellent judgment.

I say all this because at this point I should also like to say that I have recently got another cat — or, rather, another cat got me. It all happened on a trip to the hallowed Boston summer resort of Martha's Vineyard. There are, of course, other than Proper Bostonians who summer here — Washingtonians and even New Yorkers, who are made reasonably welcome as long as their money is not too new and they do not have too much of it or show it too much or they are not Yankees fans.

The reason for my trip was that I was to lecture on Martha's Vineyard and, needless to say, in this lecture I stressed the importance of being born, if not actually on the Vineyard, at least in Boston. That night after the lecture Marian and I stayed with an old friend, the distinguished artist Ruth Emerson, and we spent as much time as possible with Ms. Emerson's beloved raccoons and skunks — which every night she regularly feeds in a way which would do credit to the Black Beauty Ranch.

All in all, it was a delightful visit up to the dawn of my last day. That day, however, I made a serious error. At the behest of another devoted animal person, Anna Bell Washburn, I visited the local animal shelter. And there, as I walked by the cages in the cattery, I suddenly felt a large paw on the back of my head. As I turned around, I saw the perpetrator — his telltale paw still out of the cage. He was, as later described by Elaine Lembo of the *Vineyard Gazette*, an "orphaned white cat with a silly, blue-eyed buggy stare" — one which, she said, turned me into "mush." And, not satisfied with that — a word, for any curmudgeon, certifiably libelous — she then went on in the next paragraph to repeat the libel.

I did not sue, but only for the reason that I was, at that time, entirely too busy with the cat. I was, indeed, from the moment he reached out to me, had. Actually, as I was later to learn, the whole thing had been a put-up job. Mrs. Washburn and her friends had, I believe, all but trained the cat to reach out anytime any likely large sucker was about to pass. Clearly they knew — and I had to admit they were right — that this cat was the kitten image of Polar Bear when I first saw him that snowy Christmas Eve. The only difference was he had blue eyes instead of Polar Bear's green, and his two front paws six, not five, toes. Those women also knew that I would not be able to resist him, but not for any mushy reasons. I am not, after all, a sled-dog driver.

Polar Star, as I named him — and before, I should add, the recent novel of the same name — was a country stray.

His summer family had just abandoned him on the incredible theory such people seem to have — that a cat can just get along somehow. And somehow this one had, at least for a while, until a kindly person had found him and brought him to the shelter. If his looks are similar to Polar Bear's, however, his personality is not. He is as outgoing as Polar Bear is the opposite. He loves everybody, and right away. Indeed most of the time he seems more like a dog than a cat.

I know that the idea of my falling for another cat will offend many people, particularly those who will remember Polar Bear's very poor attitude toward other cats. I wish, however, to state my side of the case. In the first place I never had the slightest idea of bringing Polar Star to my apartment. Although Polar Bear has grown less hostile to the occasional stray who passes a night or a weekend with me, I really believe this is because he now knows through experience that they will be transient and not permanent guests. In the second place, the place to which I did take Polar Star was not to my apartment but instead to my office at the Fund for Animals, where he would join our other two permanent office cats, Benedict and Little Girl.

It was, I should admit, at first not an idyllic arrangement. Indeed, both Benedict and Little Girl immediately took very dim views of the whole idea and were, from the very first day, very mean to the then-small newcomer. In vain I warned them that, small as he then was, he would get bigger. And, by the size of those six-toed paws I could see he would be very much bigger than they were, and in fact this is just what has happened. And Polar Star now returns in full measure just what they, in the beginning, did to him. Maintaining even short periods of peace has not been easy, but the armed truces now outnumber the actual wars and, as my battle-scarred multi-catted friends Jeanne Adlon, Jane Volk, and Jennie Lester assure me, all will, in the end, work itself out.

One important lesson I've learned from Polar Star is that there is a large and basic difference between city strays and country strays. And this is that, generally speaking, the former are wary of people, since people are the ones who have usually done bad things to them. The latter, on the other hand, are most wary of other animals because it is with those other animals that they have had their problems. Certainly Polar Star, who loves people, does not love other animals — and this unfortunately, at least at present, seems to include other cats — but at the same time, no cat I have ever known is better loved by almost every person who comes across him.

I was well aware that no matter how I explained why I adopted Polar Star — or rather allowed him to adopt me — it would still not satisfy some people. One of these would, I knew, be Rosa, the cleaning lady. Since Rosa also cleans the office, she knows both Polar Bear and Polar Star intimately — and, totally possessive as she is of Polar Bear, she was at first almost as bad about Polar Star as the other office cats were. I remember well, on one of Rosa's worst days about the whole situation, she called me from my apartment. "Mr. Amory," she said in a voice which I knew boded no good, "Polar Bear is very difficult today — he won't eat a thing." I told her that Polar Bear was very difficult many days, and that that was what a curmudgeon cat was supposed to be. I also added that, as for his not eating that day, this was not bad but good news. Rosa, of course, was not about to buy my explanation. "The reason Polar Bear is difficult," she said, "is that he knows perfectly well you have another white cat down there. He's seen the hairs on your clothes." I told her that Polar Bear could not possibly know I had another cat, and that as for the hairs, that I had had hairs of various animals on my clothes since before she was born. "But," she added sternly and firmly, "what if he thinks you love another cat as much as you love him?"

This time, equally sternly and firmly, I told her there was no way he could think such a thing because he was a smart cat, and he was certainly smart enough to know it could not be true. I even went so far as to tell her that I did not believe I would ever, in my entire life, have another cat I loved as much as Polar Bear.

Rosa was, at last, at least partially satisfied. Nonetheless, she had one last question. "Mr. Amory," she asked, "are you going to write about Polar Star?" I knew immediately that she was going to be very cross if I said I was, and so I decided to beg the question. When it comes to a difficult question I am usually as brave as a lion but once in a while I think that begging is a better policy. This, clearly, was one of those times.

Just the same, after the conversation was over, I did some good hard thinking about the whole matter. And, as usual, I came to the right decision. I would indeed write about Polar Star, but I would not do so until the very end of the book. For there, I was sure, it would be safe from Polar Bear as safe can be.

He had sniffed and even eaten some of my first book, it is true. But he had never, after all I had done for him, done me the courtesy of finishing it.

ACKNOWLEDGMENTS

The author wishes to thank first of all Marian Probst, his longtime assistant, under whose incredible memory for irritating facts he has, with the patience of Job, long suffered. He also wishes to thank Sean O'Gara, whose love of computers and other modern nonsense was not only baffling to the author but also annoying to Polar Bear. Then too he wishes to express his appreciation to Lisa Adams, his illustrious illustrator, who proceeded at tortoise pace to produce the cover and drawings, meanwhile studiously ignoring every one of his masterly suggestions. Finally, he wishes to acknowledge the all too pointed criticism of two particular writing friends — Cynthia Branigan, who early understood that the best way to handle curmudgeons is at a distance, and Paula Deats, who pinpointed the distance at 3,000 miles.

Bedsides these, the author wishes to acknowledge the professional and personal encouragement of four colleagues at Little, Brown and Time Warner — Fredrica Friedman, his editor, whose belief in this book from the beginning was, even to Polar Bear, catalystic; Kelso Sutton, whose support was, at crucial times, critical; Jennifer Kittredge, whose charm was such that it overcame even her constant mention of other authors; and finally Glea Humez, copyeditor extraordinaire.

Finally, the author is grateful for permission to quote from the letters excerpted in the second chapter, as well as from the following works:

Kinship With All Life by J. Allen Boone. Copyright 1954 by Harper & Row, Publishers, Inc. Reprinted by permission of the publisher.

Cat Astrology by Mary Daniels. By permission of the author.

Catsigns by William Fairchild. Copyright © 1989 by William Fairchild Publications, Ltd. Reprinted by permission of Clarkson N. Potter Inc.

How to Learn Astrology by Marc Edmund Jones. By permission of the Marc Edmund Jones Estate, P.O. Box 7, Stanwood, WA 98292.

Linda Goodman's Sun Signs by Linda Goodman. By permission of Taplinger Publishing Co., Inc.

Your Incredible Cat by David Greene. By permission of Bantam, Doubleday, Dell Publishing Group, Inc., and Joan Daves.

"The Story of Webster" from *Mulliner Nights* by P. G. Wodehouse. Copyright 1930, 1931, 1932, 1933 by P. G. Wodehouse, © renewed 1958, 1959, 1960, 1961. By permission of the Estate of P. G. Wodehouse and Scott Meredith Literary Agency Inc.